This All-at-Onceness
A Memoir of Hope and Satellites

Julie Wittes Schlack

Pact Press

Published by Pact Press
An imprint of
Regal House Publishing, LLC
Raleigh, NC 27612
All rights reserved

https://pactpress.com

ISBN -13 (paperback): 978-1-947548-51-0
ISBN -13 (epub): 978-1-947548-52-7
Library of Congress Control Number: 2019934824

All efforts were made to determine the copyright holders and obtain their permissions in any circumstance where copyrighted material was used. The publisher apologizes if any errors were made during this process, or if any omissions occurred. If noted, please contact the publisher and all efforts will be made to incorporate permissions in future editions.

Interior and cover design by Lafayette & Greene
lafayetteandgreene.com
Cover images © by VT_Studio/Shutterstock

Regal House Publishing, LLC
https://regalhousepublishing.com

Printed in the United States of America

Disclaimer

This book spans almost sixty years and touches on the shames and sorrows of real people. To save them from unsolicited attention, I have in some cases changed their names.

I have more systematically disguised the facts in one chapter in this collection, "Beacons." Because I cannot definitively identify some of the people in it, let alone give them a chance to assess the accuracy of what I've written, I've chosen to fictionalize this account by making up the names of people and organizations, changing the sex of some key players, and occasionally putting words into peoples' mouths that aren't literal transcripts of what they said. So read this chapter as fiction—not absolutely factual, but fundamentally truthful.

Contents

To Mark

Prologue (1962)

In 1962, the city bus stopped directly in front of my house in Cote St. Luc, then a suburb, and now a neighborhood of Montreal. When I lived in that brand-new split level, with a patio and lilac bushes and crabapple trees in the back yard, I was still too young to venture more than six or seven blocks from home alone. But having proximity to a bus stop, such an essential gathering place, was a badge of honor. At the age of eight, I felt that it afforded me a certain prestige, as if the city and transportation commission had quite intentionally chosen my house to safeguard its vital property, a bus stop sign with detailed information about when the 161 ran and where the route ended.

Better still, it gave me the chance to watch others unobserved. A tall and narrow pane of ridged glass ran floor to ceiling next to our front door, and standing behind it, I could peer out at the sidewalk. Through the thick and wavy window, the commuters—some mothers, the very occasional father, but mostly bigger kids and cleaning ladies—looked as though they were under water, having silent but animated conversations as they waved their arms about. And when they leaned wearily, arms folded, against the black metal sign post, or methodically bounced a tennis ball on the sidewalk, I felt I was an invisible participant in something very private, as they stood exposed in their solitude.

That sidelight window illuminated the border between inside and outside. It was where I learned and liked to live.

"What we have done over time with electronic media is to place our nervous system outside ourselves. This means that every private operator can own a piece of your nervous system as if it was a box or a hunk of bread, and he can stand on your nose, your heart, your head, and manipulate your inner being by these external means."

- Marshall McLuhan[1]

W Dallas (2015)

Today I pored through the cell phone usage data of twenty-four male high school athletes who had given my company permission to passively monitor everything they did on their phones. Our client's hope—and every marketer's fantasy—is that they'll be able to predict consumers' behavior based on the data that smart phones capture about where their owners are, how long they stay there, what they do when they're at a given location, and in what proportion.

Not surprisingly, fourteen- to sixteen-year-old boys spend a lot of time on Instagram and ESPN. They use apps for tracking their workouts and performance. They listen to rap and heavy metal, play Angry Birds and Greedy Pigs. One apparently amuses himself and others with Fart Soundboard.

We can't read the words of their text messages or emails, can't eavesdrop on their phone calls, but we know what ball field or Burger King they're at when they're tapping and swiping.

My job is to bring people together in private online communities and get to know their needs, frustrations, passions, and opinions— all so that my largely Fortune 500 clients can better assess what consumers want, what they're likely to buy, what they're willing to pay for it, and why.

In my office, we spend our days hearing from tens of thousands of people around the world in chats and discussions, via Skype and surveys, in English and German and Mandarin translated in real time, through the videos they shoot on their smartphones and the collages they create, in the shopping receipts they scan and send us, in the voice mail messages they leave us.

We ask them questions, sometimes banal, sometimes profound; we text with them as they go bra shopping and show us what they're seeing on the racks and what they overhear sales people saying to each other. Now and then we send them ten dollar Amazon gift certificates and, in exchange, they record their daily snacks, their children at play, the contents of the Valentine's Day card they long to get. Thirteen-year-old girls take photographs of used sanitary pads so that the manufacturer can see the saturation patterns that will inform their next animated commercial. Newly diagnosed diabetics record their daily readings so that pharmaceutical companies can come up with the innovative insulin pump that will crush their competitors.

Over the years I've learned that everyone likes strawberry yogurt, while passion fruit (and strangely, pineapple) are polarizing flavors. I know that while the sound of laughing babies brings the most joy to the most people, many find quiet happiness in the hum of a refrigerator, the regular thump of clothes tumbling in the dryer, the beeping of a garbage truck as it backs up to the dumpster. I've seen the pictures that people upload to describe how they feel about their appearance—desolate women from Picasso's blue period; fat, crumb-covered cats; and photographs of broken toys and abandoned café tables in the rain.

My job is both mercenary and inspiring. I'm supposed to care about my clients' business success. What I actually care about are the people (referred to in my industry as "consumers" or "shoppers") who go to such extraordinary lengths when they believe someone is actually listening. Everyone wants to be heard. To be known.

I was reminded of this at a recent meeting of market research providers for a major food company, held at the W Dallas hotel. I'd arrived the night before. Loud trance music pulsed in the tiny lobby, and the check-in desk was barely visible in the dim light. In a black-lit room that I took to be the bar, chrome or platinum stalactites hung like fractured Mobius strips. Young men with moussed hair escorted bosom-boosted, spaghetti-strapped female colleagues in and out of the martini den; an occasional older woman whose fashion sense vastly exceeded mine strode past while speaking in urgent tones into her cell phone.

My room—well, it was hard to hate the room, with its excellent flat screen TV, its Eurasian contours, all black woods and burnished pewter-like moldings. The half-bottle of red wine, the honor bar that thoughtfully catered to one's hankering both for a Snickers bar and a Power Bar. Other than the bed, sublimely comfortable, the room was a triumph of form over function. The bathtub sat out in the open, the showerhead suspended from the ceiling, as if inviting the bather to rotate under it like poultry on a vertical spit, for the viewing pleasure of whoever reclined on that bed.

While waiting for my Wonderful, Winsome Caesar Salad, I noticed that everything around me was in some way branded and purchasable—the bedding, the pillows, the impossible-to-set clock radio, the CDs with their remixes and anthologies of carefully chosen mood music and clever titles like "W Hotels Warmth of Cool–Overture" and "W Hotels Rhythm and Muse." It was as if the experience didn't count unless it could be commoditized, but in that mass customization way, giving the illusion of choice, the patina of identity, by letting me choose the pillow firmness or music genre or shampoo scent that uniquely defined me (and the tens of thousands of other people who presumably made the same choices).

Whatever.

I felt ridiculously homesick, slept badly, and awoke eager for the day to be over.

This event, the "Research Odyssey," was convened to get some ostensibly innovative companies together to listen and explore ways we might collaborate to achieve new consumer insights. And what is a consumer insight?

It's the unmet need.

The decision tree.

The nostalgic attachment.

5

The influential recommendation that, if properly understood, could drive the engine of commerce toward a brand, a store, a purchase.

Our insights into female potato chip buyers with at least one child aged six to twelve, for example, illuminate the fact that chips are not primarily about potatoes. They're not even about salt. They're about tamping down road rage when stalled in traffic on the way home after work, about turning the sad predictability of another evening in front of the television into an intentional, festive event; about placating their children for pennies by the ounce.

Our brainstorms about flavors and scents in general with female Millennials (aged twenty to twenty-six) reveal a nostalgia for products that smell like bubble gum and cotton candy, for the sweet pink sensations that remind them of earlier years when they were hopeful and easily pleased. Their mothers, in contrast, are past nostalgia, drawn to shampoos and detergents and deodorants that smell of burning citrus or violent rain, of musk and wildness.

But for all of these people, these "market segments"—the Style-Leading Gen Y males and the Tech Savvy ones, the Health-and-Wellness-Focused Boomer women and the Food-as-Labor-of-Loves—consumer products are prompts and markers. They are both a feature and a symptom of their lives.

There are times when I actually feel that I'm doing something of value in using the anonymous intimacy of the web to enable people to connect in ways that start out superficial but evolve, their relationships taking on greater meaning and depth. The rest of the time I feel as I did when the working session began and our client Arlene, a perfectly nice and smart Dallas soccer mom and PhD in quantitative sociology, shared what she'd been working on for the past six months: How would consumers respond if, instead of getting two large boxes of crackers for $5.99, they were offered two large boxes, each containing 20 percent more crackers, for $7.99?

All of the data indicated that they'd take it in stride. Our community members perceived this new approach as still offering value; large-scale quantitative studies suggested no decline in intent-to-purchase scores. And in virtual 3D simulations of the shopping experience, focus group members, after scanning the shelves, would readily click their cursors on the more expensive boxes. Based on what they knew so far, the snack food company was poised to make the change. While Arlene felt this was the right thing to do, it was still a little scary, given the financial consequences if consumers turned to a cheaper store brand.

During the break, I headed toward the panel of multi-colored light bulbs flashing to the Europop-beat in the dim hallway, and went into the granite and steel bathroom. I hid in the stall as other attendees re-applied their lipstick, speculating about what would be served up as a W lunch.

They left and I stayed, welcoming the solitude. Unlike the pulsating barrage of sound in the hallways, the bathroom's muzak was a recognizable tune. I was listening to a highly processed techno version of "Sound of Silence." I found myself grinning. This was the step aerobics version of the song. I wondered if it was also playing in the W's fitness center, where one could no doubt purchase a W leotard—a Weotard?—and mindlessly Stepmaster in rhythm, going nowhere.

For a moment I was cast back to the front seat of my mother's turquoise Dodge Dart in the winter of 1966. We were parked illegally in front of the Kroger on West Stadium Boulevard in Ann Arbor, Michigan. I was staying in the car while my mother ran in for a few groceries because, she believed, my presence would somehow discourage a cop from ticketing her. I was twelve years old, listening to the radio. Paul Simon's voice quivered with reproach at our worship of a neon god, and though I didn't know exactly what he meant, as a bookish, friendless, relative newcomer to the United States and to the cruelties of middle school, I felt the song's meaning. Surely there were other kids like me bending close to the radio, bored by Sonny and Cher, who shared my sensibility. I leaned in, listening to Simon and Garfunkel's wrath and hope, finally believing that I'd find my tribe, people who understood me and would recognize me as one of their own. Hugging myself against the cold that seeped into the car that night, feeling my nose and cheeks warm from the faint churning of the tinny defroster, in that moment I heard what I believed to be the future. Mine.

Photoshocked (2015)

This week, an editor in need of my photo breezily told me, "No need to send one—I'll just find something online." Curious to see what she'd retrieve, I went to Google images and typed in my own name.

The first six images on the page were headshots from my corporate website, a timeline of my increasingly middle-aged hair styles and colors from the past decade. The hundreds that followed made up a bizarre assemblage of conference logos and pictures, book covers, people who possibly knew other people I might have met—a motley collection including:

- A *Boston Globe* photograph from July of 2013 showing an aerial view of workmen exhuming the grave of Albert Desalvo, the Boston Strangler;
- Covers of Haruki Murakami's *Kafka on the Shore*—a book I'd reviewed in 2005—in eight different languages;
- A picture of a Hispanic woman in a gray Nike sweatshirt and handcuffs;
- A single photograph of my husband, uncharacteristically bound in a buttoned-up white shirt and tie;
- A stunning photo of Jon Hamm playing Don Draper, and less handsome images of Hillary Clinton cleaning her glasses and Barak Obama in khaki shorts, driving a golf cart;
- The logo of the Alabama Crimson Tide;
- An empty road running alongside a foggy river;
- A newspaper drawing of Indian and Asian teens sitting cross-legged in a circle, accompanied by the caption: "Talking together is an effective way to develop good communication skills";

- An annotated paragraph from a book chapter titled "Advanced Potion Making";
- A grainy family photo of three women, their arms slung around each other's shoulders, associated with an article titled "Three Sisters: Joined at the Funny Bone";
- Army photos, family reunion photos, and obituary photos of a man I've never met.

I've been ruminating about this last set of images, copious and more personal than the others. The Army private looks dapper and crisp, though in the black-and-white portrait taken what looks like a decade or two later, he's a bit doughier and less somber. The family reunion shots in faded color show a genial man surrounded by children and grandchildren, sunburned and dressed for Florida. They look just like the hundreds of photos of my parents and sibling, cousins and children, taken over years of ski trips, birthday parties, and eventually winter vacations in Sarasota.

But they're not my family. The man in the photos was the father of a professional acquaintance named Pete, an ad agency executive who was an early champion of blogging and Facebook and LinkedIn. I'd met Pete at a couple of conferences, friended him when that was a new verb, and offered some perfunctory condolences when he posted news of his father's passing. His prominence in social media since its inception has swept his family photos onto my Google image page, blowing those scallop-edged images of his dad posing for the camera (when it was a camera and not a phone) far and wide, like pollen in the wind.

Though it's not Pete's fault, I'm resentful. If Google is going to serve up a faded photo from the 1940s of a young man in an army uniform, I want it to be my father. If I'm going to see an elderly man reveling in the glow of his sun-painted grandchildren, I want those buttery little girls to be my daughters. But my father is absent from these pages and pages of images, as are my mother, brother, my daughters and granddaughters.

I should be glad that my online privacy settings are holding fast. Instead, these grainy, predictable, and precious photos of other people's families arrayed on page after page make me feel misrepresented and strangely robbed of my own past. If my name is going to be associated with pictures, shouldn't they be pictures of my own choosing, my own people? If it's only my public life that's durable, shouldn't I be posting more often, with care to crafting my online legacy rather than leaving it to Google's associative prowess?

But then I hear my daughter's gently mocking reproof in my head, calling me by my childhood nickname, telling me to "Simmer down, chooch." My life did, after all, begin long before the social web, and its dearest moments are rendered much more vividly in my mind than they could be in any visible image. Photos will never tell the story of how this life has felt. And, I suddenly realize, despite the cheap longevity promised by online storage in the cloud, they'll never make it eternal.

Signs (1961-1962)

Many of my grandmother's errands on Saturday afternoons involved visits to frightening people. My eleven-year-old brother and I would climb onto the massive, marshmallowy front seat of her 1959 yellow and white Plymouth with the push-button transmission and head downtown.

The first stop was usually at the newspaper and tobacco store run by my great uncle, who took a tender, devoted interest in my grandmother after my grandfather's early and sudden death a few years before I was born. One-armed since the age of six when he was hit by a streetcar in Winnipeg, Uncle Charlie wasn't dashing, nor did his eyes twinkle from behind his thick, black electrical taped glasses. He and my grandmother would chat, and before we left, he'd press a damp nickel into my hand in honor of my sixth or seventh birthday, direct me to pick a treat from one of the big, dusty penny candy jars on the counter, giving me a quick, surprisingly firm squeeze around my shoulders with his stump. The contact ended like a cruel joke, as if his elbow and lower arm had been yanked away like a chair someone was about to sit in. Much as I loved candy, in every visit I dreaded that moment, ashamed of my squeamishness.

But more disturbing than Uncle Charlie's stump were the arms of some of the other people we visited, arms that had blue numbers tattooed on the insides of their white wrists.

"Don't stare at them," my grandmother warned my brother and me, thereby guaranteeing that we would. Why did they have these numbers, we'd ask. What did they stand for?

"They got them in concentration camps," she told us.

This was an answer, but not an explanation, so we continued to stare. We'd sum the numbers, look for patterns in the sequence of digits. (Were they always odd, even, odd?) There was little else to do in these small, stuffy apartments on the east side of Montreal, as my petite, stylishly coiffed grandmother, with her tinkling voice, strained to make conversation with these pale people in faded house dresses and lumpy suits, immigrants whose speech was guttural and thick.

These visits melded, but I remember one distinctly. My grandmother, as usual, came bearing food. Carefully climbing the circular, external wrought-iron steps that adorned the front of every building in this neighborhood, I carried the bag with the kimmel bread and the still-warm cheese and cherry danish. Behind me, my brother gripped a casserole full of my grandmother's stuffed cabbage, while my grandmother led the way, one hand on the winding banister, the other clutching a bag of store-bought smoked meat and several pounds of homemade brisket, baked for hours and still steaming in its foil girdle.

In a square living room stood a couple in their sixties with pale blue eyes that matched the room's pale blue walls. They smiled as their daughter opened the door for us, excitedly gestured us to come in and sit on their plastic-covered couch. They spoke to their daughter or to my grandmother in short, loud bursts of Yiddish, their speech forced out of exaggeratedly shaped mouths, their words largely lacking in consonants and difficult to understand. The food smelled wonderful, they seemed to be saying with a mix of signs and sounds; we needn't have come but they were so glad we did; would we stay and have lunch with them? I was afraid that my grandmother would say yes.

She declined, but the twenty minutes that we were probably there felt like hours. I was terrified of this perfectly friendly couple with their strangled voices and wildly waving hands. Just as the occasional sighting of a kid with misaligned eyes confirmed that we shouldn't cross ours even for a minute because they might get stuck, these people and those other grim ones with the numbers on their wrists seemed to have been placed in my path as a warning that terrible things could happen to innocent people.

Years later my mother explained that this deaf couple was related to someone who had worked for my grandfather in his vending machine business. The concentration camp survivors were probably receiving aid from the Combined Jewish Philanthropies, for which my grandmother volunteered. These visits were nothing more than my grandmother's acts of kindness toward people who were on the periphery of her daily life.

But for me, my brother, my cousins—for most of us born in the early 1950s to Jewish families in Montreal—they were living, breathing evidence that bad things happened, really bad things. We could walk and talk freely in our cloistered suburban neighborhood, but there was danger surrounding our anglophile, Semitic island in a province where, fueled by general anti-English sentiment, support for the pro-Nazi Vichy regime in France lived on well after the war had ended. We knew from snatches of overheard adult conversation, and from the war movies and spy movies that alternated with the Westerns on TV, that Nazis and Communist spies could still be walking among us.

While we owned the streets and yards of Cote St. Luc, our minority status became ever more apparent with each mile we traversed out of our neighborhood.

The drive from Montreal to our house on Lac La Croix took a few hours. My brother and I sat in the back seat, playing *Ghost* and *Geography* and willing the car to break clear of the rush hour traffic and out onto the first, newly completed stretch of highway. When the city stopped, the autoroute started. We'd look for cars like ours and count the toll booths, where my father, distressingly careless about rules, would casually flip the coins into the bin without even looking, his eyes still on the road in front of him.

At Val-David the highway turned to a paved strip bordered by gas stations and hot dog stands. We always stopped at Marcel's, an asbestos-shingled hut with a huge red and white sign out front. On it, the words *Chien Chaud* formed two arcs joined in the shape of a giant hot dog. *Frites*, painted like long thin French fries, jumped out from each end like hot spitting oil. These and a few other French words—translations for *please, thank you, help, God, pie* (and the name of every kind of berry that was put in pie), *milk*, and *lake*— were all my brother and I needed to know. They were the words on the signs, on the delivery vans that drove up to our house, the substance of our lives during these summer days. At home, in our neighborhood, we needed no French. And if we were outside the English neighborhoods, our parents were usually with us.

At Marcel's we'd sit down at the picnic table and eat hot dogs in the pink dusk. Then back in the car, my brother and I would pull the blanket up from the floor and curl up, our feet doggedly bumping together. As our parents' voices became softer and more directed to each other, I'd lie with my head on the arm rest, looking out the back window, focusing on a single star and trying to figure out how it stayed in the same place no matter how far and fast we drove.

I'd check off the milestones: the beaver dam, the huge silhouetted billboard for Santa's Village, and the arrow pointing toward *Au Petit Poucette—Jambon Fumee* (smoked ham—I knew that too.) Then came the sign for Mont Gabriel, and next to it, a neon cross, bigger even than the one in Montreal on top of Mount Royal. I wondered about the crosses that were everywhere but in our neighborhood (except for the one on Beth Bailey's lawn). I understood they were symbols, that they stood for the crucifixion of Christ who, if you were a Christian, you thought was God's son. But so what? How did the crosses help anyone? They seemed to me to be like those little air raid shelter signs that had recently sprung up on phone poles and building walls, that told you that there was a shelter somewhere in the neighborhood, but didn't tell you exactly where, or how to get to it, or guarantee that they'd even protect you when the Russians dropped the bomb.

After a spiraling climb up the mountain, we could look down at the sign tiled into the hill below us. It lay like a giant mosaic—*Camp Val-David*, each letter on its own big wooden square. My brother and cousins and I had heard our parents refer to it as an "adult camp," which we'd interpreted to mean that it was a nudist colony. We would imagine naked people playing volleyball and frying eggs for breakfast.

But on one trip past the sign, my mother said to my father, "Bryna told me that a realtor up here told her that it's some kind of right-wing retreat."

"I've been hearing that since the war," he answered. "Rumor had it that somewhere around Saint-Sauveur there was a colony of Nazi sympathizers just waiting for their chance to—well, I don't know what they wanted to do. But I wouldn't be surprised if they're still there."

"Nazis?" my brother asked. "Like Hitler?"

"Probably not Hitler," my father answered, "but anti-Semites who agreed with the Nazis about some things, people who've never met a Jew in their lives and have all kinds of crazy ideas."

"But it could be Hitler," my brother insisted. "I heard he was hiding out in the mountains of Argentina. But it could have been the mountains of Quebec. Or he could have come here because he was about to be discovered in Argentina."

"Hitler's dead, hon," my mother said. "It's just that they couldn't kill his ideas with him and some people—not many, but a few—still believe in them."

Hitler. I'd heard him once. Some World War II-related anniversary and one of his speeches was being broadcast. My father had turned up the radio and called my brother and me over to listen.

"This is what I heard," he said, "sitting in my parents' kitchen when I was sixteen. I didn't know German, but I knew this man was a maniac, that he was filled with hate."

And I heard the same thing in this harsh and horrible voice screaming out of the radio. The sound felt like it was bruising my skin. The rough fabric stretched over the radio's speaker trembled. I lay my fingers on it and felt the vibration as millions of people cheered. Hitler got more and more wound up, yelling and pounding the podium. And I felt like I *was* my father twenty years earlier, sitting in his Outremont kitchen with the Yiddish-speaking grandparents I never knew, knowing there were millions of people sitting in millions of kitchens, hearing this voice broadcasting to the whole world.

I looked back at Mont Gabriel, so busy and glistening in winter but now bereft, sitting muddy and bald except for the tufts of trees around the edges, its ski lifts small and frail. I scanned the hills. These mountains were the oldest in the Appalachian chain, probably the oldest in North America and the world. They'd survived dinosaurs and the ice age. Hitler could easily be hiding there. He was an army guy—I had always seen him in uniform. He'd know how to make campfires no one else could see, how to travel by night, how to lie on one of the dull gray rocks and aim his rifle at the passing cars below.

But how would he know which cars to shoot at? Ours wasn't a Jewish car; it was a Rambler. He needed spies, informers. Maybe the people hiding under the Camp Val-David sign kept track. Every weekend they could see who drove on this road, who stopped at a house with a cross and who kept going, farther into the mountains to finally turn into a house with a little mezuzah on the door frame. They would get to know all the cars, follow people. They could. None of the year-round people were Jewish. It was only the weekend people they had to watch.

It was late when we pulled into the driveway of our house on Lac La Croix, but the house was dark. My aunt and uncle and cousins weren't arriving until the next day. I remember my parents unlocking the door and unloading the luggage while we waited in the car. I kept them fixed in my sight, watching lights turn on one after another as they walked through the house. Then my father reappeared, opened the car door, and we followed him into the house, our feet crunching the gravel. The stars were very bright and the air was cold and blue. I wondered if there was an animal—a raccoon or a mink—in the milk crate trap we kids had put in the gully last weekend before we left.

We went straight to bed, but I couldn't sleep. I lay there, listening. My parents were upstairs. My brother was on the top bunk, breathing just loudly enough for me to hear him. There was only me to guard the house through this endless night. Here, with the family asleep out in the middle of nowhere, Hitler wouldn't need a rifle. He could sneak up with a knife. I listened hard for the sound of footsteps. If he came, I would stand behind the kitchen door with the cast-iron frying pan and hit him on the head as he came in. But what if he didn't come in the kitchen door? There were four other entrances to this jumbled house.

There was no choice. I would have to go out after him, not wait inside. But still I lay in my bed. I tried to imagine slipping out into the dark, sneaking up behind someone—even Hitler—and hitting him on the head or thrusting a knife into his back.

But I knew I couldn't force a knife through anyone's flesh. I lay there thinking, *This is how it happened.* This is how all those people let themselves be dragged out of their houses and put on trains and sent to concentration camps. Would I be any different from them?

The next morning, I was the first one up. I slid quietly out of bed and out the kitchen door. I walked outside barefoot, around the house, then down the gully, sliding but not falling in the tangled roots and scattered rocks. The milk crate trap was empty. But the biggest frog I'd ever seen was sitting on the rock we tied the boat to. I picked up a stick and tapped it against the base of the big spruce that held our tree house, feeling it bounce back gently in my hand, more branch than weapon. In my pink and turquoise flannel pajamas, I threw it into the lake, as far out as I could. At dawn, in the valley of mountains that enclosed my world like stadium walls, I lay one foot in front of the other, heel-to-toe, heel-to-toe, and paced the perimeter of our property.

Detectives (1962-63)

I'm not sure why I chose Howie Herschorn to be my partner in solving mysteries. Perhaps it was because, a year younger than me (a mere seven years old to my eight) and living one very long block away, he dwelled outside my everyday social circles of classmates and family. Or perhaps, in his freckled blondness and quiet dreaminess, I recognized both the exotic and the familiar.

Our first case involved Mrs. Alter, the woman my parents had hired to come to our house two afternoons a week to cook and clean while they were at work. She was a broad, lumbering Polish woman in her early fifties, with wide shoulders and thick ankles that ballooned out of the tops of the black-laced boots that she wore on even the hottest of summer days. A thin layer of greasy perspiration coating the broken blood vessels in her nose and cheeks gave her clenched face a red and glistening veneer. Her light blue eyes were locked in a perpetual squint, and when the sun streaming into the house struck the wire frames of her glasses, they seemed to emit predatory daggers of light. Swollen and sagging, the bosom that strained against her flowered dress created the impression of someone both inflated and defeated at the same time. Or, as I thought then, mean.

Beyond the fact that she spoke very little English, Mrs. Alter was profoundly foreign, smelling sourly of cabbage and sweat, and always grumpy. She'd scrub the counters with a frightening vigor, as if expecting to uncover gold dust beneath the robin's-egg Formica. Then she'd take a break and sit down at one end of the narrow kitchen table, a glass of hot tea in front of her, with a tablespoon resting in it, she explained, to "eat the heat." Pressing a sugar cube to her front teeth with her tongue, she'd take frequent, short sips, imbibing in loud, hissing bursts that reminded me of a snake I'd seen on a TV show, inhaling a live mouse.

19

My brother and I complained about her to our parents. Why did we need her? How come she smelled so bad? Why did she only make stupid hard cookies with poppy seeds instead of soft ones that oozed with melting chocolate chips?

"Don't be mean just because she's different," my mother would chastise us. "Mrs. Alter doesn't have an easy life."

That brought our complaining to a dead stop. We were supposed to feel bad for people who didn't have easy lives. We were to treat them with kindness and respect, and help them if we could. But what was so hard about her life?

"Her son's a no-goodnick," my mother said to my father over dinner one night, "and her daughter-in-law's even worse. It's not like they're hurting for money. Who puts their mother out to work cleaning other peoples' houses if they don't have to? It's not just unkind. There's something, I don't know, unseemly about it."

"Unseemly" sounded criminal to me. If Mrs. Alter's son and daughter-in-law were mean to her, surely they were up to other nefarious activities as well.

Our love of detective stories wasn't unique to us, I now realize. Children are still drawn to *Nancy Drew* and *The Hardy Boys* and *Encyclopedia Brown*, to *Judy Moody* and *Timothy Failure*. These characters have physical courage but also smarts. They're spunky, with a sense of their own agency that all kids aspire to and lucky ones have. But there's more to it than that. Adult interactions are encrypted. Grownups use code words for sentiments that are too impolite to explicitly express, small gestures like shrugs and eye rolls to convey who is to be pitied, scorned, or simply ignored. They borrow phrases from other languages, exchange long and opaque gazes when someone has transgressed by being too noisy or too quiet, too demonstrative or too restrained, too smart or too stupid. Kids understand that to grow up, they must first decipher, then adopt the code. So they learn to love looking for clues. They seek triumph in the face of the dangers they have invented.

Howie and I started, as all good detectives do, with footprints.

In 1963, Cote St. Luc was a neighborhood expanding into a suburb as it strained ever westward, and even the four-block walk from Westminster School to my house revealed its striations. The two-block area surrounding the school comprised bungalows and small ranch houses built immediately post-war. When we moved into our split-level ranch house in 1956, we were its first occupants, and Howie's family was the first to inhabit their semi-detached townhouse. But just a couple of blocks south and west of mine, new roads and large brick homes—free standing and almost palatial with their arched doorways, multiple floors, and garages that opened and closed with the push of a button—were being built in what had been empty fields.

And in front of them were freshly poured sidewalks, rich with clues. Despite being cordoned off by thick red string, the rectangles of wet concrete held imprints and etchings. Howie and I tried to decode them as we patrolled the new streets, looking for footprints. Some, my father had told me—the ones with neatly stenciled arrows and letters like *SW* or *30V*—indicated where water lines and electrical cables met in submerged junctions. Others—the messy scrawled initials, five- and six-pointed stars, and the handprints—were clearly made by other kids.

We ignored the handprints, and after only a couple of forays, found signs of steps. But they were never more than one or two consecutive footprints, traces that trailed off like an unfinished thought.

"They must be trying to escape detection," I told Howie. Still, we stayed on the trail, scouting the newly named Wolseley Avenue, speculating as to why the evil daughter-in-law and weak-willed son wanted Mrs. Alter out of the house. It might have been so that they had time and space in which to sort their stolen jewels, or so that they could counterfeit their money in peace. Or perhaps, given the proximity of the train yard, they were smugglers.

Besides being the possible site of the Alter family iniquity, the train yard held another fascination. With its lack of houses and people, its expanse of nothing but track, dirt, and a handful of mute, permanently parked freight cars, it was the most likely site in Cote St. Luc for quicksand. I knew all about quicksand, having seen not just the *Lassie* episode in which Timmy gets stuck in it, but also the *Sky King* episode in which, thanks to some mighty fine piloting by Sky King, Penny is able to toss a lasso down from the low-flying, circling Cessna to the robber who is sinking fast below them. As the viscous sand laps him in, the robber faces a choice: throw away the satchel of loot that he's stolen from the bank in order to grab hold of the lifesaving rope that will lift him to safety, or be swallowed alive, a victim of his own greed. For that was the nature of quicksand—it didn't distinguish between the good, like Timmy, and the bad, like that stupid robber, and it was indistinguishable from solid ground.

We went to the train yard prepared. I wore my red pedal pushers so that I wouldn't get any quicksand on the cuffs of my pants, and though I had no lasso, I did bring my yo-yo. As usual, Howie was sitting outside on the front stairs to his house, and silently joined me as I parked my bike in front of my aunt and uncle's. We had walked to the dead end of Westluke before, but this was the first time that we'd ever actually stepped over the rounded curb and onto the hard-packed dirt, studded with bottle caps and rounded bits of glass. As we neared the tracks, we turned left and, eyes to the ground, paced slowly in parallel to them. But if there were footprints, we couldn't discern them in the mottled mix of hardened mud and tufted weeds. The rusty CNR freight cars had no hobos sleeping in them, nor were there small bands of white slaves or fugitive Nazis cowering beneath them. Even now I'd like to say that there were bills of counterfeit money blowing forlornly in the late afternoon breeze, or that we'd found the papery skeleton of a rabbit or a lost cat. But we saw little besides rocks and puddles, and the naked sides of the last houses on each block.

It was nearing dusk, and the blue-grey sky was made darker by rain clouds blowing in. Thunder growled nearby, and as we headed back, first jogging, then in a flat-out dash, the skies opened up and we were blasted by rain. The already damp ground turned instantly slick and I slid, falling flat on my chest. Howie helped me up; we kept running. The hard-packed dirt loosened under the pounding, turning into a sticky, oozing mud, and a minute later, one of my canvas sneakers got stuck in the muck and my foot lifted right out of it. I stopped for a second to try to retrieve it, but Howie kept going, and I was afraid to stand still, panicked that the ground would grasp more than my shoe.

I was covered in mud by the time I got back to my bike. Howie was already in his house. He'd left me alone on the abandoned block. When I got home, my mother made me strip off my dripping clothes in the foyer, despite the fact that Jerry Marcus was there playing floor hockey with my brother. She wrapped me in a bath towel, and as she marched me through the house to the tub, Jerry, the friend of my brother whom I most despised, poked his head out from the top of the basement stairs and, in his best Woody Woodpecker voice, cawed *Uh uh uh AW uh*. My humiliation was complete.

That was probably the last of my adventures with Howie. Years later I heard that he'd become a dentist, and that his mother left his father for a failed affair with Sheila Goldstein's father down the block. I can no longer hear his voice, let alone anything he may have said. I remember his fair complexion and his placidity, which I now recognize as sadness. He was my uncritical companion on those still afternoons when we strayed from the familiar onto brand-new blocks, where nobody was known, nobody knew us, and everything but the inscrutable faces of the houses themselves was imagined.

Were we just like any suburban kids, living at any time in any place? Or were we attuned to the zeitgeist, sensing if not knowing that 1962 held some very real, very big secrets?

Three years earlier, the United States' satellite program had been launched, not to promote communication, but to enable surveillance. An orbiting Corona satellite would shoot photographs of secret facilities around the world, then jettison the film canisters. Fifty thousand feet over the Pacific, as the canisters delicately drifted downward—their flight slowed by a brightly colored parachute—a crew of ten skilled pilots, lassoers, and winch operators would snatch the film capsules out of mid-air and reel them in to their aircraft. After landing, they'd place the film on another aircraft that would transport it to Maryland for analysis. This process, making it possible to see what was going on around the globe in an operation that required mere days to complete, demanded an extraordinary meld of engineering, logistics, and human skill. But of course, it wasn't publicized, let alone celebrated.

During the 1962 Cuban Missile Crisis, provoked by satellite images of Soviet missiles ensconced in Cuba, there had certainly been nothing festive about our family's abrupt mid-week excursion to the country house in St. Adolphe. Secretly warned by the head of the Canadian military—brother of a Canadian Air Force friend of my Uncle Herbie's—that nuclear war was imminent and we should get out of Montreal, our parents loaded up the cars with my cousins, my brother and me, and cases of canned goods, and fled the city. Though the five of us kids often played soldier, marching in lockstep while chanting "Left, Right, I had a good job and I Left, Right…," on that October day we filed silently between house and cars with suitcases, lanterns, jugs of detergent, milk, bleach, and a lone can of maple syrup.

Our first afternoon there, we sat on the porch steps, and looked across the grey lake to the Franklin's, a house long-abandoned and most probably haunted. After a brief caucus, we decided that after all these years of wondering, it was time to finally explore it. We piled into the boat. As my cousin Paul rowed toward the house across the lake, we girls sang. "Just you wait, 'Enry 'Iggins," investing it with as much Cockney malice as our skinny throats could summon.

But our song faded as the boat neared shore. We scrambled up the barren rock, climbed soggy, leaf-covered steps, and pushed open the unlocked door to the Franklin's house. Splinters of fading light slanting through gaps in the walls illuminated a couch with a broken leg, spewing out mildewed stuffing. A brown, straight-backed chair had fallen on its side. An empty, greasy, blackened pan sat atop a cold wood stove. Next to it, the delicate carcass of a mouse was still clamped in its trap.

Walking cautiously through the dank room, I kicked something and looked down. A soggy game board lay littered with animal droppings, and strewn about the floor, in garish oranges and blues and greens, were the shriveled remains of popped balloons and faded Monopoly money.

Children had lived here.

Silently, we left. We girls tried singing on the boat ride back. "You'll be broke and I'll have money. Will I help you? Don't be funny." Our song sounded like a whimper.

I was only eight and remember little of that time—just that first and last trip to a house that would never be lived in again; the sound of our parents listening to the radio; we kids playing desultory games of *Sorry*; the two families' dogs writhing in the damp autumn leaves.

Our house was cold and after a couple of days of awaiting the apocalypse, we decamped and went back to town.

"We probably just told you that we were taking a fun school vacation," my mother says when I ask her how she explained these events to us.

"And why were you advised to leave the city?" I press her. "Why would the Russians have bombed Montreal?"

"I don't know why he told us to leave. Maybe he thought there'd be rioting or pillaging." She pauses. "Now that I think about it, our going to the Laurentians made no sense. If anything was going to be bombed, it would have been the NORAD radar towers in Morin Heights, right near St. Adolphe."

"But you didn't realize that then?"

My mother looks perplexed. "I guess not. I don't know if we were panicked or just incredibly passive back then. It simply didn't occur to us to ask those kinds of questions."

But my parents, and many parents of the 1950s and '60s, were acutely afraid and thus deeply angry in the face of such madness. This was not what so many of them had risked and lost their young lives for in World War II. Some of them managed their anxiety and rage at how their lives had shrunk so soon after blossoming, with Valium and Librium, what the Rolling Stones would later call "Mother's Little Helper." Some doubled down on their denial. They pursued stability and wealth, and when their children revolted, dismissed or, in severe cases, disowned them. And some, like my parents, looked for the other closeted malcontents who shared their restlessness.

For a few years, Jack Kennedy served as the vessel for their vague ambitions. For them and so many of their generation, JFK's inaugural address was more than lofty rhetoric. Since August 6, 1945, they'd known that "the world is very different now. For man holds in his mortal hands the power to abolish all forms of human poverty and all forms of human life." They felt that union of hope and terror every day.

But that ended on November 22, 1963. Just before school ended that day, Mrs. Bailey told us that JFK had been shot and killed.

Susan Feinberg and I dawdled on our walk home. It was a slow, leisurely journey, past new street signs and stop signs, each block bearing its own landmarks. (*That's the poet's house*, I'd recite to myself. *There's where that girl Ruth with the mustache lives. On this street used to live the man that disappeared—killed or a runaway, nobody knows.*) As we walked, we discussed what would happen next.

"Do you think the Russians will take over?" I asked Susan. As third graders born and raised in Montreal, though our airwaves were dominated by American culture and politics, we knew nothing about American laws of succession.

"They might," Susan answered. "Or they might not. I mean if they tried, the U.S. might drop the bomb on them."

"Americans would never *start* a war," I protested.

"Wouldn't they?" she answered archly. With her brassy voice and already budding breasts, she struck me as very mature. "They're very bossy."

I'd seen televised Russians at their May Day parades. With their jowly faces, in their square suits, they looked grumpy and mean. But they seemed too glum to terrorize anyone. In fact, they looked not so different from John Diefenbaker, until recently Canada's own petulant Prime Minister. (And his successor, Lester Pearson—well, he seemed friendly, but was named Lester and therefore couldn't be taken seriously.) Besides, it was the Americans who had dropped the two atom bombs, right?

When I got home I found my mother in the basement, crying and painting. The canvas showed faces streaked and blistered in strokes and pools of brown and beige, faces ravaged and weeping like hers. I'd never seen her use such dismal colors, or apply the brush with such sweeping violence.

We spent lots of time in the basement for the next few days, as that's where our brand-new television was installed, its bulbous glass eye gazing out from the knotty pine paneling of the wall. We were there, planted on the scratchy blue couch, when Lee Harvey Oswald was escorted through the basement of the Dallas City Jail, obscured by a gauntlet of police and reporters in suits and trench coats carrying wired microphones attached to portable reel-to-reel tape recorders hanging from their shoulders. We were probably still digesting the bagels and scrambled eggs we usually had for Sunday brunch when we saw the back of a man in a hat lunge into the frame, then heard the pop of Jack Ruby's gun. Two men grabbed him and wrestled him to the ground.

"There seems to be a scuffle of some sort," an unseen broadcaster said. Then we heard cries of "He's been shot! Oswald's been shot!" Bodies crowded around something or someone, the viewers' line of sight obscured by jostling men. The correspondents gathered around Pierre, a man with a French accent who witnessed a flash coming from the gun of a man in a black hat and a brown coat. Bob Huffecker, a flustered KRLD reporter breathlessly announced the arrival of an ambulance, the sight of the victim looking "ashen and unconscious." The video suddenly shifted to the exterior of the jail, an announcer said we'd be going "back to Harry Reasoner in New

York," but we didn't. Instead, paralyzed and mesmerized, we gazed at big cars pulling out of the garage and speeding down a Dallas street.

At least that's what I imagine now, as I watch remastered footage of the event on YouTube. In one video, Oswald's right arm hangs off the stretcher and trails along the basement floor before he is hurriedly lifted into the ambulance. Bob Huffecker (who, with no earpiece to provide a guiding voice, persists in referring to the victim as "Lee Harold Oswald") struggles to be centered in the camera's frame, but police and other reporters walk to and fro in front of him as he interviews a Dallas police officer. Hands grab the jackets of those blocking the camera and yank the offending men out of the way.

"Does he look like he's dying?" Huffecker asks the officer.

A long pause. "I wouldn't want to say."

The blocked visuals, the wrong names, the dead air—it all looks so amateurish, nothing like the aerial view of O.J. Simpson's white van from the CNN helicopter in the blue sky. But on November 24, the botched production values give events an immediacy that's re-evoked even now, over fifty years later. Millions of North Americans were sharing in the same televised experience.

It was a murder.

On November 29, 1963, after a fevered bidding contest, *Life* magazine published thirty black-and-white frames from the 26.6 second, color, eight-millimeter movie that Dallas resident Abraham Zapruder took of the presidential procession. It would become the most studied film in history. Over time, its 486 frames have been reproduced as 35 mm slides and as black and white photos. They've been color corrected, slowed down, and sped up. Missing frames have been identified and 16-millimeter copies of the film have been made. The Zapruder film has gotten almost six million views on YouTube, alongside the dozens of other videos showing other assassination-related footage (including one claiming to document Texas governor John Connally pulling a gun out of his jacket pocket at Love Field in preparation for shooting the President a little later on their sunny drive through Dallas).

Some conspiracy theorists denounce the Zapruder film as a fraud, buttressing their case by citing photographic consultants who point to gaps, unnatural jerkiness, and other anomalies in the film.

And today that's what we notice—the production values of the lives (and deaths) streaming to us in real time. Visual information no longer floats down to us under a brightly colored parachute; it's not snagged from mid-air by skilled and ingenious experts. It inundates us. It washes into our consciousness like a seaweed-clogged tide. Slow motion, instant replay, high definition—whether we're watching a running back dive into the end zone or a jet fly into a skyscraper, we're tempted to feel that by manipulating the image, we can understand the reality.

But back then, when Howie and I had gone looking for footprints in the newly poured concrete, events suddenly made it clear that there were big, invasive mysteries beyond our brand-new sidewalks.

Who or what could be so powerful as to make our parents weep?

Children playing detective is a timeless activity, but the clues they find and the narratives they construct from them are historically specific. As kids, my parents had pretended to be rum runners and cops, Eskimos and Arctic explorers. They'd played store, enacting the most mundane transactions that signified rescue for their immigrant parents.

But my generation looked for hints to how the world worked in the unmediated impact of real-time events. We began to recognize that adults weren't always in control, at least not the ones we knew. Mothers and fathers got divorced. Presidents could be killed. Prisoners could be killed, even when surrounded by police.

The blocks we patrolled were like postage stamps, colorful and square-edged, rich with detail magnified by our imaginations. But beyond their borders lay train tracks and wilderness, quicksand that would swallow both the robber and Timmy if either entered it alone. There were large forces at work, glacially cold and transformative, that not even our parents understood.

Our Wed and Unwed Mothers (1962)

Despite her restlessness, up until 1962, my mother had been like all the other mothers in our still-growing suburban neighborhood. When we got home from school, she'd be in the kitchen talking to her friend Babs on the black rotary phone that anchored the counter. But my father's business selling dish detergent and frozen foods was struggling, and though nobody said we were poor, my brother and I knew that there were many things we couldn't afford "right now." So, with characteristic practicality, my mother decided to go to art school.

Actually, her plan wasn't totally ridiculous. Montreal's Museum of Fine Arts offered a one-year certificate program in art education, and with the long tail of the boomer generation filling elementary schools as quickly as they could be built, teaching jobs were still plentiful.

That's when Nola came to live with us. In 1962, Canada had fewer than ten million people. Montreal, Toronto, Winnipeg, Edmonton, and Vancouver were the five large beads in a vast but sparsely populated chain stretching three thousand miles from east to west. People from small rural towns came to the cities for jobs, for a once-a-decade vacation, or to hide out and ride out their illegitimate pregnancies.

Nola had lived on a farm about fifty miles from Calgary, Alberta. I can't fathom why she came roughly two thousand miles from there to Montreal. But like Lynn, who would come after her, she had somehow found the Catholic agency that would place unmarried, pregnant women with local families for the duration of their pregnancies, scoop up their babies for adoption, and ship the women back on the train to wherever they'd come from.

Of course I understood none of this in that year, when I was eight.

Nola did not yet have a belly, and as far as I knew, she was living with us to occasionally cook dinner, do the laundry, and mostly, to babysit my brother and me while our mother was in school. She had beige glasses and dirty blonde hair that started each day in a hopeful page boy, greeted the afternoon with the limpest of waves, and ended it yanked and bound in bristly curlers. She wasn't fun, but she wasn't mean. Her non-live-in predecessor, Mrs. Alter, had a clenched red face and hands with a glistening veneer of sweat. Nola had soothing, cool hands and pale, almost transparent skin. She didn't frighten me.

I liked to go into Nola's small basement room, which was narrow and smelled new. Usually she would be sitting on her pillow at the head of the bed, her back against the wall, leafing through an issue of *Chatelaine*, but sometimes she would just be gazing at the square of light that snuck in the basement window on the opposite wall. These visits were short, as I never knew what to say to her, and if my bed was already made and my face was free of peanut butter, she had little to say to me. But on Wednesday, Friday, and Saturday nights, her boyfriend—the cabdriver she met as he drove her from the train station to our house when she first arrived—would come pick her up, and Nola would emerge from her cubby of a room, hair gleaming, eyes bright behind her glasses, smiling lips garish against her pellucid face.

I don't remember the arrivals of our unwed mothers, only their departures. Lynn waddled out of our house about five months after she'd come, escorted to a black Rambler by my mother, who carried her two suitcases, and a lady I'd never seen before holding her elbow. They looked strangely festive to me, as if they were hustling Lynn to a party at which she was the cake.

Nola left within a couple of months of her coming. I have one vivid memory, though, from the week before her boyfriend drove her back to the Canadian National Railway station from which she'd come. The memory is this: While my parents confer quietly outside her door, I peek in and see Nola lying in her narrow bed under a pile of blankets, her face white and clammy. Nola is sick, my parents tell me. Don't disturb her.

31

Of course, Nola wasn't sick. The prior night, she and her boyfriend had gone to the town of Ste. Agathe des Monts, about sixty miles north of Montreal. With an off-season population of about eight thousand people that practically doubled in the summer, Ste. Agathe was one of the largest towns in the Laurentian Mountains. It had three movie theatres—the year-round French one and the two English-language ones only open in July and August. It had a tuberculosis sanitarium and a Catholic hospital that served all the small towns within a forty-mile radius. Spas, summer cottages, ski hills, and a year-round paper mill created a steady stream of laborers and service workers, transient young men, and young women likely to get in trouble. They were served by a handful of backroom specialists who took only cash.

I don't know how much Nola paid to have her uterus scraped in someone's second-floor kitchen in Ste. Agathe. I only know what my mother told me just recently, when I finally thought to ask about this scene that I've remembered all these years—that very late on Saturday night, Nola's boyfriend phoned my parents' house in a panic. She'd had an abortion, he told them, and started to hemorrhage almost immediately. He'd taken her to the hospital in Ste. Agathe, but the nuns refused to admit her. She was now lying in the back of his cab, bleeding out onto the seat as he stood in the phone booth at the Texaco station just off the autoroute. He didn't know how he'd clean it, how he'd get the blood out of his cab. He was afraid Nola would die, and he didn't know what to do with her. Could he bring her home, by which he meant, back to our house?

Of course, my mother answered. Then she called her gynecologist to see if he would admit Nola to the Jewish General Hospital in Montreal. No, he told her. He couldn't take the risk of being associated with an abortion, even one he didn't perform. Instead, he wrote my mother a prescription for an antibiotic and instructed her on how often to give it to Nola. He told her to apply ice packs to Nola's belly.

The tableau imprinted on my mind's eye—Nola waxy and scared, my parents secretive and grave, my father leaning in close to my mother as he stood with one foot resting on the leather seat of our toy chest—must have been from the next morning, after they'd stayed up with her all night. I knew nothing of that. I just knew that my father's foot barred entrance to my holster, my tutu, to the wood-burning set with which I painstakingly etched out pictures of trees and clouds and children, the sweet smoke rising from the wood, the outlines emerging from its smooth, flat surface.

Until 1967, it was a jailable offense in Canada to publish or otherwise transmit birth control information. Any discussion of contraception on the airwaves had to be cleared in advance by the Board of Broadcast Governors, and it was illegal for drugstores to sell condoms (though they carried them under the counter). Indeed, the words "condom" and "penis" never appeared in the press. Any married couple engaging in fellatio could be jailed for practicing "gross indecency," and while that couldn't be enforced, the law barring homosexuality could be and vigorously was.

"We were all having premarital sex," my mother tells me now, "or at least most of us, and we could all get diaphragms from our doctors. But nobody talked about it. It wasn't something we'd admit to even our closest friends. Ruth was pregnant when she married Lou, but we all just nodded and clucked with concern when she told us that Stacy was born prematurely."

Though 90 percent of the earned income in Canada went to men, the government did award a monthly stipend to all wives with children. And just as well, because, as Canadian journalist Pierre Burton notes, married women "could rarely open a bank account, apply for a credit card or even a library card without their husband's signature."[2] Abortion was, of course, illegal, and a divorce was almost as difficult to obtain. "In British Columbia [a woman] could have obtained a divorce if she'd been the victim of rape, sodomy, or bestiality. In New Brunswick, frigidity and impotence were grounds; in Nova Scotia, consanguinity (blood relationship), impotence, or cruelty. In Quebec and Newfoundland there were no divorce courts; she would have had to petition Parliament through a private member's bill. In the rest of the country she would have to prove adultery."[3] To get divorced, many couples agreed that one of them would falsely admit to adultery, hiring professional co-respondents to serve as their "lovers" in court. My mother knew of such cases, but the bizarreness of the situation—the pretend Protestant restraint of marital sex, the winking lies of divorce—only strikes her now, looking back from a different normal.

At the point that we left Montreal in 1964, I knew two divorcées. My mother's cousin Eleanor had won a divorce after her pharmacist husband decided when she was in labor that he really didn't want a child, after all, and moved out as she was giving birth. ("He brought shame to the Levine name," I overheard from more than one neighbor and relative.) Then the mother of my friend Jane, who lived right around the corner from us, got divorced. Nobody knew why; her mother never invested her pruriently interested neighbors with the secret. If Jane had wanted to talk about her parents' split, I doubt she could have. I was one of her best friends, and though I was curious, I was not alone in believing that discussing her parents' divorce would cause her unbearable shame. I was still allowed to play at her house, but it was a quiet and darkly sour place, as if the divorce had left a stain that time could never lift. Mrs. Kaleb moved through it like a ghost, nearly invisible.

For my first few years of elementary school, it seemed that our mother was always tethered to the phone when my brother and I got home from school. Sometimes she'd be on the kitchen telephone, more often sitting on the couch in our finished basement, an occasional Salem cigarette burning in the ashtray next to her, talking to her childhood friend Babs.

I thought Babs was a really odd name, but fitting for Mrs. Abrams, whose voice, both breathy and loud, accessorized her large frame and brassy personality. She was bossy—not quite my mother's type—but not perfectly manicured and coiffed and tight-mouthed and angry like so many of our neighbors—also not quite my mother's type. Still, I couldn't understand what they could possibly have to say to each other day after day.

When my mother went to art school, the daily conversations with Babs stopped. While she spent her days at the museum, the other mothers kept chatting on their newly upgraded wall-telephones in pink and green and beige. While they paced their kitchens, the long, curly cords of their new phones draped behind them like wedding dress trains, my mother was downtown, mixing paints and breathing in turpentine and modern art.

Years later, I would find myself sitting on a couch, talking on the phone. Every weeknight after dinner, I'd get a call from Rosie, my daughter's babysitter, ostensibly to tell me what Katie had done that day. I resented those calls, which encroached on my scant and precious after-work time with my daughter. But Rosie was simply starved for conversation, and as I sat squeezing and releasing the spit-curled phone cord, I pictured the smoke from Rosie's Newport curling upward from the beanbag ashtray next to her, and recognized her trapped and frantic tone. Her days in her small, dim row home were structured by children—her own and those she babysat—and at night, if only for a few minutes, she wanted to abandon the cooing and coaxing and calming that consumed her days and simply hear her own, adult voice.

My mother had a wildness about her, and an eagerness too, that made her different from the other mothers. Her salads were big and bright, the peppers and carrots chopped large enough to ensure that their green and orange stood out against the pastel iceberg lettuce and their crunch was audible. She put pineapple in the tuna, copious garlic in the soup, made peanut butter and banana sandwiches instead of peanut butter and jam. She listened to Miles Davis records when the other mothers were enduring Perry Como, and when Rodolfo and the dying Mimi sang their last duet in *La Bohème*, she'd sit my brother and me in front of the record player with her so the three of us could weep together. When we got into the car, we could never drive directly to our destination; she would insist that we try out a new route, or stop for a small gift to bring to whomever we were visiting, or take advantage of the Open House that we were passing to see the interiors of homes we would never be in a position to buy. When she played piano, her fingers were not delicate on the keys, and lying under it, I could feel the floor tremble.

In other ways, my mother was just like the other mothers. She would never leave the house without first applying lipstick, and her purse swelled with folds of Kleenex adorned with red, fuzzy, crescent-shaped kisses. She cooked Swedish meatballs in a sauce made from ketchup and grape jelly, stabbed them with toothpicks, and served them to visiting dinner guests from a chafing dish that sat in the middle of the dining room table atop a glowering flame. She dutifully lit Shabbat candles every Friday night, though the ritual meant little to her, and went to meetings of Jewish philanthropies, where they planned fund-raising parties to support good deeds. The fact that we'd had some of our own furniture repossessed and could have used some philanthropy ourselves was not discussed there.

Indeed, it seemed to me that my mother invested tremendous energy in keeping up appearances. For every uncomplicated hug that she gave, she also tortured me with her clenched-teeth attempts to pass a hairbrush through my curly hair, with her insistence that I be corseted into a stiff, abrasive crinoline beneath my party dress, or wear shiny patent leather shoes instead of my beloved red canvas sneakers. To look presentable was to be subject to scratchy clothes and tugged hair, to be victimized by what I felt to be small, daily acts of violence.

"Were you just trying to conform when you did that?" I asked her recently as we discussed life before the women's liberation movement.

"I wasn't trying to conform," she answers, startled, in fact, wounded. "I was just proud of you." Then, after a pause, "I suppose I would have been embarrassed if you'd looked awful." She is eighty-four, and one of her front teeth has broken off, making her mouth suddenly sunken and *embarrassed* sound like *embarrathed.* "I think every mother feels that way. Didn't you feel that way?" She's right, of course, and suddenly I am deeply ashamed.

In those years that my mother was in art school, our finished basement got messier. Now, besides the toy chests, the brand-new television built into the wall, the stacks of records, the plastic-covered card table to be used for all, and that meant *all*, chemistry projects, the plastic bowling pins, the cases and cases of unsold Glee detergent, the two industrial freezers stuffed with cartons of Sara Lee cheesecake and Chef Lee Chow Mein, we had oversized art books on every surface.

My favorite was *The Private World of Pablo Picasso*, with text and copious photographs by photojournalist David Douglas Duncan.[4] In the photos I studied most often, Picasso painted, chatted with a visiting friend, read a newspaper—all while wearing a white boatneck shirt, horizontally striped clown pants, knee-high argyle socks, and white loafers. These pictures left me dumbstruck. I'd simply never seen a grown-up dressed like that, not even in a movie. While my mother pored over his paintings in the companion book that sat on the end table next to the couch, I studied the pictures of life at La Californie, Picasso's French villa.

A gleaming sculpture of a small-breasted, wide-hipped woman sat on a shelf, her long neck widening at the top to serve as the opening for a vase. Below her, on crates and palettes and squatting on the floor were other women, some with off-kilter heads or enormous rounded breasts. The breasts were always smooth and gleaming in contrast to the rough stone or plaster of their torsos and arms. In one room of the house, a live goat sat tethered to a doorknob, a box of straw on the floor behind its stubby tail. In another photograph, the goat stood in a garden, leashless and erect, facing off against a sculpted bronze dog.

And throughout, there was Picasso—in the bathtub, ebullient, scrubbing his back with a loufa, playing a xylophone made of coconut shells and strips of wood, or twirling on his bedroom balcony, hands overhead and gravely clapping, fingers snapping, wearing his wife's petticoat and an ancient African war helmet that looked like a birthday party hat, dancing a flamenco.

One sequence of photos began with a picture of him sitting at a table at the end of a meal, sucking on the remains of a fish.[5] In the first frame, he placed the perfectly intact spine, feathered by delicate ribs, on wet plaster, and painted a hand-thrown plate on a stool in the next. Then, in the final frame, he tenderly laid two plaster casts of the skeleton of the fish that he had just thoroughly, voraciously consumed onto the dish he had just painted.

Though his images were not realistic, there was nothing ethereal about his art. It was as corporeal as a tongue lapping up bits of moist flesh from the carcass of a fish, as shocking as a gash of wet paint on a dry plate. And though his villa was enormous, it was cluttered with canvases, sculptures, animals, children, costumes, and visible noise.

It wasn't just the impropriety of the place that enthralled me. It was the bedlam. For me, Picasso and his peers were grown-ups acting like children. They suggested the nearly unthinkable notion that adults could simply play.

But for my mother, this art signified the possibility of no rules, of making your own rules. "It was only when I stood in front of his canvases that Picasso moved me," she tells me. "But for years before that, I was intellectually thrilled by him. What he was doing—what he showed me you could do—was deconstructing something instantly recognized, something familiar, and then reassembling the pieces to make something entirely new."

"... instead of tending towards a vast Alexandrian library the world has become a computer, an electronic brain ... And as our senses have gone outside us, Big Brother goes inside."

- Marshall McLuhan[6]

The Czech Exhibit (1967)

In 1967, at the age of fourteen, I finally got to ride the 162 bus unaccompanied by an adult, though the brick house behind the bus stop was no longer my home. But in the hiatus between school and summer camp every year, I would come back to Montreal from Ann Arbor and stay with my Auntie Anne, Uncle Herbie, and my three cousins, whose house was one long block from my old one.

When we moved away, my aunt and uncle had to give up the country house, and Anne's misery at being stuck in the city was almost palpable. Those summers in the country had been a beloved necessity. Anne was happy there, playful and free. She rarely talked about her childhood, which ended on the last Kindertransporte train out of Vienna when she was fourteen, and never about her parents, who had been killed in the Holocaust. But when out in the woods, she would reminisce about going mushroom hunting with her grandmother. She'd bend close to the ground, hold an imaginary magnifying glass to her eye, and tiptoe through the underbrush. "It was like searching for gold, delicious gold you could eat." We kids would hold our breaths in those moments, and silently follow her.

But once those summers in the country were yanked away from her, we heard no more reminiscences about visits to her grandmother in Czechoslovakia. "Prague was a fairy tale city," she'd once half sung, half soothed, with the tone and cadence of a bedtime story, "with a castle like Walt Disney's." But by the summer of 1967, on the rare occasions that she spoke of going somewhere, it was to wail at her kids, "You're driving me to Verdun," which was the local mental hospital. The summer days were long and slow, and she spent many of them in a darkened bedroom, crippled by migraines.

My cousin Carla and I would dawdle over breakfast (especially since Anne allowed Frosted Flakes and Kix in her house, cereals that were forbidden in mine), then ride bikes to the brand-new neighborhood swimming pool. When we didn't abandon ourselves to the sheer mindless pleasure of splashing and diving, we'd flirt, watch, bicker, sigh, and judge the other kids our age doing exactly the same thing.

After an enervating day in the sun, we'd pedal home in slow motion, slump exhausted on the interior green carpeted stairs between the main level and bedrooms, until one of us roused ourselves to go put a Beatles record on. Then, in a twilight made magically ours by the cooling of the air, we'd set the table and whisk my aunt's homemade steak marinade ("The secret's in the wodka," she'd say in her piercing Viennese voice. "Yeah, we know, it's wery important," we'd answer, never pausing for one instant to marvel, even to think about, how quickly and thoroughly she had learned English.) That far north, the evening sky stayed violet until after nine, and we'd lie in the back yard or sit on the stoop, nursing popsicles, waiting for our lives to start.

Then, in the last two weeks of June, 1967, they did. Montreal's World's Fair, Expo 67, had opened on April 28, and it became for Carla and me, the irresistible center of the universe.

Late each morning, Carla and I would walk down Westluke to the corner of Kildare, and stand in front of my old house, awaiting the 161 Bus. We'd ride it to the Plamondon stop on Montreal's brand-new Metro, which had only opened the previous year. Like Moscow's, its stations featured enormous, original works of art—stained glass murals and ceramic mosaics —and the brand-new trains, with their rubber wheels, were immaculate and silent. We'd take the red line through downtown Montreal, then transfer at Berri to the yellow line, which carried us a few short stops to the Jean-Drapeau station on Ile St. Helene, one of the three islands in the Saint Lawrence river that served as the site of the fair.

When Montreal won the bid to host Expo 67, Ile Ste. Helene was the only island in the St. Lawrence adjacent to downtown. But clever planners realized that they could take the twenty-five million tons of dirt excavated in the effort to build the Metro and use it both to enlarge Ste. Helene and to create the brand-new, artificial Ile Notre Dame. This was recycling at its finest, though that term had yet to be coined. Then they called it Ingenuity, or Modernity.

Across the two islands, a span of roughly sixty-four city blocks held radically styled buildings—inverted pyramids, metallic tent-like structures, round glass-shingled buildings, and a geodesic dome. Unlike the pulp science fiction comics of the 1950s, where domes and towers dominated the landscape, Expo 67 suggested that the future would be made of triangles.

Of course, the question of what to wear to the future loomed large for Carla and me as we rifled through our dressers in her floral pink bedroom.

"Too childish," she ruled when I held up my favorite beige pedal pushers and red striped shirt for her inspection. She twirled around in the red bowl chair at the foot of her bed. "We're going to La Ronde tonight, remember?" La Ronde, an enormous amusement park at one end of Ile St. Helene, was, for that summer, the social hub for everyone in the city under the age of eighteen.

Eventually we settled on uniforms of jean skirts, sandals, and the cotton peasant blouses that were just coming into vogue. That was just one of many looks in the eclectic fashion parade at Expo, where the different styles represented the diversity in generations more than in culture. For the older visitors, both the locals and the tourists from around the world, Expo was like taking a trip on an airplane, something for which one dressed up. Alongside the young people in bell bottoms and Peruvian vests were men in Fedoras and suits, women in matching skirts, jackets, and pillbox hats. Hemlines ranged from mid-shin to mid-thigh; some men's shirts were ironed and white, their necklines sharply angled and held in place by collar stays; others were paisley, wrinkled and limp in the summer heat. But every outfit told us stories.

Fifty million people came to Expo; over ninety countries exhibited there. Standing in line for a train or an exhibit on any given day, we swayed like seaweed in a sea of people from around the planet. Though we couldn't understand much of what was being said in the multi-lingual conversations around us, we could look at the clothes and find our peers, and with our privileged, heady parent-free status, show instant solidarity in a meaningful glance with some other fourteen-year-old from halfway around the world whose anxious mothers and fathers were trying to educate and uplift them.

Each day, the Montreal papers would list the notables visiting Expo. I remember Anne's gregarious and overly enthusiastic neighbor, Eleanor, planting herself at the kitchen table while my aggrieved aunt slammed a coffee cup down in front of her, hoping to get the forced schmooze over with as quickly as possible.

"Princess Grace is coming today!" Eleanor exclaimed.

"Who?" Anne asked. She undoubtedly knew the answer.

"Princess Grace! Of Monaco!"

"Monaco. Is that like Nabisco?" As withering as Anne's resentment could be when turned on Carla, we took unhealthy pleasure in seeing her aim it at someone else.

"Don't be ridiculous. Monaco is…it's in Europe someplace. Princess Grace used to be Grace Kelly. Surely you've heard of Grace Kelly!"

Anne didn't bother to answer. "We haven't," Carla piped up in a rare act of solidarity with her mother.

Sighing, Eleanor once again peered at the paper. "Oh, and so is some Maharajah, Maharishi…some yogi."

The Beatles guru, Maharishi Mahesh Yogi, was joining Princess Grace in the odd registry of visitors to Man and His World. Later that summer, so would French President Charles de Gaulle (who won the lasting enmity of the English-speaking Canada for yelling *Vivre Quebec Libre!* to a crowd of nationalist Francophiles who had lined the streets to greet him) and Ethiopian Emperor Haile Salasse. The cultural performances were equally eclectic, from The Supremes and Tiny Tim to Thelonious Monk and Jefferson Airplane. But no matter—*all* were celebrities, and like the nerd who finally gets an actual date for the school dance, the nation stood up straighter and got a little strut in its step.

But beyond confidence, Expo 67 exemplified enlightenment. When my brother returned from his visit to the 1964 World's Fair in New York City—a joint bar mitzvah present from my mother's three New York City cousins who paid for his train ticket, put him up, "schlepped him around," and made me almost sick with jealousy— his stories were about the moving armchairs at the General Motors exhibit, the "World's Largest Cheese" in the Wisconsin pavilion, and the enormous Belgian waffles sold for the extravagant price of three dollars apiece. While generating near-ecstasy in a thirteen-year-old boy, the New York City fair was largely and accurately characterized as a commercial extravaganza that coupled few examples of the visionary with many of the tawdry.

In contrast, Expo 67 was a cultural exhibition, not primarily a commercial one. Of course all of the national, provincial, and cultural exhibits were rich in business and trade industry sponsorships, but that nuance was lost on me then. No, Expo 67 was fundamentally about social progress. Its logo was based on a primitive representation of "man"—a vertical line with arms diagonally outstretched to create a Y-shaped figure. But in the graphic designed for the fair and adorning every flag and municipal sign in Montreal, the figures were linked in pairs to represent friendship, and eight pairs formed a circle to suggest friendship around the world.

The Quebec City newspaper, *Le Soleil*, which, like much of the French language press, generally tilted in favor of the separatist aspirations of some in the province, embraced the inherent internationalism of the event, though in a Quebec-centric fashion. "Isn't this the best possible way for Canadians to get to know one another—what other event could attract to Québec so many of our compatriots from the nine other provinces?—to make ourselves known to the rest of the world and at the same time to realize how much progress ties all nations together?"[7]

Expo 67 was clean and humane, worldly and welcoming, so unlike my experience of the United States. I'd moved to Michigan at an age when my curly hair, budding breasts, and shyness would have made daily life excruciating anywhere. But those routine agonies of early adolescence were compounded by the fact that I'd skipped a grade upon moving, had a funny Canadian accent, and was clueless about what an "ice cream social" was, why paper bags were called "sacks," and why Michiganders had such an aversion to pronouncing words containing double o's as they were meant to be articulated, choosing instead to refer to "roofs" as "ruhfs" and "roots" as "ruhts." Not only did I have trouble understanding my new schoolmates, who throughout sixth grade and junior high school seemed almost uniformly stupid and cruel, but even worse, I felt completely misunderstood by them.

With the Cold War still rumbling and the Vietnam war festering and about to explode, America's emerging status as the self-satisfied but aggressive cop to the world was entirely consistent with my own experience. For me, already a reluctant expatriate and already politically aware, Expo's celebration of diversity and culture, of friendship and internationalism, rather ironically aroused a national sense of Canadian pride—more than pride, superiority—which I would come to find obnoxious, but that struck me then as purely deserved. It confirmed that those conformist American kids whose cliques I could not penetrate really *were* jerks. Even *Ca-na-da*, the song that became the unofficial anthem of the Canadian centennial and of this event—a relentlessly upbeat number composed by a jingle writer named Bobby Gimby and sung by a chorus of Toronto schoolchildren—made me feel that my native home had all the healthy goodness that my adopted one, with its ignorant bullying boys and maudlin Midwestern homilies about God and country, did not.

The Metro was new, the islands were new, and in this, its centennial year, Canada as a whole was in the mood for self-reinvention. After a nationwide design contest, the red maple leaf, whose very color I

44

found shocking the first time it appeared in the heretofore exclusively black-inked Montreal newspapers, had displaced the British ensign on the new Canadian flag. Though technically still belonging to the British Commonwealth Realm, my homeland was no longer an English colony, and it was certainly not American. To be a supremely self-centered fourteen-year-old Canadian at Expo 67, in the year of the Canadian centennial, was to feel that my environment was simply, naturally mirroring my internal state—festive, independent, and fresh.

The minutes, and sometimes hours, dragged as we stood in the vast but orderly queue outside the Canadian Telephone pavilion. But the anticipation was sublime. Upon passing through the turnstile, we were greeted by two women standing in front of a small stage, dressed like stewardesses, in tailored short skirts, matching jackets, and pillbox hats. One speaking English, the other French, they took turns demonstrating the phone of the future. The Anglophone dialed, the Francophone answered, and we spectators saw their faces displayed in a split screen on two giant monitors as they carried on an animated conversation.

"It is so annoying when you miss a phone call, either because you are already on the line or because you are not home," one said with rehearsed frustration.

"Yes, but in the future, you will never have to miss a call!" the other answered with soothing optimism. "In the future, you will be able to switch from the call you are on to an incoming call. And when you leave the house, you'll key in the number of the place you're going to, and the phone will ring for you there!"

This vision of perpetual connectivity was at best, puzzling. Telephones were for our mothers. Who wanted to be on the phone when you could be out in the world?

As we were funneled through a second set of the turnstiles and herded into a large, round theatre, our excitement grew. As fifteen hundred of us stood enclosed by waist-high metal rails, the lights dimmed, and a green but dusty parade ground appeared on screen all around us. Then, amid the sound of thundering hooves, dozens of Mounties, lances pointed, charged toward us from all sides, their scarlet uniforms lurid against the horses' gleaming flanks and brilliant blue sky.

This was the start of *Canada 67*, a short film executed in the revolutionary new, panoramic *Circle-Vision 360!* Nine projectors, concealed in the narrow gaps between nine enormous screens, projected a completely circular image, while twelve synchronized sound channels enveloped us in sound. Of course I didn't know these technical details then. I just knew that as the film took us on a whirlwind trip from east to west, each archetypical Canadian scene made my heart race and my skin, cooling in the air-conditioned dark, tingle. We hurtled down an ice slide at the Quebec Winter Carnival, then stood tense and ready in the goal at one end of the Toronto Maple Leafs' rink, sandwiched between the crowd noise behind us and the slashing whistle of blades on ice as three Detroit Red Wings bore down on us. We flew over Niagara Falls, and as the plane banked, we gasped and grabbed onto each other or the rails to keep our balance. And when we found ourselves on a bucking bronco in the Calgary Stampede, our hamstrings tensed, we drove our feet into the floor, and experienced all of the heaving with none of the risk.

As exciting as it was, *Circle-Vision* was just an appetizer. The Czech exhibit was the main course, where all of the magic that I'd already associated with Prague was on display.

Illusion—both the technology and the politics of it—lay at the heart of every exhibit in the pavilion. And the high point of the Czech pavilion was Kinoautomat—which as best as I can determine, is Czech for "interactive cinema."

The movie (dubbed into English from the original Czech) called *One Man and his House*, begins with a flaming house—one in a block full of tenement row houses—then flashes back to what had given rise to this situation. Mr. Novak is alone in his apartment, his wife having gone out on an errand. The doorbell rings, and he opens the door to discover a young woman, a neighbor, clad only in a towel. She has locked herself out of her own apartment and asks Mr. Novak to let her into his home. Mr. Novak wants to be a good neighbor, of course, but she is rather young and scantily clad, and his wife is due home any second. What a quandary!

As I remember that moment (and not quite as it actually occurred), Mr. Novak steps out of the screen and onto the stage. (In fact, the actor playing Mr. Novak simply walked on stage from the wing as the movie frame appeared to freeze.) "What should I do?" he asks the audience in what I would later learn was memorized phonetic English, of which he knew not a word. "Should I let her in?"

Each of us picked up the small remote control tethered to the arm of our seat and pressed either a red button for *No* or a green button for *Yes*. A border of 127 lights surrounding the screen lit up in red or green, the audience's verdict was displayed, and then the movie continued down the path we had chosen for it.

We had nine such decision points in the movie, some involving Mr. Novak, some involving other characters. The votes were usually close (except for one occasion that I recently read about, in which a large contingent of nuns occupied all 127 seats and all commanded *No* at every opportunity). I don't know what was more thrilling—the illusion of live people stepping in and out of the film, or the almost plausible hope that we, the audience members, were actually determining the course of events on screen.

But we weren't, no more than the citizens of the Czech Republic were in command of their own country in 1967. The fact was that the outcome was pre-ordained; the movie always ended as it began, with the flaming tenement. It had been scripted such that regardless of how we voted, each of the two branches ended up at the same decision point. To have done anything other than that would have been logistically daunting and cost-prohibitive. (Years later, as a computer game designer, I would come to appreciate the exponential complexity introduced by choice.) In the projection room, two perfectly synchronized movies were running—one showing the action caused by each *Yes* vote, the other showing the action caused by a *No*. The projectionist would simply put a lens cap over the projector to obscure the road not taken at each given juncture. The on-screen action never actually stopped and then began anew as if we, the audience, were inventing what would happen next. Those moments of frozen time were just a filmed static image, hundreds of frames of stillness exquisitely timed to contain the duration of each vote before the "live" action resumed.

As with the *Canada 67* movie, we felt like active participants. But we weren't, not really. We were still just consumers with illusions of our own agency.

And in these dark days dominated by dueling likes and hashtags, I wonder if like blind, cave-dwelling animals for whom sight no longer confers any survival benefit, our ability to take material action is becoming nothing more than the quaint vestige of a time when what we did actually mattered.

Our World (1967-2015)

I logged into my work email account today with the obligatory fourteen-character password containing at least one special character—@lluneedi$love. Then, as is my habit when goofing off at the office, I wiled away far too much time at wefeelfine.org, where brightly colored circles and dots swirl around like confetti. Click on one and you'll see a randomly selected phrase that someone, somewhere, has just written about their inner state. *I feel like I am falling into a lie*, someone posted six minutes ago, at the same time that someone else wrote *I feel closer to my heavenly father who knows the end from the beginning*. I can spend hours exploring the postings lying behind the pink or yellow dots, the green or blue squares. *I mentioned to him at some point that perhaps when you couldn't see it, you felt more separation anxiety*, reveals one. *I feel like a mime because I am trying to bridge the language gap*, says another.

You can see why I do this, right? The posts are so voluminous and so profoundly serendipitous, that like the Kabbalist who believes that the voice of God could be finally understood if *pi* was calculated to the last digit, I keep clicking and clicking, hoping that some pattern will eventually reveal itself. That's completely irrational, of course. Even if there is an underlying connection, it's unlikely to be made visible in a random aggregation of postings, some of which are made simply because *I feel like I have nothing to do*. But the hunger driving me isn't irrational. It's programmed, this search for affinity, as hard-wired as our ability to sniff out pheromones or detect snakes.

Growing up, I knew what community meant. My parents, first-generation Jewish Anglos who came of age during WWII in a city of French Catholics, transmitted both their knowledge of clan and their hunger to break free of it as ineluctably as their genes for crowded jaws and thick hearts. I entered my teens in 1967, during the Summer of Love, and my tribe comprised what felt like an entire generation whose common convictions would, we were sure, stop war and remake the world.

But sometime early in this twenty-first century, I lost sight of the difference between a crowd and a community, and between simultaneity and an actual shared experience. The millions of people whose status updates float into my line of sight on wefeelfine.org are taking simultaneous action, but the sheer volume and velocity of these expressions almost ensures that nobody is undergoing a common experience.

Ironically, this disconnected digital concurrency had its roots in what was probably the largest shared encounter in modern history. In June of 1967, the first live satellite-enabled television broadcast was aired. Roughly ten thousand technicians and producers worldwide not only wrote scripts and shot footage, but coordinated transmission among four satellites across the International Date Line. Over 1.5 million kilometers of cable were used to quite literally link up the planet and enable the broadcast of *Our World*, a three-hour aggregation of short, wide-ranging documentary segments, to thirty-one countries.

I'd made a mental note to investigate *Our World* after hearing a radio clip about it, thinking it a nice bit of cultural adornment that I could weave into a story sometime. Then recently, having gone online to win a debate with my husband about some obscure bit of pop music trivia, I came across a clip from the broadcast. It was The Beatles singing "All You Need is Love." I didn't love that song when it came out. But watching this performance, I found myself close to tears, moved by its goofy self-consciousness and absence of cynicism. I started googling, and after much searching, I was finally able to get a copy of the show in its entirety.

The ground rules that the *Our World* producers set for all participating countries were few and clear. No politicians or heads of state could be involved or featured, and all material was to be presented live, not pre-recorded. Each country would have its own

50

announcers, and translators would provide voice-over for the native audio when not in a country's native language.

I was thirteen when the broadcast occurred, in a year of big historical events and cultural milestones—the seminal Monterey Pop Festival, the Summer of Love in San Francisco, and the Expo '67 World's Fair in Montreal. But the entire effort was nearly derailed four days before the June 25 broadcast when, in an act of protest against Western coverage of the Six-Day War in the Middle East, the Eastern Bloc countries—the Soviet Union, East Germany, Hungary, Poland, and Czechoslovakia—withdrew from the effort, taking their crews and one of the four communications satellites with them.

The transformative nature of that war, the festering and spreading impact it would have on peoples, ideologies, and governments for the indefinite future, was obscured by its speed. But in speed, in near simultaneity of experience, the show's producers saw the potential for unity. Dismissing the Soviet complaints as a piece of "vintage Cold War rhetoric," *Our World's* American anchor, Paul Nevins gravely voiced the team's vision. "For the moment we're going to ignore our differences and focus on what we have in common," he declared in the U.S. introduction to the worldwide broadcast, as maps of the continents were linked by curving, glowing lines on screen. " ...For we are, in a sense, electronic Magellans, on an exploration without precedent."

With those words, the simulcast began.

Watching the opening to *Our World* now, it seems like a frantic, crowdsourced video collage. In grainy grayness, fountains spurt, geysers spew, volcanoes erupt, and the Vienna Boys Choir sings as the phrase "Our World" appears in dozens of languages, one at a time, then dissolves.

The sequence ends as abruptly as it started, and suddenly we are looking at a pastiche of pedestrian scenes from around the world, in real time. We're in Linz, Austria, watching steel workers steer something indistinct into something equally indistinct, but fiery. Then we're in a traffic helicopter, flying over Paris at dawn, while a barely audible male voice, muttering like a demented golf announcer, comments on the sparse traffic down below. Then we move yet again, this time to a narrow street in Tunis clogged with shoppers. The montage continues—a snippet of fishermen off the coast of Huelva, Spain; the exterior of a house in Glassboro, New Jersey; a farm in Ghost Lake, Alberta; a sparsely populated beach in Vancouver; a tunnel in Tokyo.

It strikes me that this choice of scenes was driven by the laudable trust that the mundane habits and sights that bore us at best in our own daily lives will somehow be invested with greater meaning when we see them occurring in someone else's, continents away. "People are people," the producers seemed to be saying. "We all go to work, raise children, enjoy a day at the beach, get stuck in traffic." By hop-scotching through time zones, by showing the daily routines as they actually occurred, they hoped that they could break through non-temporal boundaries as well.

The three-hour show consisted of an aggregation of short, wide-ranging segments grouped into five major themes. "This Moment's World" panned the planet showing babies who had just been born, literally making their first entry into our world. "World Hunger and Overcrowding" examined the challenges these children were likely to encounter as they grew, featuring a diverse set of civil and social engineering projects—from shrimp farms to planned communities—intended to address them. In an earnest celebration of human potential, the next two sections, "Aspirations of Excellence" and "Artistic Skill," displayed athletes and famous dancers and musicians training, racing, rehearsing, and performing. The final portion, "The World Beyond," returned to the lofty ambitions of the opening proclamations about the show's purpose, featuring the scientists and technicians leading the efforts to explore outer space.

It showcased giants of the twentieth-century art world—people like Calder and Miro, whose legacies have endured. And it showed ordinary and anonymous people—Japanese subway workers and Canadian cattle farmers, Spanish fishermen and Australian ticket-takers, Swedish rowers and Mexican dancers—people whose daily lives were fundamentally no different from those of the people watching them.

For the artists, technicians, and journalists involved in its making, *Our World* was not only a technical marvel, but a social elixir. Narrative voice-overs between the show's segments offered urgent expositions of humanity's challenges, framed in hopeful explanations of how technology would help us address them. *Our World* was to be the pixelated proof that through the efforts of "ingenious men on five continents," led by educated humanists, mankind could transcend its political divisions and enlightened liberalism could harness our efforts to the greater good.

An estimated 400 million people watched *Our World*, the largest television audience to that date. But more significantly, this was probably also the broadest and most concurrent experience of any sort in human history. Other natural events—climate changes, epidemics, and wars—had a much more profound impact, but they unfolded much more gradually over time. Multinational and democratic, *Our World* represented the birth of what media scholar Marshall McLuhan dubbed, "the global village." He believed that the simultaneity enabled by this technology would create empathy and mutual responsibility between peoples and cultures.[8]

The rational progress envisioned by the show's producers and participants wasn't immediately realized. The show aired on the cusp between two transformative years. In 1967, idealism and technology briefly merged to stoke the belief that through large-scale, electronically enabled experiences, humanity would finally understand that we shared a single, sprawling but unsteady home, and join together to remodel it.

But if 1967 was a year infused with promise and hope, 1968 was its opposite. Martin Luther King and Bobby Kennedy were assassinated, the police riots at the Chicago Convention went unpunished, and the flares of freedom in Czechoslovakia were doused with dispatch by Soviet tanks. In 1968, after peaceful protest was met with violence and the embodiments of hope were literally shot down, many of us sighed, brooded, grew up, and channeled all that hope into building happy little homes.

It's always fascinating to look into the past at projections of the future, exploring which prophecies were and weren't realized, and why. Some of the *Our World* segments—such as an overhead view of the morning commute in Paris or a brief glimpse of Austrian steel workers on the job—were mundane. Others, though—such as an in-depth look at Habitat and Cumbernauld, two large, planned communities that exist to this day—offered bold predictions that didn't pan out. Some of the musicians featured—people like Leonard Bernstein and The Beatles—have legacies that are not only extraordinary in their own right, but that informed and reflected the times they lived in. Others, though, like the long-forgotten stars of Zeffirelli's *Romeo and Juliet,* had careers that flared and then fizzled over the course of mere months.

And yet look around. McLuhan's 1967 vision of an electronically enabled global village, one where signs of suffering and calls to action are passed from person to person and nation to nation almost instantaneously, has finally come to fruition.

But corporations are making it happen, not governments, not journalists. As I write this, Facebook has just announced that it is sending up a satellite to beam broadband Internet access to sub-Saharan Africa. It will be sent up on a Falcon 9 rocket owned by SpaceX, Elon Musk's commercial space launch firm. Once in geostationary orbit, Facebook's satellite will be operated by Eutelsat, an international communications company that already manages thirty-nine other satellites for media and telecommunications companies. And Facebook isn't relying just on satellites. In May 2014 the company bought Ascenta, a British maker of high-altitude, unmanned, solar-powered drones capable of beaming Internet access to suburban and urban areas.

Are these examples of visionary entrepreneurs stepping in to meet the human needs ignored by lumbering, self-serving government bureaucracies? Or are Mark Zuckerberg, Elon Musk, and their Silicon Valley buddies motivated by purely commercial aspirations as they seize first-mover advantage, making the land grab that will leave media-addicted consumers (increasingly fearful of being left alone with our own thoughts) with no other dealers to turn to?

Are we at the gates of the digital Promised Land? Or are we exiles wandering in the desert with only tweeting Kardashians for company?

The answer is both. We are alone in crowds, straining for a tenuous connection with others through our relentlessly tapping thumbs. But the Internet also enables us to create a sense of community—however transient and illusory, sometimes through expressions of sympathy and support, more often through the exposure and humiliation of others. We use social media to both exercise and condemn our most anti-social impulses.

"We shape our tools and thereafter our tools shape us," explained McLuhan's friend and colleague, Father John Culkin.[9]

One way they've shaped us is to confuse simultaneity with shared experience. Yes, we can now digitally display our meals and vacations, and the far more significant sights and sounds of war and mass migration, to our friends or the world at large. Imagination, empathy, and electronic imagery are now inextricably braided. Still, as each of us looks down at our personal device, we weaken the capacity to empathize that is generated largely by live, oral, interpersonal conversation. We lose sight of the fact that we're all occupying one subway car, the same sprawling city. Balkanized and personally branded, we can too easily forget that we're all on this, our only planet, together.

As a child of the 60s, my sense of connection was almost tactile. Many of the most moving and transformative experiences of my life were spent in large groups of people. In protests and marches and music festivals, I found not just emotional but sensory validation that beyond my immediate circle of friends and family, I belonged to a tribe, one organically formed out of experiences that were literally shared.

I'm not just being nostalgic. We weren't stupid to value communality. Society's refusal to acknowledge that we're on this gorgeous, faltering planet together has enabled the climate change that will demand radical, unwelcome adjustments in how we legislate and live. No community has gates impermeable enough to shield the lucky few from the pain of collapsing ice shelves and mass migrations. But mobilizing and sustaining the necessary fight for social and political overhaul requires a sense of "we," demands physical gatherings and raised collective voices. Movements are not made of "likes," but of actual people coming together as a corporeal whole.

As early as 1967, McLuhan recognized that the boundary between active engagement and consumption was beginning to blur. In June of that year, as he helped to introduce *Our World*, his newest book had just been released. A typo on its cover reportedly delighted him. Mistakenly titled *The Medium is the Massage*, the collection of photographic collages, brief and cryptic pages, pages printed backwards and meant to be read in a mirror, even pages left intentionally blank, fascinated me. I had no idea what it meant, and I suspect that even many of its adult readers, like my parents, didn't either. With its bold and demanding design, the book was undoubtedly cool.

But its herky-jerky vitality belied its meaning. McLuhan was not offering a celebration, but a warning. In 1962, he argued that electronic technologies are an extension of the human central nervous system, that "instead of tending towards a vast Alexandrian library the world has become a computer, an electronic brain... And as our senses have gone outside us, Big Brother goes inside." His uncanny predictions couldn't be understood until the changes he anticipated actually came to pass. And when they did, anyone living in the developed world in the twenty-first century couldn't help but agree with his dire prognosis.

I sometimes think of 1967 and *Our World* as representing the fulcrum between *before* and *after*. But on good days, I think that perhaps it is also a story about *still*, not just about the flare-up and extinction of idealistic energy, but also about its gestation, and the speed at which it travels through time and culture. On good days, I start to believe that what I remember isn't over.

The compromises that adults make cause much of the suffering in the world, or, at best, fail to deal with the suffering. Acceptance of one's lot—maintaining a silence about what can't be said, lowering your expectations for your own life and for others, and understanding that nothing about the way the world works will never change—is the very marrow of maturity, and no wonder the newly fledged children look at it with horror and know that it won't happen to them—or turn their backs on it for fear it will.

- Jenny Diski, The Sixties[10]

More Love (1967)

The one segment of the *Our World* broadcast that endures on YouTube is the one that makes me cry now.

A camera swoops down and in over the backs of trumpeters and trombonists playing the stirring opening strains of *"La Marseillaise,"* pauses for a second-long medium shot of three men on stools, then zooms in on the still-angelic face of Paul McCartney, headphones on his ears, crooning, "Love, love, love" in an earnest falsetto into his tootsie-pop microphone, strumming his upside down bass.

"Nothing you can do, but you can learn how to be you in time. It's easy," John Lennon sings. He is wearing an ornate, brocaded Sergeant Pepper jacket and jeweled barrette planted on his forehead like a third eye. "All you need is love."

A bouquet of balloons in the corner of the studio strains to break free of its leash. The studio floor is drizzled with flower petals, and seated on the floor around the lads is a Who's Who of English rock and roll—Keith Moon, Mick Jagger, Marianne Faithful, Graham Nash, and others, heads bobbing, singing along. Paul, legs crossed and bouncing, seems to single-handedly propel the formally clad orchestra musicians, muscling through their parts as though they were playing Stravinsky. And behind them all, Ringo, resplendent in a silk Indian coat, placidly lays down the simplest of beats. Incongruously, in the pause between lyrical lines, all but George appear to be chewing gum

As the tune progresses, John, Paul, and George can't help but exchange smiles. What they are doing is so surpassingly fun. At the end of the song, as the orchestra plays a snatch of "Greensleeves," a small group of festively festooned luminaries enter the studio wearing sandwich boards, extolling *Love, L'amour, Liebe,* любовь. A burst of confetti rains down from the ceiling.

This broadcast, this song, effectively inaugurated the Summer of Love in San Francisco, six months after the Human Be-In event in Golden Gate Park had announced that there could be a new way to live. That thirty-thousand person "Gathering of the Tribes" had danced, smoked, swayed, chanted, and exhorted one another into the conviction that we didn't need to revolt, or even persuade, that we could instead simply come together and live in a different way, alongside but against the prevailing culture. Inspired by that event, a volunteer group of anarchists who called themselves The Diggers collected unused and discarded food from markets and restaurants, then gave it out; the founders of the Free Store did the same for clothes, shoes, sofas, and plates. For a heady few months—before the tourists and the professional hippy merchandise vendors, before the exploited runaways and drug-seeking addicts clogged Haight-Ashbury—it seemed stunningly simple and clear to many that it was true, that really all we needed was love, and the rest would take care of itself.

In 1967, three weeks after the *Our World* broadcast, I sat on a bench in the rec shed of the Shaker Village Work Group, a highly non-traditional summer camp, where a town meeting had been convened to decide what to do about Eric. Separated from his Scarsdale drug dealer and desperate to get high, Eric had astonishingly chosen to believe another kid's assurance that if you took enough of it, you could get stoned on Midol.

Crampless but buzzless, with nothing to show for his novel experiment but extreme nausea, Eric now hunched over, peering anxiously out from under a cascade of wavy red hair, waiting for his fellow campers—about sixty other thirteen- to fifteen-year-olds—to decide whether to send him home for violating the no-drug policy, or to give him another chance.

"This isn't about the rules, man," one of the staff said. "It's about the bigger mission of the group. It's about not being busted or shut down."

"He took Midol, man," Jon drawled. In his orange bell bottoms, a paisley shirt, and dark granny glasses, he was conspicuously cool, and a good six inches taller than all the other boys his age. "The Staties aren't going to barge in here just because some guy took chick pills." Jon would later become one of the founding members of the Glam-Rock band, Twisted Sister, where his fashion sense and simple, bombastic guitar playing would be richly rewarded.

"Yeah, but this place is about acting in the greater good. Getting high—I mean people should have the right to do what they want…" Amy, freckled and earnest in her Indian print blouse, began to falter. "But getting high is against the rules—I mean not because they're rules, but just because well, you know, technically it's illegal or something…" She finally summoned her thought. "I'm just saying we're here to prove there's a different way to be, you know? Not so individualistic or something."

Of course it was a foregone conclusion that we'd allow Eric to stay. His public humiliation was punishment enough. And besides, probably half the people in that room had smoked the innocuous herbal mix called Shaker Tea by then, in a similarly hopeful but futile quest.

Investing a community of adolescents with this kind of decision-making authority was one of many features of this experiment in temporary utopia, one that began on the heels of World War II. In 1946, a labor lawyer, Jerry Count, and his wife, Sybil, bought the land and buildings occupied by the rapidly dwindling community of Shakers living on Mount Lebanon, New York, just over the Massachusetts state line, in the heart of the Berkshire Mountains. A year later, they opened the Shaker Village Work Group on the property.

On the surface, an aging New York lawyer and his chain-smoking English wife were an unlikely pair to preside over a camp of about two hundred white hippies and black urban refugees, and in the latter half of the 1960s, the Shakers were an unlikely choice of role model. But while their celibacy and religious ecstasy were lacking in "relevance" (that quality teenagers in the late 1960s cherished most), many elements of their philosophy and life style had a distinctly counter-cultural quality.

Jerry and Sybil's vision was to update and enact many of these values in the new Shaker Village. It would function as a democratic, egalitarian community, and use the full tuition payments of some to finance the scholarships of many others. While the program would allow time for recreation and relaxation, we were there to work—maintaining and improving the property, growing food, and producing items to sell in the crafts store to visiting tourists.

Though I didn't know his exact age, to my adolescent eyes, Jerry Count was old. He had white hair that shot straight up like tender leeks, and wore a lumpy red cardigan sweater regardless of the temperature. He had come of age with the Russian Revolution, and drew his inspiration for Shaker Village from a seemingly disparate set of sources—from the work camps established by the Civilian Public Service during World War II to provide conscientious objectors with an alternative to military service, to the United Society of Believers in Christ's Second Appearing, or "Shakers," themselves.

Every Monday through Saturday morning, Jerry would lead a meeting on the lawn in front of the old Shaker chair factory. Dazed by daylight, some of us breakfasting on single-serving boxes of Frosted Flakes, we'd sit cross-legged on the grass as Jerry or our villager-elected Mayor made announcements and then tried to engage us in a discussion of something that mattered. Often it was a matter of Village policy. Should people be allowed to smoke cigarettes anywhere on the premises? Was it improper for us to buy our own products, the boxes and oven mitt holders and brooms we'd made, from the crafts store?

Jerry didn't say much during those meetings, but stood stock still, hands in pockets, listening intently. And when he did speak, it was usually to share some insight from Prince Peter Kropotkin, the nineteenth-century Russian anarcho-syndicalist who was his intellectual idol, and apply it to the most mundane of matters. "In *Mutual Aid: A Factor in Evolution*, Kropotkin argued that it was an evolutionary emphasis on cooperation, not competition, that enabled all species, including the human species, to thrive," he'd say as casually as if sharing the score of the previous night's Yankees game. "So as you formulate your strategies in Capture the Flag tonight, you may want to bear that in mind."

Just before we embarked on the annual blueberry harvest, Jerry would hold up a berry-filled branch he'd snagged from one of the bushes that surrounded the village, then, with the relish of a gourmet shucking a fresh oyster, demonstrate how to pluck the berry and drop it into a metal milk bucket without damage to either the tender blue sphere or its branch. "You've got to be careful," he'd warn us cheerily. "Blueberries are a renewable resource that supports almost all of our jam production. And that's important. After all, as Kropotkin always said, 'Local production obviates the need for central government.'"

I'd ended up at the Village largely by accident. My parents, now both graduate students, had no money to send my brother and me to summer camp. But they both devoutly believed that summers in the country were as essential to our wellbeing as food and polio vaccines, so every year my mother cobbled together enough camp sessions and visits to friends and relatives with country homes to ensure that we got at least some mosquito bites, campfires, and dawn swims in bracing mountain waters. That year, while scouring the classifieds in the *Saturday Review* magazine, my mother had found an ad for Shaker Village indicating that they granted scholarships. That was all she needed to know.

Two months later I found myself side by side with middle-class Jewish hippies from Long Island and working class black kids from

Detroit and the Bronx, learning to can and to weave, though few of my bunched and skewed place mats made their way to the store to be sold next to books, sachets, and Shaker paraphernalia. I learned to dig potatoes and pick beans and milk a cow—horrified and thrilled by the sensation of wringing each long teat, the warmth of the watery milk shooting out, the torrential sound it made as it hit the base of the metal bucket. I learned to craft Shaker brooms and boxes—gleaming oval baskets with slender, dovetailed joints, held together by glue and wooden tacks—to make jam from the strawberries and blueberries we picked at the start and end of summer, and can Bread-and-Butter pickles. And, because paid tours and craft store sales helped subsidize the program, I learned enough about Shaker history to escort visiting tourists around the South Family village.

"The Shakers were founded by a woman, Mother Ann Lee," I told my small party one afternoon, a collection of middle-aged socks-and-sandals-clad refugees from New York City, who had come to the Berkshires for cooler air and culture. "She came here in 1774 with eight of her followers and began to preach. She was fleeing a violent husband in England, and perhaps that helps to explain her belief in celibacy." Young and involuntarily celibate as I was, I smirked a little when I said this. "Mother Ann Lee also believed in equality of the sexes. Every village, or 'family,' was led by an Elder and an Eldress, and they had equal authority." I did not smirk when I said this. Other than Golda Meir, I'd never seen any woman besides a teacher in a position of power.

"You hear that, Hal?" a blonde woman muttered to her husband. "*Equal* authority."

"Why not?" he answered with expansive geniality and a broad shrug. "We're already celibate."

While tour guide, with its transient authority, was one of my favorite jobs, that wasn't what made Shaker Village a keystone in my life, even now. It wasn't the Shakers' invention of the clothespin or the broom, or the fact that the Shakers were the first to sell seeds in paper packages that excited me. No, what mattered is that they were pacifists. *More love*, went one of the Shaker hymns we learned to sing. "More love, the heavens are blessing, the angels are calling, Oh Zion, more love." Self-sufficient men and women, the Shakers found righteousness in peace, succor in work, togetherness in song, and ecstasy in dance. And in 1967, we aspired to do the same.

I hadn't known that the summer had an official name until one afternoon I read a three-month-old newspaper that I was using to wrap ceramic cups in the gift store. The article quoted an April press conference held by The Council for the Summer of Love. An amalgamation of people from an anarchist group, an underground theatre company, the *San Francisco Oracle* underground paper, and about twenty-five other locals, The Council had been formed to prepare for the anticipated rush of runaways, hippies, and seekers expected to descend on the city once school let out. Working with churches, food banks, and doctors, they tried to create a Haight Ashbury infrastructure that would support the imminent population explosion. Of course I had no appreciation for their practicality, only for their rhetoric. "This summer," they declared, "the youth of the world are making a holy pilgrimage to our city, to affirm and celebrate a new spiritual dawn....This city is not a wasteland; our children will not discover drought and famine here. This city is alive, human and divine..."[11]

On the day that I read this, Gray Line Bus tours began their Haight-Ashbury District Hippy Hop tour, "the only foreign tour within the continental United States." That irony was not lost on my friends and me as we sat outside the craft store three thousand miles away, waiting for tourists of our own to guide, intently leafing through *Life* magazine's gaudy photos and *Time*'s breathless dispatches from San Francisco.

The July 7, 1967 cover of *Time* magazine featured a psychedelic picture of musicians—what looked like an amalgam of Jefferson Airplane's Paul Kantner and Gracie Slick, Joni Mitchell, and some grinning guy in paisley who could have been Dennis Hopper—amid swirling flowers and swooshes in purple, blue, and gold. "The

Hippies: Philosophy of a Subculture" read the angled banner at the top right.

"Hippies preach altruism and mysticism, honesty, joy and nonviolence," the cover story explained. "They find an almost childish fascination in beads, blossoms and bells, blinding strobe lights and ear-shattering music, exotic clothing and erotic slogans. Their professed aim is nothing less than the subversion of Western society by 'flower power' and force of example. Although that sounds like a pipe-dream, it conveys the unreality that permeates hippiedom, a cult whose mystique derives essentially from the influence of hallucinogenic drugs."[12]

With its translations of common hippie words and phrases, the article read like a parody: "Though hippies consider any sort of arithmetic a 'down trip,' or boring, their own estimate of their nationwide number runs to some three hundred thousand.... They feel 'up tight' (tense and frightened) about many disparate things—from sex to the draft, college grades to thermonuclear war."

Even reading it today, I find myself taking umbrage at its patronizing dismissal of "the unreality that permeates hippiedom." Not everyone who aspired to those values was a devotee of hallucinogenic drugs. (Idealistic but fundamentally timid, I certainly wasn't at the age of fourteen, or ever.) While some kids—too many—ran away from home or dropped out of school and ended up sleeping in doorways in Haight Ashbury or St. Mark's Place that summer, most of my peers went where our parents sent us, and at least went through the motions of leading the lives we were supposed to lead. Like tourists on the Hippy Hop bus, we were in some respects just passing through, acquiring the tchotchkes of hippiedom while keeping a safe distance from it. But just as one visit to Paris or one swim in a still black lake on a moonlit night is enough to lodge itself in your heart forever, the hippy ethos penetrated us like sunlight, coloring our skin and making our bones stronger.

What I remember best is dancing—not the stomping but geometrically pristine Shaker dances that we'd re-create on parents' night—but the nights in the barn when we'd get to dance to our music. Though it hadn't been used as a barn for decades, the sweet-scented warmth of horses and hay had infiltrated every dry-aged board. Simply standing in that sun-bleached and listing structure, I felt the tender attention of past generations. Dancing, I felt that I was channeling their energy, mingling it with ours. We'd sway to "Lucy in the Sky with Diamonds" and ruminate over the lyrics ("It's clearly about LSD, man."). We'd shout with The Chambers Brothers —"Time, time, time!"—our voices fusing and frenzied, delirious with possibility, and close out the night with The Doors. The songs started slyly, with a sexy wink and grind from Jim Morrison to the mass of gyrating youth in the stunned and creaky old barn. Ray Manzarek's organ, compressed and insinuating, squeezed out the notes as we belted out the words: "We want the world and we want it...now."[13]

Dropping out, simply establishing a parallel, self-contained society of just and peaceful people, seemed possible. It wasn't even a stretch to imagine it. That we were living in a worthy and self-directed community of teenagers seemed not so much unusual as simply *appropriate*.

The fact that this was just a summer, one that our parents had paid or borrowed or applied for, was lost on us. We were young, as naive as we thought we were worldly. At least most of us were.

There was one camper at Shaker Village in 1967 who wasn't in the least bit naive. Then fifteen years old, Ben Chaney was a celebrity of sorts. His older brother, James, had disappeared in 1964 while en route from Philadelphia, Mississippi, to the town of Meridian, along with two white Freedom Riders from New York City who had gone South for the summer to help register black voters. Their families raised a ruckus, and when the FBI finally found the bodies of James Chaney, Michael Schwerner, and Andrew Goodman in an earthen dam forty-four days later—pistol-whipped, mutilated, and shot—the press descended on Meridian, the Chaneys' hometown, to cover the funeral.

Nine years younger than James, Ben had idolized his older brother. And for good reason—James had been like a father to him, and brought him along as he organized prospective black voters in the weeks leading up to the Freedom Summer. When twelve-year-old Ben had himself been arrested for demonstrating for civil rights, it was James who had obtained his release. In an interview over forty years later, Ben would say of James, "He treated me like *I* was a hero."[14]

I'd seen the picture of Ben that had been taken on August 7, 1964—the day of his brother's funeral. His mother, wearing a black straw hat and black veil that covers her downcast face like chicken wire, cups Ben's temple, holding his head to her chest. His white shirt collar is brilliant; it seems to illuminate his face and make the tears on his cheek glisten. He looks like the child he was, grieving and haunted.

Soon after the funeral, Ben's family began to receive death threats. The Goodman and Schwerner families raised money among their network of friends, family, and supporters in New York City, and their financial support enabled the Chaneys to flee the South. By the time I met him, Ben lived in New York and attended the predominantly white Waldorf School as the first recipient of the Andrew Goodman Memorial Scholarship. With the aid of well-wishing benefactors, he was spending his summer in a similar milieu at Shaker Village.

He didn't say much about his history, at least not to me, and I didn't know how to initiate that conversation. I was intimidated by his celebrity, by the horror in his life that had earned it.

Of course my female friends and I talked endlessly about him. We talked endlessly about all the boys—the ones we liked, the ones who liked us, the ones we'd made out with in the woods the night before.

"So after he felt me up, Howie told me to start shaving my legs," Michelle said as she brushed out her curly blonde hair in preparation for straightening.

"What did you tell him?" Ruth asked. She licked her finger then quickly touched the flat of the iron she was about to apply to Michelle's hair.

"I told him he was a sexist piglet. I said, 'I'll shave mine when you shave yours,'" she answered from behind the curtain of hair that now fell in front of her face. Then, arms akimbo, she bent over and carefully touched her head to the edge of the ironing board.

Ruth fanned Michelle's hair out, then laid a damp towel over it. "I bet he didn't tell you to start wearing a bra." She firmly swiped the iron just inches from Michelle's forehead. "Assuming he noticed."

"Oh, he noticed," came Michelle's muffled response.

Ben probably figured into one of those conversations. By the end of the summer, practically every boy there did. I know we danced together in the Rec Hall and played with the camp cook's mangy dog—a bandana-clad mutt that softened Ben's raucous, angry laugh. But my most vivid image of him is silent. He is on one side of the dirt road that led up to the Village, at the edge of the meadow where I liked to sit and dream. He is wearing his usual outfit—blue jeans and a bright white T-shirt—smoking a cigarette. He stands apart as we congregate on the other side of the road. I sense the gap between us; I *see* it, but don't know how to bridge it. Nothing in my experience equips me to make sense of his.

As the FBI investigators dredged rivers in their search for the missing men back in 1964, they found the bodies of other black men and women who had been murdered. These were the unnamed, uncelebrated victims of racist violence. They were not icons. Most of us knew nothing of them.

But Ben did. I recently found another picture of him taken on the day of his brother's funeral, one that *Life* magazine chose not to run.[15] The Chaney family is in the limousine that would carry them to the cemetery. His parents sit in the front seat, gazing out the front window, their faces sober and empty, depleted. Ben's three older sisters sit in the back seat, looking straight ahead. But Ben, perched in the corner of the back seat, his head disproportionately large as it juts out over his slender torso, stares directly at the camera. His face is hard to read, as if he is looking inward and out well beyond the lens at the same time. He seems to be looking into the future, and it is bleak.

Ben didn't return to Shaker Village in 1968, and by 1970 he had joined the Black Panther Party in New York City. That spring, on the way home from a trip to Florida with two New York friends, Ben was arrested in South Carolina and charged with four first-degree murders and other crimes in three Deep South states. All the alleged murder victims were white, and Ben faced the death penalty in the electric chair.

Hearing about his arrest at the time, I felt unsurprised, and ashamed of that fact.

While he had been present when the murders took place, Ben was found innocent of murder.

He did his prison time once again back in the South. A newspaper photo from this time shows him standing in a cell, still wearing blue jeans and a bright white T-shirt. His face is in shadow, bifurcated by bars. He has a sparse mustache and his hand, hanging by his side, is holding a cigarette. His eyes, pained but alight, seem to be saying *Of course.*

I recently discovered a Shaker Village alumni group on Facebook, where someone posted a photo from my second year there, the summer of 1968. About 120 of us are arrayed on the ground in front of the old chair factory, the largest building on the property. Built into the hillside, the building now housed a dirt-floored theatre for camp-wide meetings and movies, and above it, workshops for weaving, caning Shaker chairs, candle-making, and building Shaker baskets. Evenly spaced windows checkered the front of the building, flooding the workshops with natural light and making the wide wooden floorboards gleam like honey.

In the black and white group portrait, most of the kids are smiling, or at least not scowling. They wear T-shirts (without logos, as all

T-shirts were then), jeans, shorts, Indian blouses, flannel work shirts. Some wear sandals, some wear Beatles boots, but many are barefoot. There's Eric, one of the Bergen twins, all red curls and braces and pompousness to make up for being short. There's the guy whose name I forget with his arm around his girlfriend —the "it" couple, because he had enough facial hair to form a robust mustache, and she had him. David, with his cupid chin and hair broader than his narrow, army-jacket clad shoulders, looks frail and yearning, which is how I remember him. Four rows up, half cropped out of the picture, is one of the many Dans, dark and glum, in the ludicrously piped sweater he seemed never to take off, dutifully staring at the camera. His boyfriend, Zach—tall and willowy, with fair skin and curls like Byron and Dylan—must have been outside the camera's frame, because the two of them were never apart. Innocent and pining, it didn't occur to me then that they were anything other than best friends.

Standing in the back row is Michael Scala from New York, gangly and goofy behind his granny glasses and untucked button-down shirt. One hand rests on the tree next to him, the other holds up a sign. *Stop the War*, it says. He is unusually tall, towering over the other kids like Abe Lincoln, but he is smiling like Abe probably never did, with the open happiness of someone who has no reason to doubt that the world belongs to him and his friends, if not now, then soon.

I look for myself in the group photo. There is a girl with center-parted long, frizzy hair four rows up, two kids away from the blond guy with big lips who I think was called Charlie. Her head is tilted to the right, the way I'm told mine often is, and her expression is grave. She might be me.

From *The Berkshire Eagle*, August 8, 1968:

SHAKER VILLAGE PAIR ORGANIZING 'PEACE MARCH'

A pair of youngsters spending the summer at Shaker Village Work Group in New Lebanon, N.Y. have organized a "peace march" for Aug. 10 from 2:30 to 4:30 p.m. in Park Square.

Michael Scala, 16, and Julie Wittef, 15, claim they already have 300 marchers—200 from Shaker Village and another 100 from the Pittsfield area—and they are attempting to recruit more. A series of peace "vigils" in Park Square last winter and spring never drew much more than 100.

PURPOSE OF THE MARCH

The purpose of the march, Scala said, is "to protest the amount of money being spent in Vietnam in view of the domestic problems that we still have in the U.S." The protesters, he said, will carry signs stating their point of view. Yesterday, the group started putting up silk-screened posters in store windows and libraries in an attempt to drum up more interest in the march. The youngsters and the adult staff members live in a communal society. Each person has one vote.

In handwriting much larger and more legible than mine is today, I'd circled my misspelled name, underlined the final sentence of this article, and next to it, written *Stupid.*

Sitting cross-legged in the grass, Michael and I had crafted the text of our anti-war leaflet a few weeks before the march.

"We've got to educate people," I said. "They don't know that the Vietnamese don't want us there."

Michael lit an L&M and dragged deeply. "No, man. We've got to show them that we grok them."

"Grok?"

"Yeah, like in *Stranger in a Strange Land.*" I looked at him quizzically. "Wait, you're telling me you've never read that?"

"I've never read that."

He shook his head. "You're the one in need of an education. *Stranger in a Strange Land* is only, like, the greatest book of the twentieth century." He reached into his back pocket and pulled out a dog-eared paperback from under his work shirt. On the cover, a man and woman, both blond, nude, and shapely, stood in waist-high water. She looked heavenward, he to the side, as if alert to danger. Both were muscled, golden against an indigo sky. "It's about a guy raised on Mars, a human, who's raised by Martians after his astronaut parents die, and comes to earth as an adult and is, like, totally freaked out by how sexually uptight and war-like and fucked up we are."

"So what's…whatever that word was?"

"Grokking. To grok. It means to empathize, you know? To so thoroughly understand someone else that you become one with them." His heavily accented Long Island voice rose in excitement. "Like merging with the whole. No more individual identity, man. No more divisions. We're all one."

We're awl one, I repeated in my head, trying to mimic his pronunciation of vowels, so exotic and earthy at the same time.

We decided to frame our leaflet as a series of questions, seeking the tone that would be the perfect blend of rabble-rousing and respectful.

Why is the United States spending three million dollars an hour, half way around the world, when forty million people are impoverished here? we asked.

Why have over twenty thousand young men—American alone—died in this immoral war in a country that does not want our support?

The questions continued, seven of them spanning two columns, each headed by a giant question mark. And at the bottom of the leaflet, in its own carefully drawn box, was this entreaty:

We plead with you to give these matters your highest consideration and to pose questions to your friends, your community, and to yourself.

While I'm sure that the summer of 1968 held the same mix of farm work and folk arts and music as the summer of 1967, it seems to me that our sense of separation—even of the *possibility* of separation—from mainstream culture, had already dissolved. By August of 1968, buffeted by assassinations, police riots, escalated bombings in Vietnam, and Richard Nixon's campaign for president enveloped in the mantle of the "Silent Majority," we were feeling like trapped and frantic members of the society we had to change.

One morning in late August, in the last week of the summer

program, Jerry Count stood in front of us and held up the front page of the *New York Times*, dominated by two black-and-white photos. In one, a procession of tanks lined a cobblestoned street in Prague, empty except for a single taxi headed in the opposite direction. In the other, a young Czech man had leapt atop one of the tanks and legs spread, held up a flag as if leading a charge. On either side of the street, clusters of people stared, and behind them, thick smoke rose from an unseen fire.

In response to political reforms in Czechoslovakia and a surge of democratic stirrings during what had been dubbed the Prague Spring, the Soviets had enlisted their Warsaw Pact allies to join them in sending two hundred thousand troops and two thousand tanks into the country overnight. By the morning of August 21, 1968, Czechoslovakia was occupied.

I think it was sunny that morning. But no light glinted off of Jerry's wireframe glasses as he stood in front of us, huddled and mute. When he roused himself to speak, he used words like "travesty" and "unforgivable."

"Any state founded on authoritarianism—socialist or capitalist—will sow the seeds of its own collapse," he railed, jabbing the offending photographs with his finger. Then his arms just dropped to his sides, sagging in his puffy red cardigan. "But oh, the people it will take down along the way."

In November of that year, all of the summer's villagers got a letter notifying us of Jerry's passing. The newspaper obituary it included spoke only of his "sudden death," and made no mention of the cause. There were rumors, never confirmed, that he'd committed suicide. As I would later feel upon reading about Ben Chaney's conviction, on hearing the news, I was sad but unsurprised.

Shaker Village Work Group closed for good in 1971, one of many physical communities, actual instantiations of utopian ideals, to come and go. But attempts to build them persist, and given both the swelling ranks of baby boomers and the emerging ethos at the time,

1967 was a banner year. That's when the planned city of Columbia, Maryland, opened, with a carefully designed layout of streets, schools, interfaith congregations, and stores on an intimate, pedestrian scale. Inherent in the plan was the belief that well-designed cities could improve not just an individual's quality of life, but promote racial, religious, and class integration.

One of the most earnest and dull segments of *Our World* is a profile of the newly opened Cumbernauld, a "visionary" town in Scotland, designed with a sunny, if unwarranted, faith in the power of enlightened civic engineering. The vision of Cumbernauld's designers was to replace urban squalor, pollution, and irrationality with a planned community in a pastoral setting, one that would eventually provide seventy thousand people with safety, fresh air, a self-sustainable economy, and, of course, accessible shopping.

But those ambitions feel very distant now as I watch a woman and her daughters traverse paved paths through Cumbernauld's empty courtyards, seemingly stranded in this still slumbering Brigadoon made of poured concrete and grand ideas. In the streaming gray video, this treeless new settlement looks barren and lonely, and I feel the aching gap between the longing for the ideal community and its sensible execution.

Cumbernauld still exists, though its pedestrian walkways became wind tunnels, and the development seems largely distinguished by having been the site of Britain's first indoor shopping mall and for having twice won the architecture magazine *Prospect*'s Carbuncle award for being the most dismal place in Scotland. Fast food restaurants abound there, and according to a BBC report, "When it won the Carbuncle award in 2001, judges compared Cumbernauld to Kabul and described its shopping centre as a rabbit warren on stilts."

Utopian ideals endure, even though every physical community erected to house them has eventually crumbled. Perhaps these are convictions that can't be constructed, only grown and carried from place to place, through time. What grew out of those last few summers at Shaker Village was organic and real, far more enduring in its impact than Cumbernauld. Though our physical congregation as a community—and as a generation—was transitory, the knowledge we acquired there sunk deep roots that have strengthened and spread. We know, and now our children know, that peace and cooperation are material and daily choices that we make. Utopia isn't built from the outside in, and it certainly can't be planned. It doesn't require great engineering minds, just verdant hearts.

As I try to summon up how I *felt* being there, what gets revived is the shocking carnality of my first French kiss, the energy stoked by being part of a group and feeling myself to be a pulsing cell in a larger organism, the completely unwarranted confidence in my own agency. What I remember from those summers is simply being an adolescent. But what I feel now is the continuity in conviction that is my past, pulling me like a tow line into my future.

Upon being released after thirteen years in prison, Ben Chaney went back to New York City and got a job as a paralegal for Ramsey Clark, the former Attorney General who had represented him at his trial. He created the James Earl Chaney Foundation, to promote voter registration and to maintain a memorial in Meridian to his brother, Schwerner, and Goodman. He gives speeches to young people about the need for nonviolent change. I'm guessing that he no longer smokes.

I've found one recent picture of him, part of a slide show of photos taken at the 2009 annual gala celebrating the life of Dr. Martin Luther King held by CORE, the venerable civil rights organization.[16] Ben and David Goodman, brother of Andrew, receive plaques in honor of the three slain men. They join a cast on the dais that includes the now ancient Delfonics singing "Lift Every Voice and Sing" and the USO Liberty Bells—three women looking like an integrated knock-off of The Andrews Sisters—singing the "The Star-Spangled Banner." Roy Innis, the Republican-leaning chairman of CORE, imposing and dapper, receives an award. Pat Boone, the now seventy-five-year-old white singer who made his fortune singing covers of R&B songs, the Christian icon who organized the first Beverly Hills Tea Party rally, emcees the event and shows a music video tribute to Dr. King. And in the audience in front of them are over two thousand well-heeled people, an even mix of black and white, clapping with what I imagine to be a mix of politeness and bafflement at this bizarre assembly.

But then comes the climax of the evening—a video greeting from President Obama. Once again, as so often happens lately when I look at the cultural kitsch of the recent past and present, I wonder why I'm laughing so derisively. I am, after all, looking at a photograph in which a group of old people who have led long lives full of pain and puzzlement are finally being addressed by a black man who is, after all, a president.

As at his brother's funeral, in this photograph Ben is wearing a crisp white shirt and a dark tie. Balding, in dark-framed glasses, he looks old beyond his years. His wildness is gone. He looks slight, almost diminutive. He and David Goodman stand side by side at the podium, comprising in their loss and their endurance, a community of two.

Aliens (1966-1968)

It was a bright, moonlit Sunday night on March 14, 1966, when Frank Mannor's dogs began barking frantically. Frank and his nineteen-year-old son, Ronnie, went outside their farmhouse to investigate. In the distance they saw lights and a faint red glow, "like a cigarette being smoked,"[17] and set off over the rolling farmland to investigate. Frank thought that perhaps a meteorite had crashed nearby, and hoped to find some fragments. Instead, what he and Ronnie saw hovering about eight feet above the swampy ground was an oval object about the length of a car, with a hump in the middle and a light at either end. Its surface was textured and rough, "like coral rock." As Frank and Ronnie got closer, the entire object glowed red. Then it went dark. When the pair got to the spot where they'd seen it, the object was gone.

Meanwhile, back in the house, Frank's wife, Leona, called the police department in nearby Dexter, Michigan. Three Dexter policemen and two Washtenaw County deputy sheriffs sped to the scene, along with dozens of nearby residents who'd heard about the sightings via the Mannors' eight-household party line.

I wish I could say that I remember hearing their sirens that night. I don't, but I could have from our house, halfway between the college town of Ann Arbor and the farming hamlet of Dexter.

Though Frank never saw the object take off, the policemen did. They reported that it made sweeps in the air about a thousand feet up—"like a pendulum," one said—its lights flashing, first white, then red. As it zipped through the sky, the witnesses described it as sounding like a ricocheting bullet, others like the keening of an ambulance. And most reported seeing three other similar objects join it, then all fly off in a tight formation. Washtenaw County Sheriff Doug Harvey ordered all available deputies to the scene. Six patrol cars, two men in each, and three detectives surrounded the area, and eventually chased a flying object along Island Lake Road without catching it.

At around 1:00 a.m., William Van Horn, a civil defense director, and dozens of students watched an object matching Mannors' description swoop, hover, and fly near the University of Michigan campus, a nearby airport and a local swamp. Starting at 3:50 a.m., the Washtenaw County's Sheriff's Department started getting calls from sheriff's deputies in Livingston and Monroe counties saying that they were seeing a formation of four flying objects diving, rising, and flying at fantastic speeds. The Livingston County officials were in turn receiving phone calls from local citizens reporting the same. The Monroe County officials called Selfridge Air Base, northeast of Detroit, and were told that they'd detected some objects over Lake St. Clair, but were unable to identify them. "The Air Base called Detroit Operations and were to call this Dept. back as to the disposition," the Washtenaw County Sheriff's Department log notes, but apparently no call ever came.[18]

For the next seven days, people saw these UFOs again in and around Dexter, Ann Arbor, and the small town of Milan, Michigan. Professor J. Allen Hynek, a Northwestern University astrophysicist who consulted with the military, was sent to Dexter to investigate. "He came into my office," Sheriff Doug Harvey recounted forty years later. "We went out to the site where supposedly this object came down on the ground. Dr. Hynek in the car said, 'There is something. We just can't put our finger on it. We've been investigating this for quite a while.'"[19]

After speaking with Frank and Robbie Mannors and tromping through the area where they claimed to have seen the object land, Hynek and Harvey returned to Harvey's office. Hynek went to a private room to make a phone call to Washington, D.C. When he emerged, his uncertainty had vanished.

"It's swamp gas," he announced.

Mannors was outraged. He'd been in the army in Louisiana, he said, and seen swamp gas often. This wasn't swamp gas. But Hynek stuck to his conclusion, and though there continued to be reports of UFO sightings in southeastern Michigan through the next two years, they became more infrequent and suspect.

Still, sitting on the damp grass on late spring nights in 1968, my first year of high school, my friends and I would scan the sky in a hopeful search for unearthly objects.

"Okay, so assuming there are intelligent beings out there, why in God's name would they come here?" Jeff asked. Though some mistook his tone for arrogance, Jeff was so much smarter than most people that he was just perpetually astonished at what came out of their mouths. "For the weather?"

"Maybe they're just being neighborly," Diana offered, "like Andy Griffith. You know, 'Howdy, friend. Welcome to the galaxy.'"

"Oh, so we should just open the door to the planet, invite them in, and offer them meatloaf?" I asked.

Diana looked at me in amazement. "Meatloaf?"

"Isn't that what you Americans eat? Okay, what, cookies? A beer?"

"Maybe they came to borrow some sugar," she mused.

"Or maybe they came to be taken to our leaders so they could haul their dumb, war-mongering asses to another planet." Though capable of humor, John rarely displayed it.

"Seriously, why would aliens come here, to this planet?" Jeff persevered. "For water? To take specimens?"

"Maybe we're the only intelligent life forms around, besides them," I offered.

"God, that's frightening."

"They're much more likely to be some new kind of low-flying bomber or surveillance plane." John, his deep voice at odds with his slight physique, doggedly stayed on track. "The kind of thing the government will never admit to."

"Spy-o-rama," Diana said. She'd recently taken to adding "o-rama" to a wide array of nouns and verbs. I thought she was incredibly witty.

"Maybe they've come to watch television?" Jeff offered.

John elaborated. "Maybe watching us is like watching television, like flipping between war movies and *Green Acres*."

Diana dreamily suggested, "Maybe they've come for a delicious Stuckey's Pecan Log Roll."

In Diana and Jeff and John, and a handful of other irreverent, and highly political kids, I'd finally found my people. We'd all come from somewhere else; none of us had lived in Ann Arbor for more than five years. We all deplored violence, hated the war, smoked just a little pot, scorned our dim and ancient teachers, mistrusted our young and "relevant" ones, and made damn sure to do well in school nonetheless. Jeff read Alan Watts, Diana read Borges, John read science fiction tomes, and I was enamored of Anais Nin. (Though I'm now the writer, they had much better taste.) And though it wasn't something any of us had aspired to, we'd been catapulted from outcast status in our respective junior highs to being the cool kids in high school.

My house, situated on a hill at the end of a dirt road outside of town, had become our default gathering spot, though "house" is an exaggeration. My parents and brother and I lived in the large finished basement of a home that an antique dealer, Leroy Darwin, had built for his wife, Mary Lou, just before divorcing her. She lived on the upper floor with their five-year-old daughter, Vicky Lou, whose name she pronounced "Vickaloo," as if she were an Indian dish. We had only one other house within sight, occupied by Lew and Judy and their daughter, Vicky Lynn, who was also five and could have been Vicky Lou's brown-eyed twin.

My mother had furnished the apartment with items bought at auction—a giant oak dining room table that doubled as a desk, a giant green leather wing-backed chair, a ramshackle wooden tea cart that my father repainted the color of a tired winter sky. Because the house was built into a hill, the basement had sliding glass doors in the living room, flanked by two life-size ceramic chickens. From the Turkish-print couch, we looked out on a lawn so large that Leroy had to mow it in his tractor. "Lawn," too, is a bit misleading. It was really just a sloping field with a giant uncultivated meadow to the right of it. The incline was so steep and the patch of trees at the base so dense that when my mother's 1963 Dodge Dart slipped out of gear, it rolled down the hill and was so thoroughly swallowed by the trees that she reported it stolen. The police came, but it was Leroy who discovered it several days later on his final pass across the lawn.

Forty miles from the Motor City, practically every high school kid with a license also had a car, and since neither of my parents got home until dinner time, my friends were there most days after school. With its rural setting and oddball décor, with its abundance of stereo equipment courtesy of my Uncle Herbie and the big starry sky outside, that house was the perfect incubator for our emerging sensibility. We were attuned to all that was ironic and all that was deplorable; we loved to ponder the Big Questions and to mock ourselves for doing so.

Our generally absentee landlord, Leroy, a wiry, belligerent guy, was an up-and-comer with the foresight to buy up big tracts of undeveloped land in anticipation of Ann Arbor's suburban sprawl. He made it clear at every opportunity that he hated Commie hippies, and our neighbor, Lew, was only slightly more tolerant of the long-haired, bell-bottomed peaceniks traipsing in and out of our house.

But their wives were curious. A farm girl from Dexter, now installed in her husbandless house on the hill and living on alimony payments whose generosity reflected Leroy's desire to show what a big man he was, Mary Lou seemed perpetually baffled about what she was supposed to do. Judy, a townie from Ann Arbor, was as down-to-earth as Mary Lou was dazed. Out in the sticks, stuck at home with Vicky Lou and Vicky Lynn all day, the two of them would whip up big batches of Snickerdoodle cookies and bring them to us as at dusk. They'd tap on the sliding glass doors when my friends and I were hanging out in the living room, then come in bearing mass quantities of deviled eggs on platters adorned with pastel-colored crepe paper. On weekends or late at night, they'd randomly offer us limp hot dogs in Wonder Bread buns. I realize now that they weren't much older than us, and perhaps a bit envious of…what? Our unencumbered state? Our knowledge? At times, it seemed what they really coveted was our certainty.

"The South Vietnamese people don't want us there," I'd explain. "This war is being fought for the benefit of Dow Chemical and Bank of America, not for us."

"Yeah, and the South Vietnamese government is a puppet regime. They've slaughtered thousands of their own people," John would elaborate.

Mary Lou would brush back her hair with a flour-coated hand, and look at us with wide gray eyes. "Really? That's terrible," she'd say, with exactly the same tone of genuine distress as if I'd told her that we were out of butter.

Judy was more skeptical. "Who gave you the inside scoop?" she'd ask between drags on her Virginia Slim cigarette. But she wouldn't listen to our answers; she was more interested in who was singing on that record we were listening to, or why Diana would want to leave Michigan for San Francisco, or how much a nickel bag of pot actually cost. She wasn't wowed by our worldliness, but she knew privilege when she saw it, and wanted to understand it better.

We already had a well-defined sense of *Us* and *Them* by the middle of our high school careers. Leroy, with his bristly crew cut and *America: Love it or Leave It* sticker emblazoned on the bumper of his Oldsmobile Cutlass, was *Them*. Sheriff Harvey, with his football player physique and practice of busting hippy panhandlers and cutting off their hair before releasing them from jail (or what the underground press referred to as "Harvey's Pigpen") the next morning, was *Them*. The farmers of Dexter, with their limp and faded American flags hanging over sagging porches and their lack of outrage at their own poverty—they were *Them*.

But our neighbors Mary Lou and Judy and the two Vickys in their tow-headed wildness were harder to silo. When Vicky Lou started first grade, Mary Lou decided to get out of the house. She enrolled in a poetry class at Washtenaw Community College, and took up with the professor who taught it. He was blind, but had once been sighted. His mass of curly hair and thick, droopy mustache seemed cultivated to resemble Kurt Vonnegut. Only the dark glasses derailed the overall look. Mary Lou took obvious delight in driving him around town with the top down on her rust-colored Mustang convertible. I'd babysit some nights so she could go out with him, and when they'd come home, she'd insist that I stay and have a glass of wine, then listen with a stillness that may have been fascination, but more likely sleepiness, as he and I talked about whether *Catch-22* was the new *Catcher in the Rye*. She was the only non-jerk in the kitchen on those nights.

Sometimes after Vicky Lou had gone to sleep, Mary Lou would join us as we lay on that vast mowed lawn, gazing up at the sky. And one night, our vigilance almost paid off. A bluish-white disc of light appeared on the horizon at around eight p.m., arcing upward until it was almost overhead, then dropping back down. At first we were mystified, then excited. But the dim and fuzzy light was just that—light—seemingly without mass. Bored within minutes, Jeff concluded that it couldn't be a UFO, so we went inside to drink hot chocolate and listen to the Paul Butterfield Blues Band. The ever-so-slight mystery of the light would be solved the next day when we learned that a new car dealer on Plymouth Road had set up a searchlight to attract people from the tri-county area to see the great new selection of 1969 Chevrolets for themselves.

I remember this specific car lot, because it was adjacent to Elias Brothers' Big Boy restaurant, a hamburger place that was very easy to find thanks to the thirty-foot tall statue in its parking lot of a big, apple-cheeked, blue-eyed boy with a bizarrely asymmetrical black pompadour. He wore red checkered shorts, suspenders, and a white T-shirt, and held aloft a plate containing three buns separated by hockey pucks meant to evoke hamburgers. "Home of the Original Double Decker" said the sign behind him. Four years earlier, my parents had left Montreal ahead of us to find and furnish our first apartment, and when my aunt, uncle, three cousins, brother, and I finally arrived in Ann Arbor after a ten-hour drive, this was the first landmark we saw. My carsick brother baptized our new home by violently retching at the Big Boy's feet, bestowing it with a symbolic value that I grasped even then.

"So what is a light year?" Mary Lou asked shyly one night.

"It's the distance that light travels in one year," Jeff promptly answered. "And since light moves incredibly fast—something like 186,000 miles per second—a light year is a really long way away, something like six trillion miles."

"They say UFOs come from places hundreds of light years away," Mary Lou continued. "How could aliens stay alive for the time it would take to get here?"

John had an answer. "One theory is that their spaceships are complete ecosystems where they can grow their own food and produce their own water and reproduce, for generation after generation."

"So they live their whole lives in a flying saucer?" Mary Lou asked.

"Sounds great, doesn't it?" Jeff laughed. "The same people, the same three meals, the same view out the porthole. 'Look! Stars!'"

"Snooze-o-rama," Diana offered.

"I dunno," Mary Lou said off-handedly. "Sounds like my life."

Though my friends and I looked for UFOs at the end of the 1960s, we were driven more by the casual desire for something new or cool than by real yearning. Life on earth was fascinating enough. We were insatiably interested in ourselves and each other, in music and connection and rebellion, in the big mysteries of existence as well as the smaller, local ones. A serial killer, for example, was raping and murdering brunettes in the area—a two-year period in which my parents were hyper-vigilant about my safety and I blissfully was not. Peter, the red-haired, really nice (and, I realize in retrospect, really gay) classmate seemed to want to go out with me one day, then not the next.

And under cover of darkness, somebody was cutting down Stuckey's billboards on the stretch of highway between Ann Arbor and Toledo, Ohio. Stuckeys—a restaurant chain popular in the South and Midwest, and at that time, in Southeastern Michigan— was almost as ubiquitous at highway exits as McDonalds is today. Perky red italics below the logo invited desperate travelers to *Relax, Refuel, and Refresh!* Behind the gas pumps, adjacent to every Stuckey's restaurant was a "world famous" Pecan Shoppe. There you could buy not just tins and boxes of nuts, but nougat-and-nut concoctions so petrified and dense that they put ancient trees to shame.

"Who are the Billboard Bandits?" asked the *Ann Arbor News* sometime in 1969, when the numerous Stuckey's billboards lining the highway began thinning out. Whoever was cutting them down sent no letters to the media; they left no message beyond the act itself. And somehow, over the course of about a year, they never were caught. Some speculated that they were engaged in some form of corporate warfare, others that these were simple vandals. Though there were far more politically or morally egregious targets out there, I felt a frisson of delight each time another Stuckey's sign hit the asphalt without the axe men being nabbed.

"It's definitely a statement," I said to my friend, Arnie. He was a quiet, quirky guy whose deeply subversive outlook was belied by his short hair, bland expression, and standard uniform of button-down shirts and khaki pants. Arnie was another regular after-school visitor, bearing spacy, avant garde LPs he thought I should listen to and love.

"What's the statement saying?" he asked.

"That our patriotic, artificial, sugary culture is coming down."

"A-plus, Julie," he said, smiling slightly. "Give that girl a gold star." Then we fell back into silence and resumed listening to King Crimson.

I never knew what Arnie expected of me in those visits, if he expected anything at all. I couldn't tell if he just liked me "as a friend"—lacerating words, though fine in Arnie's case, since that's how I liked him—or if he was simply too shy to "make the first move" (another term repeatedly used in frustrated or despairing conversations with close friends, as in "When is he going to make the first move?"). Sometimes I just thought he liked the quiet surroundings of my house, or our record player, or my parents' jazz collection.

But whatever his motives, Arnie was reliable. He'd join our contingent at local anti-war rallies, hand out leaflets supporting our Student Union candidates for the Pioneer High School Student Council, and author well-researched articles about enfranchised minors or progressive education for our high school underground newspaper, *The Foundation of Every State.*

"No pedagogy which is truly liberating can remain distant from the oppressed by treating them as unfortunates and by presenting for their emulation models from among the oppressors," he earnestly wrote, quoting Paolo Freire in one of our last issues before graduating. "The oppressed must be their own example in the struggle for their redemption."[20]

We'd had a showdown with Mr. Eastman, the Assistant Principal, over that issue. The first page featured a photograph of a bare-bottomed woman at the top of a stairway, bent over and peering between her legs. Her ample derriere filled most of the frame, and I was inordinately proud of the headline that I'd written to accompany the image: "Looking Back on a High School Education."

"If it goes out, so do you," the normally, if falsely, jovial Mr. Eastman declared. My fellow editors and I, all a semester away from college, having variously been suspended for smoking or walking out in protest of the war, or, in the case of my friend Carol and me, for wearing pants to school in defiance of a dress code, were unwilling to face another suspension.

"So much for being our own example in the struggle," Arnie muttered as we skulked out of Mr. Eastman's office. That was as close to being visibly angry as I'd ever seen him. But despite his lack of flash, Arnie seethed inside.

I never knew how much until a slate-skied evening at the end of that year, when he invited me to look at something in the immaculate white Plymouth Valiant parked outside my house. The air was damp, and the creak of the hinge was the only sound as he opened his trunk and pointed. Nestled inside were a gas-fueled power saw, an axe, and a sliver of a Stuckey's billboard.

In a stand-up routine from the 1980s, comedian Joan Rivers wondered why aliens always chose to reveal themselves only to drunken hunters and farmers. Unlike today, rural people didn't yet signify the Heartland and all that was right and pure with America. The fashion until the Reagan administration was to typecast them as ignorant crackers, a stereotype shockingly apparent in the derisive tone of the 1966 *Life* magazine article about Frank Mannors, the Dexter man who had set off the first in the series of UFO sightings that year.

"Frank should have been born in the days of Dan'l Boone," it begins. "Since he wasn't, he's on the unemployment. Still, he's a happy man." The article goes on to itemize the Mannors' home—an ancient refrigerator with an external cooling coil on top, an outside water pump and privy, and four junked cars on cinderblocks out front. It paints Mannors as a bad-tempered Gomer Pyle, with none of the homespun wisdom.

"That wasn't no foxfire or hullabillusion," Mannors insisted two weeks after his UFO sighting. "It was an object. Maybe it'll come back if all these people would stay away and we could get a picture and have verification of it. Anybody wants to give me a lie-detector test, I'll take it."

Nobody wanted to test Mannors' veracity. But Sheriff Doug Harvey believed in it. Forty years later, he'd say, "Dr. Hynek was sent in from the U.S. government. He came into my office. We went out to the site where supposedly this object came down on the ground. Dr. Hynek in the car said, 'There is something. We just can't put our finger on it. We've been investigating this for quite a while.' He was on the phone for quite a while, which I found very enlightening. He came out and I said, 'Well, Dr. Hynek. What do you think?' He said, 'It's swamp gas.' He tells me one minute he has no idea what it is. And then he makes one phone call to Washington and comes out and gives a statement that it's swamp gas. Very strange."

"They did see something," Harvey told an interviewer. "I'll believe this to the day I die. Somebody has kept something quiet, and nothing more ever materialized. So we don't know if it was the government experimenting, or was it really a UFO. I don't know."[21]

Jailer Doug Harvey, overseer of Harvey's Pigpen, short-hair enforcer, head-busting keeper of the peace, is no longer emboldened by certainty. Forty-six years later, he now believes in government cover-ups. He and the Billboard Bandit turn out to have something in common. Arnie is now one of the country's foremost authorities on the Freedom of Information act. The Sherriff who was an arm of the State has become a Libertarian, alienated from the authorities he once served; the boy I knew who thrived on subversion has become an authority himself, albeit one who champions transparency and Americans' inalienable rights.

And what of Vicky Lou and Vicky Lynn? Did they marry at eighteen, surrender to the powerful pull of the familiar, and disappear into silent woods? I don't know. But as I've become ever more rooted with age, I like to think that their mothers' unruly curiosity took seed in them, blowing them to new, alien landscapes.

Social Studies (1971-2015)

"Call me Sheila," Mrs. Faigenbaum cheerily demanded one Saturday morning in August of 1971. I was living in her house for a few weeks before starting college, there to babysit her sons Aaron and Elliott. "You're a young lady now and I'm not your teacher anymore."

Only half of that sentence was true. I was not a "lady," not prim and coy and helpless. I was seventeen years old, recently returned from backpacking around Europe, and convinced of my own worldliness. I was a *woman*. Just not a woman comfortable calling my former Social Studies teacher "Sheila."

Her cursive script on the blackboard on the first day of eighth grade had been firm and unbroken, the loops in the *l*'s and the *e*'s uniform and tight—*Balance of Power*, underlined three times. Turning to face us, hands on hips, she'd asked, "Okay, class, does anyone know what this means?"

Bill Case, who would grow up to kill himself at eighteen but was then just a nice and probably gay boy whose voice was lower and upper lip fuzzier than the other boys in class, raised his hand. "Something about equality?" he ventured.

Mrs. Faigenbaum nodded approvingly. "Something like that." She turned back to the board, and scrawled:

Liberty vs. Security
Stability vs. Revolt

"Do you detect a theme?" she asked us.

Bill once again raised his hand.

"Does anyone besides Bill detect a theme?"

"I don't know…contradiction?" my best friend, Pam, suggested. The "I don't know" was for show; if Pam lacked anything, it was uncertainty.

Mrs. Faigenbaum craned her neck, her eyebrows expectantly raised. "Yes, contradiction and…"

We stared at her. I wondered how long she could hold that inquiring face.

"How do you resolve contradictions?" she asked, allowing just a hint of exasperation into her voice.

Betsy raised her hand. "You go to your room?" Friendly and dim, she smiled in confused gratitude when several of us burst out laughing.

"Revolution," Kenny declared. Long in hair, short in stature, that was his answer to most questions.

"Sometimes," Mrs. Faigenbaum acknowledged.

"Compromise," Pam announced, not bothering to stick her hand in the air. "You resolve contradictions through compromise."

Mrs. Faigenbaum beamed. "Exactly." She set down the chalk, folded her arms, and leaned against the desk. "Contradictions are inevitable, so to solve them, you make trade-offs. You say, 'I'll do the dishes, if you take out the garbage.' The Supreme Court says, 'The states have sovereignty over a, b, and d, and the federal government is in charge of c, e, and f. Society says, 'We don't want segregation, but we recognize that integration will happen gradually.' So much of American history is just a repeating process of conflict and compromise, of choices and trade-offs. And that's what we're going to study this year."

She nodded, this time to herself, satisfied with her own synopsis. It was the first time I'd seen a teacher as engaged with the material as she wanted us to be.

Now she stood in her kitchen, which was immense and gleaming. Though she'd always seemed so solid and immovable in front of our eighth grade class, so tirelessly in charge, here, in her own home, four years later, she looked lost. The tall, chrome doors of the new refrigerator dwarfed her big-bosomed frame. And it wasn't just the fridge that dwarfed Mrs. Faigenbaum. Her husband, Marty, seemed to diminish her as well. Hirsute and muscular, he bristled with sarcasm behind his Nixonian five-o'clock shadow. Whether loosening jar lids, tightening the knot in the tie he donned every morning before heading off to his job as a Xerox machine sales manager, or hoisting his son onto his shoulders, he seemed coiled and ready to spring. I didn't understand what Mrs. Faigenbaum saw in him.

"Oh, you know," she answered vaguely when, one morning at breakfast, I asked her how they'd met. "Friend of friends. We'd see each other at parties, or out for pizza and beer. When you're twenty-one and still living with your parents, even ordinary guys look pretty enticing." Hearing herself, "Not that Marty's ordinary or anything. I just mean that when you're ready for a relationship, you're ready." She took a studious swallow of coffee, then met my eyes again. "How about you," she asked brightly. "Are you ready?"

What did she mean? Pam and I had talked endlessly about if and when we'd be ready to sleep with a boy. When Pam did in our Junior year—Pam, who I thought would be last—I was ready too, and did, the first chance I got. But she couldn't possibly be asking me about that, could she?

"Well, there's a guy, a sort of summer romance thing," I answered. "But actually, I think it's just as important to maintain my friendships with my women friends."

She contained a smile and raised her coffee cup in a toast. "Here's to women friends."

I assumed Mrs. Faigenbaum had them. I'd hear her talking to people on the phone—including my ninth grade French teacher, Mrs. Harrat, or Marie, as she'd call herself to my great unease. But there was no sign of them in this oversized, splendid new house in the outskirts of Ann Arbor, not even on the weekend, which stretched out long and quiet as an abandoned playground.

Weekday mornings, though, were hectic. By the time I rose from the guest room in the basement at the ungodly hour of seven a.m., Mrs. Faigenbaum was dressed in some floral below-the-knees dress, her lips reddened, her eyes bright behind her tortoise-shell glasses, her son dressed for nursery school, and her husband reading the paper over his morning coffee. Marty left the house first, giving Aaron a quick peck on the forehead, and denying Mrs. Faigenbaum even that. She left soon after, scooping up Aaron in one arm, her purse and briefcase in the other, and staggering out the door in her cream-colored patent leather flats.

In the half-hour or so that I typically had before the baby woke up, I'd try out different items for breakfast—Laughing Cow cheese on rye crisps with real English blackcurrant preserves on top; cottage cheese with pineapple and chocolate sprinkles on top; cocktail pumpernickel squares with corned beef rolls and pimento-stuffed olives on top. The capacious kitchen, its exotically stocked fridge, the Mr. Coffee carafe—a breakthrough alternative to the bubble-topped electric percolator—felt luxurious.

As I ate, I read Mrs. Faigenbaum's dog-eared paperback of *Couples*, the John Updike book that had been published three years earlier. Set in a toney New England town occupied by brokers, lawyers, and polo people, it told the story of four married couples and their intermingled, prolific, and kinky sex lives. It catalogued acts, such as oral sex, that I'd yet to experience and struck me as gross. But it went well beyond the standard repertoire of intimate practices, into territory that I didn't recognize and couldn't fathom—"golden showers" and, as I recall, sado-masochism (which I'd probably heard about, but only as such a costumed, bizarre, and accessorized activity that I lumped it in with *The Adams Family*).

By the time I sat in Mrs. Faigenbaum's kitchen, I'd slept with one boy a couple of times, and messed around with many. But *Couples* absolutely floored me. It seemed to epitomize the creepy lasciviousness of the mainstream, adult manifestation of "sexual liberation," as suburban couples donned Nehru jackets and mini-skirts, and, according to *Time* magazine and other disapproving chroniclers of cultural trends, engaged in "swinging" or "wife swapping." (A few months later, I'd hear someone comment on the fact that it was always the wives being swapped. Like putters, I thought, or lawnmowers.) In an interview, John Updike had said,

"The book is, of course, not about sex as such. It's about sex as the emergent religion, as the only thing left."

I didn't (and still don't) understand the grandiosity or the desperation behind that equation. There was nothing I recognized in *Couples*. Still, more than titillated, I felt sad reading this book that my no-nonsense teacher abandoned on the big, oval, faux oak table each morning. It seemed to speak to some longing in her that I pitied.

A few months later, at the first Ann Arbor Women's Liberation conference, I heard a name for Mrs. Faigenbaum's condition. Several, actually. "Domestic slave" and "objectification of male fantasies" are the two I remember, but those two long days in Rackham Auditorium were electric with slogans, phrases, and disputes that have had even more staying power.

In 1968, I'd watched news broadcasters ridicule a group of women who had picketed the Miss America pageant in Atlantic City, chanting "Up Against the Wall, Miss America" and "Miss America Is a Big Falsie." I was delighted by the protest—after all, the baton-twirling Tricia Nixon wannabes were already laughably retrograde to those of us who had (temporarily) stopped shaving our legs and wearing our bras—and unsettled by the sneering condescension of those hosting and reporting on it. ("Pretty girls don't have those problems," host Bob Hope said of the demonstrators.) But not much had happened to advance the movement in the intervening three years, so when my mother suggested that we go to this conference together, I let my curiosity get the better of my embarrassment about going anywhere with her.

The auditorium was packed and hot and tumultuous. "Processing" sessions followed each major address, in which audience members would stand up and comment on what they'd just heard from the dais about "the road ahead" and "the correct line," matriarchy vs. patriarchy, lesbianism vs. heterosexuality, about whether our mothers were our sisters or our oppressors.

("Did you think it would be good for me?" I recently asked her.

Now eighty-five, she paused before answering. "I thought it would be good for *me*. I was a generation older than all the women I worked with, and they treated me like the enemy. I was trying to figure out if I was.")

"The solution to our oppression doesn't lie in navel-gazing," shouted one woman in an incongruously frilly-necked blouse, "and so-called 'consciousness-raising' is just that—self-indulgence." With her wispy hair plastered to her sweaty forehead, she looked like some Pioneer woman in the throes of delirium.

"So you're saying we shouldn't consider our own feelings or learn from our own experience?" Someone right in front of me stepped out into the aisle to confront the person who had just spoken. She sounded like a woman, but with her short hair and button-down shirt and work boots, she looked like a man. I was intrigued; I'd never seen anyone who looked like her before.

"I'm saying that inserting a speculum and peering into a mirror to see our own cervixes isn't going to change the material conditions that give rise to our oppression," retorted Pioneer Gal.

"Our bodies *are* ourselves," someone in front of her leaped up to say. A handful of people started to clap, but were quickly drowned out by the woman in front of me.

"Men's hands on the speculum, men's laws governing our bodies—those *are* the material conditions of our oppression!" She cupped her palms to her mouth and blew in them, as if to cool them.

The wispy-haired woman rolled her eyes. "Of course we should have female doctors. Of course we should have free access to birth control and abortion. Stop obfuscating!" Stop *what?* "I'm just saying that how we *feel*—about ourselves, about our bodies—is an individual issue," she continued. "You want therapy? Fine. You want to talk to other women about it in a consciousness-raising group? Go ahead. But don't mistake that for political struggle."

Two women in front of her jumped to their feet and shouted, practically in unison, "The personal *is* political!"

Waves of applause began undulating through the auditorium,

94

as the moderator on stage tapped the microphone with her finger over and over again, pleading "Can we please have order? Everyone deserves the right to be heard. Can we please have order?"

This was amazing. All this talk about menses and placentas and orgasms and vulvas! All this yelling about rape and pornography and clitorises! And all of it in front of my mother! Like listening to an argument in the next room, I understood the odd word or phrase, enough to get a sense of what the debate was about. Was our oppression self-imposed or a direct consequence of economic exploitation? Could women change themselves without changing society, or would one flow out of the other? Was heterosexuality just capitulation to male dominance, or were egalitarian sexual relationships possible in a patriarchy? But the questions I was posing to myself and would continue to wrestle with for my first few years in college were much more prosaic. Should I take women's studies, anti-imperialist studies, or both? Could I start shaving my legs and armpits again? Should I spend Saturday night with my boyfriend or my women friends? Was it okay for anyone to be on top when having sex, or did we have to always try to do it sideways? And what about make-up? Was it ever okay to wear make-up?

I wasn't sure it was. A year earlier, still in the throes of my high school infatuation with her, I'd seen Anais Nin speak in that same auditorium. From a distance, in her black dress and red shawl, with her raven hair and crimson lips, she looked as exotic and bold as I imagined her to be. But when she autographed my book—Volume 283 or so of her diaries—I was shocked. Her face crumbled beneath a crust of foundation and rouge, and her eyes darted around beneath lids that were like a child's drawing of a peacock's tail, grotesquely painted in thick strokes. She was an old lady who looked like a harlot. This wasn't the face of a free woman.

Later in the fall of 1971, I'd catch glimpses of a philosophy professor who would provide a different look. Tall, with close-cropped hair and scholarly wire-rimmed glasses, Lois Harrison was a maverick, fashion and otherwise. Her academic studies had led her to Marxism, her politics and sexuality to lesbian separatism, and her admiration of how Czech citizens subverted the Russian invaders in 1968 through the clever use of ham radios led her to community college, where she studied television repair.

"There's Lois," one of the sophomores would announce in an excited whisper as she strode through the lobby of the Residential College in her navy blue mechanic's jumpsuit. Materializing out of nowhere, her acolytes, the students in her women-only philosophy seminar, would fall in behind her like a military flotilla of ducklings. Most of them became lesbians, then reverted to liking boys the following year when Lois quit her teaching job and moved to Detroit with her partner. (There, in a sad and ironic twist on the usual story, she worked fixing televisions to put her partner through nursing school, only to have that woman leave her for a man a few years later.)

On this day in 1971, though the fashion was eclectic, the women in that auditorium all seemed to be expressing who they were, not who someone wanted them to be. Some looked almost glamorous with their high suede boots and geometric earrings, others frazzled and seething in the close, smoky air.

But other than my mother, none looked like my mother. Their hair was longer or shorter, straighter or blonder, and they lacked the density that the older women in my young life all seemed to have, the rootedness that let them sway and dip but never leave the ground.

They looked nothing like my grandmother, who belied her age with the furious vigor and muscle behind each pass of her yellow, rubber-gloved hands as she scrubbed and dusted and polished. She was small, my grandmother, and her high, rounded cheeks, silvery hair, and manicured nails made her look like one of the dainty china figurines from her curio cabinet come to life. But when she cleaned she looked as tough as the gum-popping Catholic School girls who stood at the bus stop in front of her building. And when she'd sent us off to another country on our last night in Montreal, a lonely widow in a world of couples, I looked back at her kitchen window and saw her silhouetted, sturdy and brave as our trusty Rambler.

These conference women in their leotards or their overalls, in their heels or their Earth Shoes, looked nothing like Betty Friedan, author of *The Feminine Mystique* and the woman who, I'd been led to believe, was the mother of the movement.

Ten years later, when I finally saw Betty Friedan at a writing seminar in Bennington, Vermont, she looked just like my mother, or her friend Babs, or her friend Nancy, or any of the dozens of women who, on the other side of menopause, had found gravity irresistible. From the bags under her dark eyes to the deep grooves on either side of her beak of a nose, from her drooping breasts to her fallen arches, her body was one yeasty, downward swoosh.

On that hot July morning in Vermont, I'd heard her give a lecture about the militancy required to be a writer, about how hard it was to carve out undisturbed time and space especially if you were a wife or mother. That afternoon, I watched her from behind as she stood thigh-high in the tiny town pond, side by side with Richard Ellman, one of the faculty members. Friedan—in her black bathing suit, with her sagging buttocks and mole-spattered, fleshy back—chattered with Ellman as they splashed their faces and chests and their rounded shoulders with water. *Shmoozing and shvenking*, I remember thinking, like New York snowbirds in a Sarasota swimming pool. They looked old to me, as warm and seasoned as my Aunt Lil or Uncle Abe.

This morning, I read Friedan's biography on Wikipedia, and realized that I am now the age she was then. Though my face isn't as deeply lined, my body is even more rotund. And while I once dove into icy Laurentian lakes without hesitation, I now inch into the placid waters of Walden Pond before submerging with a gasp. I know that on those rare occasions when my daughter is with me there, she regards my receding form as I splash off to the opposite shore with a sort of protective amusement, seeing me not as a mature woman, not as someone known and respected in professional or political circles, but simply as a lovable, essential, and somewhat comical fixture in her life. She sees me as many of us see our mothers, as admirable and annoying, as well-intentioned and intrusive, as needy but hopefully, still buoyant.

The word "buoyant" doesn't appear in Sheryl Sandberg's *Lean In,* which may be the most highly promoted and read book about feminism since *The Feminine Mystique.* Neither does "resilient," or "durable." But "power?" Twenty-nine times. "Leadership?" Fifty-two.

Still, as I sit in my corner office, a senior vice president of a company with a female CEO and a predominantly female leadership team, I find myself unmoved by Sandberg's book. I don't question her sincerity, but can't overcome my sense that this is essentially a book about how women can find and retain their place in the 1 percent.

And those in the 99 percent? I've been meeting a lot of them lately—mostly Haitian, Brazilian, and Jamaican women—as I interview home health aides for my mother. I see more and more of them in her Independent Living facility, where old white women and men are wheeled or led by the hand by younger women of color. They wipe traces of dinner off the residents' faces, put on their clients' shoes with the same oddly supplicatory competence that they show their own children. Some show the infantilized elderly the same sort of affection, too, placing a comforting arm around their shoulders or gracing their papery cheeks with warm kisses.

They are in the business of caregiving, these women, sharing leads and shifts among themselves, their in-laws, and their non-English-speaking mothers. And though they are leaning in as far as their tired frames and beat up cars will take them, there are no au pairs or corporate jets in their futures. Their confidence or willingness to be outspoken, their husbands' readiness to be equal partners—none of this matters much as long as they're still living hand to mouth, scrambling for day care and housing, taking two dollars less an hour for cash payments rather than checks. They are just the latest wave of immigrants to do the work that we value so much and pay so little for.

Looking back, it seems to me that the sexual liberation movement ended up being more dramatic and enduring than the women's liberation movement so often confused with it. In her masculine clothes, with her masculine job, Lois Harrison was a complete anomaly in 1971. Now she's married to her partner of sixteen years, lives on a farm in Ontario with her cats (Alice B. Toklas, Gertrude Stein, and Zami) and dogs (Pride and Morgaine de Fey). She grows vegetables, makes beer and wine, and shares these facts with the world via Germantown High School's online alumni scrapbook, right next to the husband-and-three-wonderful-children life stories posted by the Class of 1957's now ancient cheerleaders.

Once in the vanguard, Lois earned the right to live in folksy anonymity, while against her will, Betty Friedan, once a lightning rod, succumbed to the tides of age and growing obscurity. The feminist movement of my day opened some doors and reduced some risks for women seeking to express and manage the consequences of their own sexuality. But the work of bathing and cleaning, of making the food and sewing the clothes, of shepherding the old people and teaching the children—this remains largely women's work. Essential, underpaid, and profound in its impact.

Mrs. Faigenbaum, the underside of her arms plump but not loose as she skated the chalk across the board, wrote *Government vs. Social Change*.

"So what do you think," she'd asked as blandly as if inquiring about the Tigers' pennant chances. "Now, in 1968, does government promote social change or stand in the way of it?"

"Well duh," Kenny had answered, without even waiting to be called on. "They stomp it out with their Nazi jackboots."

"Can you give me an example?" Mrs. Faigenbaum asked.

"Vietnam," Kenny said, leaving the "you moron" unspoken.

"How about in Little Rock, Arkansas, in 1957? What role was the Federal government playing then?" Her eyes were bright; she was clearly enjoying this.

I know what became of Kenny. He went on to become one of the country's leading documentary film makers, chronicling American history with a passion and fascination that had at least some seeds in that classroom.

I don't know what became of Mrs. Faigenbaum, but I suspect that unlike Lois Harrison, her life didn't end up violating her expectations. As with all of the adults who populated my adolescence, she is frozen in time. I picture her home in her high-waisted jeans in 1971, or out doing something—shopping for wallpaper, maybe, or Aaron's first pair of ice skates. Did she feel abandoned during those years, stuck back in the kitchen reading about sexual adventures while a generation of women eight or ten years her junior was having them, maybe while her husband was having them? Or did she feel relieved?

For all I know, she was at the Women's Liberation conference in 1971 too. And if she was, I don't think that her eyes would have widened in shock at the lurid language and raging slogans flying around Rackham Auditorium. I picture them glinting behind her glasses as her Bahama Coral-glazed lips formed the words that caused the women around her to pause, to question what they thought they knew, and want to know more.

In one of my imagined lives for her, she leaves her husband in 1972, moves into a commune with other single mothers and their kids, raises Aaron and Elliott to become a chef and feminist historian respectively, becomes Secretary of Education for the State of Michigan, and to this day, writes impassioned letters to the editor about the stupidity of standardized testing. In another scenario, perhaps the more likely one, she simply keeps on. Marty, mellowed by two heart attacks and chastened by a series of professional demotions, drops dead at their rented condominium just outside Tampa. Mrs. Faigenbaum, having become Chair of the Social Studies department, retires two years later, moves to Florida full-time, and devotes more time to quilting. Aaron has stayed in Michigan, Elliott has left, but both are dutiful and kind to their mother. She also volunteers at the library, where she recommends books, shelves them, and—driven by a curiosity both eclectic and unashamed—devours them.

Power Lines (1969-1972)

In the summer of 1969, men walked on the moon, Charles Manson and his band of followers went on a killing spree in Hollywood, Mary Jo Kopechne drowned in Ted Kennedy's car, and, to my everlasting chagrin, Woodstock happened without me.

It was also the summer that I met Ian, a fellow Counselor in Training at a camp in Michigan called Circle Pines. He was tall and rangy, barely kempt and badly shaven, masculine without a hint of machismo. He had blue-gray eyes that always seemed to look just beyond whomever he was talking to. I was smitten with his bow-legged gait, his tan cut-off corduroy shorts and purple paisley shirts, with his frizzy brown ponytail and his artistic aspirations.

After a month of almost constant companionship, my tenacity paid off. Ian had become my boyfriend, my first romance to last more than a few weeks. ("My boyfriend," I'd casually and inappropriately drop into conversations, as in "Oh, you're from Chicago? So is my boyfriend!" or "My boyfriend likes orange juice, too"). We revived our romance each summer, and exchanged long, moony letters between them. Ian's came in envelopes that he'd psychedelically illustrated with precise and goofy cartoons of himself squatting in a bubble, his guitar on his shoulder, floating through streets, classrooms, and the L train.

The front of my envelopes were unadorned, the letters inside dense monologues comparing the My Lai massacre to the Holocaust, reveling in the size and solidarity of the anti-war moratorium in Washington D.C. ("My first major protest," I'd actually written, as though I had just lost my virginity, "and I'll never be the same....") But on the back of every envelope I'd write song lyrics as if they were a secret code, as if the words of Joni Mitchell or the Jefferson Airplane carried some veiled meaning known only to us. *Oh, won't you stay, we'll put on the day, and we'll talk in present tenses,* I wrote one damp February night after the summer of 1969.

Over time, my choice of lyrics got more pointed. *We are all outlaws in the eyes of America,* I wrote after the following summer, not sure what Gracie Slick had meant but sure she was right. But Ian's dispatches from the University of Illinois changed little. "I've made my first record," one said. "It's in a capella choir. We sing early temperance music. What a goof."

By the end of August, 1972, in what would be my last summer at Circle Pines, my infatuation was waning. The humidity was oppressive. Earlier that week we'd seen a tornado in the distance, swooping down on a distant farm, and on the second-to-last day of camp, that same heavy stillness was in the air. Finally, just before dinner, it broke. Thunder roared, lightning cackled, and the rain pounded down, turning trails through meadows and woods into small rushing rivers. Kids and counselors alike hooted with joy. We were about to be released—from the heat, from bells and dining halls and bugs, from each other. We ran and slid barefoot in the soaked grass. Kids painted each other's faces with mud, giving them all the same tear-streaked gutter snipe look. We—the alleged grown-ups—looked on at this wet childfest. Matted hair, filthy clothes, none of it mattered. They were going home tomorrow.

As the downpour tapered off into a drizzle, we began to gather up the kids for dinner. They sloshed into the dining hall, looking forward to their half-frozen chicken parmesan patties, powdered mashed potatoes, and corn niblets with renewed gusto. I did a couple of head counts, but kept coming up one kid short. Chevonne was missing.

A ten-year-old from Cabrini Green, which was even then notorious as one of the most dangerous and abandoned of Chicago's housing projects, Chevonne was one of the many campers attending Circle Pines on scholarship. She had never been out in the country before and was terrified of insects, especially spiders. The dark silence of the woods made her shudder, and on nights when the sky was a bowl of stars hanging luminous over the big meadow, she crossed her arms and gripped them in a terror so deep she left gouge marks in her skin. But indoors, in fights, on top of roofs, and when playing Light as a Feather, Stiff as a Board, Chevonne was fearless. Wiry and strong, her processed hair flaring around her face, she scampered and jumped, laughed and yelled, and when I intervened to say you have to stop this, you have to do that, she looked at me with a fixed smile and opaque gaze.

Chevonne did what she wanted. When it was time to set up the dining room for dinner, she hid behind the barn and made miniature campfires of dry grass, or sauntered back to the cabin for a little pre-dinner nap. If she didn't want to go swimming, she'd sneak off the path en route to the lake, double back through the dreaded woods, and melt into some other unit's game of soccer or Capture the Flag. I spent anxious, exasperated time almost every day tracking her down. She was indifferent and uncontrollable as the wind.

While Ian shepherded the kids to their tables, I went outside and called her name. No answer, only a heavy dripping from the trees and a few tentative chirps from the stunned birds. Walking toward the Rec Hall, I bellowed her name again. And this time, I heard an answer, a faint, jolly "Here I am!"

I stopped and looked up, first at the roof of the office, then at the roof of the Rec Hall, and then at the stand of trees between them. Chevonne sat straddling one of the highest boughs, halfway out from trunk to tip and clutching a small branch.

"Are you all right?" I asked stupidly.

"Yeah, I'm all right." Her voice was thin—not trembling, but flat and hollow as a movie set facade. "I want to get down now."

"Now wait a second, Chevonne," I yelled. "Don't move yet. Let me go get a ladder and some help." The bough she sat on was wet and sodden and bent under her modest weight. The trunk of the giant elm was black, slick, and bare for its first fifteen linear feet. I had no idea of how Chevonne got up there, on that bough that grew higher than the power lines and Rec Hall roof.

"I don't really want to wait for no ladder." Her tone was saucy, but her voice, filtering out between the thick clumps of leaves, seemed separate from the small figure in the yellow slicker, green shorts, and red sneakers.

"It'll take me just a few seconds. Now please, sweetie, I know you don't want to stay up there but I just want to get you down safely. Can you hang on for a just a little while longer?" I pleaded. "I'll be right back. I promise you. Just hang on."

I ran back to the dining hall for help. When I returned, Chevonne was lying on her stomach, her arms and legs wrapped around the bough.

"I'm back, and Fred's coming with a ladder. Just hang on."

I heard a lazy rustle and saw one red sneaker drop a few feet, and get stuck in a tangle of branches lower down the tree. I looked frantically around the base of the tree, trying to find a toe hold or rock to stand on that would put me within reach of the first climbing branch. How the hell had she gotten up there?

"No, I don't care to wait," she said, her little voice now furry as a peach. "I don't much like it up here."

Then there was another brush of leaves, a sudden gush of water. Chevonne began slowly falling past the branches that jutted out like impatient arms on the hips of the giant elm.

"Oh my god," I heard the camp director, Billie, gasp behind me as we watched Chevonne float down and reach with her small pink palms toward the power line. She caught it and hung for what seemed like minutes, suspended like a piece of laundry on a still, muggy day. Then she dropped straight to the ground.

I can still see Chevonne's return to camp the next morning in a glistening white sling, a band-aid on her forehead, and watch the other kids crowd round her with new respect, exchange addresses and hugs and goodbye kisses. I see it like a long-ago Saturday matinee, not as anything connected to me. But that moment when Chevonne, through some miracle of will and coordination, firmly grabbed hold of that potentially lethal power line was as startlingly real as birth.

I'd thought I was finally an adult, but I was wrong. I'd been gawking at Ian, gazing at the moon, contemplating my own place in the universe, looking everywhere but at the child in front of me who had spent her life slipping from a high, wet branch. Now I felt foolish and impotent, but also awake.

When camp ended, Ian came back to Ann Arbor with me. My parents were moving to Boston, and my father had already left in mid-August to start his new job and meet the moving truck on its arrival. The plan was for Ian and me to pack up my mother's car with the final batch of items to be moved, drive her to Boston, paint my parents' new house, then take their car on a road trip through New England before going back to school.

Ian didn't drive, though, so I offered a ride as far as Boston to Mark, a guy I'd met in my Advanced Narration class. He wasn't really my type—short, acerbic, and as combative as Ian was mellow—but I admired his writing, wit, and political passion. And he had a driver's license.

We'd really gotten to know each other a few months earlier in a production of a college musical, *The Persecution and Assassination of Jean-Paul Marat as Performed by the Inmates of the Asylum of Charenton Under the Direction of the Marquis de Sade.* Rowdy, sexual, revolutionary in both its form and content, *Marat/Sade* was a play-within-a-play in which mental patients in 1808 perform a pageant enacting the assassination of French revolutionary, Jean Paul Marat, under the direction of fellow inmate, the Marquis de Sade. As members of the inmates' chorus, Mark and I spent every dress rehearsal and performance clad in torn institutional pajamas, cementing our friendship as we simulated sex while gaily singing "And what's the point of a revolution/without general/general copulation, copulation, copulation" (performed as a round, of course.)

When we weren't on stage, we were talking poetry or politics. Mark had joined the Attica Brigade, and encouraged me to join his study group in Marxism/Leninism, which I saw as a sort of graduate program after majoring as an undergrad in mere anti-imperialism. Dialectical materialism, cultural revolution, women holding up half the sky—these were weighty ideas. This was "scientific socialism," with all of the objectivity and inevitability that "science" implied to scientifically ignorant, would-be poets like me. It's what you embraced, I was starting to believe, if you were committed to social and economic change, and not a mere dilettante.

It was early morning when Mark, Ian, and I set off on what would be a very long drive with my mother. The trunk and roof bin on the turquoise Pontiac Catalina moaned as we forced them shut, and the tail pipe tickled the gravel as we drove down the dirt road away from our house in Ann Arbor for the last time. We'd decided to take the northern route through Ontario to shave an hour or two off the sixteen-hour drive. Crossing into Canada was no problem, but predictably, getting back into the United States at the Buffalo border was another story. Never once in those years, when I regularly travelled back and forth between the U.S. and Canada, was I allowed to pass through freely if accompanied by a long-haired male. We'd gambled that my mother's presence in our entourage would spare us the customary search of our car and persons, but no such luck.

"Where you headed?" the border guard asked.

"Boston," Mark answered. We'd made the mistake of not having my mother at the wheel for this portion of our trip.

"Where is your residence?" he asked.

"New York, Ann Arbor, Illinois, and she's moving to Boston," Mark answered, pointing to himself and each one of us in turn.

The guard smirked a little, then jerked his thumb toward one of the inspection bays. "Pull in there," he ordered.

"Excuse me," my mother piped up from the passenger seat, "but we had quite a job packing this car up."

"And now you're going to have to unpack it," he answered.

"Officer, we don't have any drugs, if that's what you're thinking." Her voice rose in exasperation.

"I'm not going to ask you a second time, ma'am." His face, pockmarked and florid, protruded through the driver's side window, forcing Mark to lean away.

"We better just do it, Mom," I murmured from the back seat. To my shame, I was far more afraid of authority than she was.

Two border guards made us unpack everything in and on the car. They opened and rummaged through the suitcases, inspected the inside of the teapot, peered in the sound hole of Ian's guitar, even tore open and extracted a few tampons from their tubes to see what was inside. Then, with a wave of the hand, one of them indicated that we were free to go.

"Bastards," my mother muttered as they blithely walked away from the pile of personal and household possessions strewn around the car. "Just because you look like hippies. It's discrimination—flat-out discrimination!"

Resigned, Mark and Ian and I reloaded the car. My mother continued her rant until just outside of Utica. We thought she was adorable.

Heading into the dusk just east of Albany, after we'd been on the road for about twelve hours, we heard a *thunk*, followed by an awful grinding sound. I pulled onto the shoulder and Mark got out.

"The tail pipe's broken and the muffler's dragging against the road," he said after a quick inspection. "We can't drive like this."

"What are we going to do?" my mother asked.

Mark looked at Ian and me. We both gazed back at him, speechless. Useless.

"I can hitchhike to an exit and get a tow truck," Mark said, "but it's going to take a while."

"We'll be here for hours!" my mother wailed. "Goddamnit! Fucking border guards!"

"Let me look again," Mark offered. We all got out. Mark lay down on his back and inched his way under the car, while my mother and I watched him. Ian carefully removed his guitar from its case, and facing away from the traffic so he could hear himself better, began quietly strumming.

Mark emerged long enough to instruct us to gather up all the belts we might have on our bodies and in our luggage. Ian was clearly reluctant to part with his woven Guatemalan belt that went so well with the embroidered border at the bottom of his jeans. Then Mark crawled back under the sagging Catalina and created a series of harnesses with the belts to secure the muffler. His handiwork held until we got to Boston.

"I like Ian," my mother told me privately a few days later, "but you can do better. He's in his own world. He just played his guitar. He didn't even try to help."

Years later I would marry Mark. Our romance began not when we were feigning sex in an avant-garde play, but on that dusky stretch of highway. Impatient to get to his destination, Mark had flexed his imagination and his muscle. However imperfectly, he'd moved us down the road.

I never went back to Circle Pines, though I visited Ian at school one last time in 1972. We went to a party that happened to be on the night that the draft lottery was held. The order of birth dates pulled out of a barrel determined who would be conscripted and sent to Vietnam. Somebody turned the music down and flicked on the radio so we could hear the birthdays as they were drawn. But the drawing took a long time, and after about 150 dates had been read, somebody yelled, "Fuck it, man. Turn the music back on."

Ian's birthday hadn't been called out yet. He grinned. "Lucky Capricorn," he yelled to me as "You're So Vain" resumed blasting out from the record player.

I shared his relief. I surrendered once again to his gangly charm as we danced. I didn't know what to say to the guy born on Christmas Eve who sat all alone on the dorm's dirty couch, his future just recast as Number 2.

In that first heavenly summer at Circle Pines—when we were all friends and our days were sunshine and mulberries and our nights were passed skinny dipping and singing—we were nostalgic for those days even as we were living them. Perhaps we sensed that the world was turning darker. Three Days of Peace and Love at Woodstock was followed only a few months later by gunshots and killings at Altamont. The Beatles broke up while Led Zeppelin had the poor taste to endure. In rapid order, the Chicago Seven were found guilty of inciting riots at the Democratic convention, and the U.S. invaded Cambodia. The year after that, on September 11, a military junta in Chile, backed by the CIA, overthrew the democratically elected socialist president of Chile, then rounded up and murdered thousands of political opponents in a soccer stadium. Many of them were students, people my age. Every day in my dorm, we read about it and wrote flyers. We raged and hated our own helplessness.

Still, we were "we."

In symphonic music, tunes aren't exactly in order because they're complete in themselves. Tunes don't cry out for development, and development is the main thing in symphonic music, the growing of a melodic seed into a big symphonic tree. So that seed mustn't be a complete tune, but rather, a melody that leaves something still to be said, to be developed....

— Leonard Bernstein, Young People's Concerts,
December 21, 1962

Early Movements (1967-2015)

A segment of *Our World* opens with the fractured face of one of Picasso's women gazing impassively down on a rehearsal room in the Lincoln Center where Van Cliburn, winner of the International Tchaikovsky Piano Competition and young darling of the classical world, and Leonard Bernstein, composer and conductor of the New York Philharmonic, practice for an upcoming performance. The piece is Rachmaninoff's Piano Concerto no. 3. They sit facing one another at gleaming pianos. Bernstein is playing some version of the orchestral score, as Cliburn, young and impossibly perfect in his posture and sculpted hair, solos over him. Bernstein, eyes squinting from the cigarette that dangles from his mouth as he plays, is also dressed in a suit and tie, but his tie is loosened and a wavy lock of hair falls over one eye, and though he is older, he is unquestionably cooler.

The Maestro does not love how Cliburn is playing. He stops, stands, and walks over to the prodigy. "At the moment, where we've just arrived, it's marked *più mosso*," he observes, his tone carefully curious," but you hold back there—"

"Yes, I think it sounds better." Van Cliburn is unrepentant. Back then I vaguely recall sneering at Van Cliburn, largely because I confused him with Liberace, but also because the only other "Van" I knew of was Van Heflin, B-Movie star of the 40s and 50s, and as square as they came. Now he just strikes me as an arrogant twerp with his clear eyes and shiny cheeks.

"Yes, but that's not what Rachmaninoff says…" Bernstein's display of benign authority is masterful.

"These are the bells, the old church bells." Van Cliburn is almost condescending in his explanation.

"Yes," the Maestro concurs with steely congeniality, "but they don't have to go so slow."

Young Turk meets Old Guard. But in this case, Van Cliburn, a church-going, right wing, closeted homosexual who, to this day, opens every performance with *The Star Spangled Banner*, was the Establishment, and Bernstein, once an icon, now strangely marginalized, was the rebel in ways I couldn't begin to fathom.

When I was a kid, my family and my Aunt Anne, Uncle Herbie, and three cousins all shared a summer house on one of the hundreds of lakes in the worn but still wild Laurentian Mountains north of Montreal. Both families were strapped for money—it is only now that I realize that this co-housing arrangement was born of necessity, and not just out of our parents' selfless desire to amplify our summer fun. The house had electricity and indoor plumbing, but was otherwise quite rustic, with wainscoted walls, Depression-era linoleum floors, a party telephone line that we shared with practically every house built around Lac La Croix, a small but thunderous washing machine, and a wring dryer that I assumed was far more fun for our increasingly muscular mothers than an electric one.

My uncle sold mid-range radios and stereo equipment, and seemed also to be able to buy LPs at discount. As a result, we had many record players in that house—a console in the living room that only the grown-ups got to use, a portable record player in the girls' room, and another in the "little house"—the wooden garage next to the house that our parents had converted into a sleeping and play space for my brother Bobby and cousin Paul. We girls had all the LPs, largely musical comedies and folk music albums. The boys had all the singles, the 45 RPM records that were the main distribution form for pop music in the late 1950s and early 1960s. While they lorded that fact over us, they routinely let us into their lair, where we'd pile on to the built-in bunk beds and take turns playing records and performing the tunes.

Choosing a good sequence of songs was an art, but actually playing them was an acquired skill. First, you had to properly insert the swirly plastic yellow disc in the oversized record hole so that the record would fit on a spindle meant for the much smaller diameter of 33 RPM album. Then, you had to place the needle exactly in the first groove of the vinyl, avoiding the pulse of scratchy static caused by a needle being stuck on the ridge between grooves, but still managing to lay it down before the song began.

And then we'd hear it, the bells, strings, and groggy cha-cha beat introducing "Johnny Angel," or the military snare drums opening "The Battle of New Orleans." The three of us girls would sing the chorus, while my brother or cousin Paul took the lead, both of them singing in a peculiar, unnatural, and unpleasant nasal tone that faintly mimicked the adenoidal stylings of the Shirleys and Lesleys and Tommys and Genes at the top of the charts. Though we couldn't have articulated why, even then we recognized the pure awfulness of early '60s pop music, with endless songs about parties ending in car crashes or heartbreak; with Connie Francis bathetically warbling about following the boys (soldiers, I now realize, but that nuance was lost on me then), and Bobby Vee, Bobby Vinton, and Bobby Van all fusing into a single pompadoured, Brylcreamed personification of teen patriarchy. It's not surprising that Peter, Paul, and Mary or *My Fair Lady* seemed downright gutsy in comparison.

While I loved belting out "If I had a Hammer" (though now the idea of hammering out love between my brothers and sisters sounds too much like a team-building exercise), it was the prologue to *West Side Story* that got under my skin and kept drawing me back. Edgy and aching, it was as far from *Oklahoma* as a musical could get. In the prologue, brassy, dissonant horns blared out a warning, then stopped, to be replaced by a cool, swinging summons from a saxophone, answered by the strings. But then it changed again—a

112

whistle, and what was an easy pace turned into a bass-driven balletic chase, bongos and timbales and blaring horns pounding out the traffic on the glaring avenues and silent runners in the alleys between them. Every turn of the music was unexpected, danger and ease, joy and fear melding together in something I found absolutely riveting. At eight or nine years old, I had no idea that I was hearing a fusion of Latin, jazz, and symphonic music. I certainly didn't know what it meant to stay *Cool*, but the snapping fingers, tense, percussive bass line, and sexy, insinuating piano compelled me to want to find out.

Take it slow, and daddy-o, you can live it up and die in bed.

I don't think I realized that the Leonard Bernstein who composed *West Side Story* was the same man whose *Young People's Concerts* I watched on television, listened to on records, and once attended live. It didn't matter, though; I loved them both. He reminded me of my father—a dreamy, reluctant and unsuccessful business man who was gentler than the other fathers I knew; he related almost conspiratorially to kids and made us feel that together, we'd find the humor in the actions of others, and nobody would notice us noticing them. And just as my father turned arithmetic into play, helping me to arrange multi-colored rods and cubes as a way to make sense of the decimal system, Bernstein made the complex swell of an orchestra both accessible and grand.

By 1967, our shared country house was long gone. My family had left Montreal and moved to the United States three years earlier. And, of course, as I got older, the men of my dreams got younger. John, Paul, and George took turns supplanting one another in my affections (though not Ringo—I wasn't looking for cute), then Eric Burdon of The Animals, with his raw voice and proletarian passion, and the bedroom-eyed, honey-toned Jesse Colin Young.

By then I'd also deemed classical music irrelevant, musicals corny, and older people trying to be hip, pathetic. (It was around that time that my father, like many fathers, grew sideburns, and my Uncle Herbie, bald his entire adult life, temporarily took to wearing a toupee and learned to play the banjo.) But though I'd stopped listening to him, Leonard Bernstein never lost his cool in my mind's eye. He was my idea of an artist. He had longish hair that didn't look stupid on him, even though it was gray. He looked like a poet when he smoked cigarettes, like Jean Paul Belmondo but with better skin. When he conducted, it was with open arms and wide, sweeping gestures, not all hunched and tight and prissy. He was not just a pathetic striver.

So it was fitting that he'd host what turned out to be a controversial news special about rock and roll in April of that year. I remember watching that show on the night that it aired. I was thirteen (*almost fourteen*, as I routinely reminded anyone who would listen). Though it was a school night, my parents let me wheel the cart holding our family's one television, a black-and-white with electrical tape holding its neurotic and volatile antenna in place, from their bedroom to mine. Thanks to Leonard Bernstein's patronage, Janis Ian, the fifteen-year-old phenom whose new song, "Society's Child,"[22] was causing a stir, was going to be on.

Until I heard the song, I didn't know what the fuss was about. But within the first two lines, the answer was electrifyingly obvious.

Come to my door, baby,
Face is clean and shining black as night

Janis Ian was thirteen when she wrote this song and fourteen when she recorded it. But though it had been released in 1966, very few people outside of New York had heard the song by this night in April of 1967. Most radio stations refused to play it, and one in Alabama that dared to was burnt to the ground.

As she stood in a spotlight in the darkened studio, wearing a black mock turtleneck shirt and a jumper that, in fuzzy black-and-white looked just like one of mine, I felt that Janis Ian could have been me. She had unfashionably frizzy hair like mine, which she wore pulled tightly back. She had full lips, which I'd now describe as Semitic but which then, adorning my own face, I thought of as simply fat. She had round, wide-set eyes that looked calmly ahead, never at her small, strumming hands, as she sang.

My mother went to answer
You know that you looked so fine Now I can understand your tears and your
shame.
She called you "boy" instead of your name.
When she wouldn't let you inside
When she turned and said
"But honey, he's not our kind."
She said I can't see you any more, baby
Can't see you anymore.

The injustice of it! Janis stood in her black stockings and her flats, exposing the adult world.

My teachers all laugh, their smirking stares
cutting deep down in our affairs
Preachers of equality
Think they believe it?
Then why won't they just let us be?

I thought of my ninth-grade Social Studies teacher, Mr. Berg, spouting all of this grand stuff about intellectual freedom and the importance of having questioning minds. But when I'd questioned *his* mind earlier that week, rousing myself from my post-American chop suey stupor after lunch long enough to ask why we were studying the history of ancient Greece instead of modern Vietnam, suddenly he wasn't so interested in inquiry. And though I personally hadn't experienced or even observed any racist attitudes firsthand, well, that's because other than Sarah, the Haitian woman who had sometimes babysat and cleaned our house in Montreal, and my parents' friend Joe, the darker half of what was reputed to be the only interracial couple even in a progressive college town like Ann Arbor, I didn't yet know any black people. Which, come to think of it, somehow proved just how endemic racism was. But that was all about to change, was already changing. People Janis's age, my age, were going to do it.

One of these days I'm gonna stop my listening
Gonna raise my head up high
One of these days I'm gonna raise up
my glistening wings and fly

Wait—"one of these days"? Not today?

But that day will have to wait for a while.
Baby, I'm only society's child.
When we're older things may change.
But for now this is the way they must remain.

She sang the refrain, this time adding as the final line, *No, I don't wanna see you any more, baby.* The plaintive melody ended; the final notes on the acoustic guitar faded into a sigh.

Then, in a completely unexpected coda, like a call to arms, an electric organ responded with one of the most memorable endings in pop music history—a bluesy, two-bar taunt, answering pathos with funk, and surrender with defiance.

If the song represented 1967, the coda announced 1968.

In that wrenching year, finally in high school, I spent my time after class in the Mobilization for Survival office in Ann Arbor, Michigan, attending meetings and producing leaflets for anti-war marches.

Hot town. Pigs in the streets, read the text above a black-and-white photo of a scowling, jowly cop in a white helmet and chin strap, leather jacket, and dark, nearly opaque shades. *But the streets belong to the people!* Below it was a clenched, black-and-white fist, and below that, *Dig it?* Thanks to the art plastering the walls—photos of Che Guevara, of Benjamin Spock marching with Martin Luther King for civil rights and against the Vietnam war, of three flower-frocked women sitting seductively on a bench, vertically bordered by text saying *Girls say YES …To boys who say NO*—the otherwise drab office breathed fire. Presiding over the Gestetner ditto machine was Black Panther Huey Newton holding a rifle; next to the coffee-maker, brittle and crusted, was a print of Uncle Sam in a jaunty red, white, and blue stovepipe hat made of an American flag, half his face a black-and-white skull, the other half bearing the invocation to *Mobilize Against the War*.

Some psychedelic and faux children's art still adorned the place, entreating us to *Make Love, not War* or reminding us that *War is not good for children or other living things*. But by the fall of 1968, such pacifism and idealized innocence were on the wane. *Fuck the War* in blaring black-and-white was more indicative of the prevailing mood. *Fuck the Draft. Fuck the Pigs.* And, in an attempt to bridge the two, was another black-and-white poster of a soldier and a policeman, each in profile, with *Soldiers out of Vietnam* above one, *Cops out of the Ghetto* above the other.

Those slogans—I could hear them—formed a noisy crowd in my head. I was generally conflict averse, and the confrontational language felt assumed, unnatural to me and to most of us in this office. The rifles frightened me, and I'd debate—mostly with myself—whether violence was ever legitimate in fighting violence. At the Democratic Convention in Chicago in August of that year, police and National Guard had beaten anti-war protestors and the journalists covering their actions. *The whole world is watching*, the crowd had chanted, but the cry seemed to only incite the cops further. *We don't give a shit*, they answered with flailing clubs and jabbing feet. So what choice were they leaving us? (Almost fifty years later, George Zimmerman gets away with murdering Trayvon Martin. Sandra Bland dies in a Texas jail cell in which she didn't belong. Police kill Eric Garner for the crime of contesting his arrest for unlawfully selling cigarettes. People respond to the outrage with hashtags and Facebook photo filters, with riots and arson, with peaceful, symbolic actions and violent, scary ones, and that quandary haunts me still.)

Watching the 1968 Chicago convention on TV from the safety of my parents' bedroom, I was not just frightened by their violence. I had never before seen such arrogance, and it enraged me. Martin Luther King had been assassinated. Bobby Kennedy had been assassinated. Two priests, Phillip and Daniel Berrigan, and three others had been imprisoned for destroying draft files at a Baltimore Selective Service

Office. Even Dr. Spock had been sentenced to jail for counseling young men to refuse the draft.

The following summer, Black Panther leader Fred Hampton, facing a two-to-five year prison term for allegedly stealing seventy-one Good Humor bars, was drugged by a police informant, then murdered in his bed by police. Unlike some people who used "revolution" as an excuse to dress tough and bear arms, Hampton was a genuine leader, having brokered peace between warring street gangs in Chicago and forged a "rainbow coalition" across numerous black and Chicano and Puerto Rican and predominantly white student groups. For this he was deemed dangerous enough by the FBI to warrant assassination. After shooting him point blank in the head, the cops pulled his dead body out of bed and dumped it on the floor at the entrance to his bedroom. Then they photographed it, supplying the press with pictures of Hampton, clad in a jacket and polka-dotted boxer shorts, lying face down on the floor in the pool of blood.

But another photo made its way out into the world from that night as well, a picture of Hampton's bed, illuminated by a floor lamp next to it that shone upward, bathing the peeling walls, tiny desk, sturdy chair, and sheetless, blood-soaked mattress in a fan of warm light. That was the picture that also hung on the walls of the Student Mobilization office in Ann Arbor, the one that, empty of a human form, haunted me the most. I could not reconcile the tenderness of the light with the savagery of Hampton's murder, and I know now that I was also terrified by what it revealed about death—a palpable and permanent absence.

I was fifteen at a time when the pace of change was fantastically condensed, like the kind of time-lapse movies we were shown in science class. But instead of budding plants or rotating planets, I was seeing leaders and movements roar by, fragile and transient as twigs in a churning river. I went from flower child to anti-Imperialist to ambivalent Maoist a few years later, uncomfortable with the rhetoric, but convinced that I had to rectify what I then saw as my own willful naiveté about political power, how to get it, and how to use it.

Every now and then, Leonard Bernstein would briefly appear in my peripheral vision, giving speeches at anti-war marches and rallies for Eugene McCarthy. He flared back into the news in June of 1970, when up-and-coming essayist and exemplar of The New Journalism, Tom Wolfe, wrote a lengthy article in *New York* magazine. "Radical Chic: That Party at Lenny's," which documented a fundraiser that Leonard's wife, Felicia, had organized and held in their penthouse apartment for the Black Panther 21s' Legal Defense Fund.[23]

Wolfe's snarky phrase, "radical chic," has since become a permanent part of the American vocabulary, at least among the intelligentsia. It's the identical twin to "political correctness," a weirdly superior sort of insult that's hurled from the left rather than the right. It bugs me, so tonight, after watching the *Our World* clip of Bernstein and Van Cliburn, I seek out that Tom Wolfe article from 1970. Midway through the first page, I'm already sickened by its venom, its smugness, its pandering to racial stereotypes under the guise of skewering white privilege. I find it appalling.

Lenny was not new to progressive causes, I argue with the page. In the years preceding World War II and in its immediate aftermath, when fighting Fascism was as American as a *Thank you for your Service* bumper sticker is today, there were unlimited opportunities to take a well-intentioned stand. With his dollars and with his words, Bernstein had supported numerous anti-Fascist organizations, raised funds for victims of Stalingrad, begun work on an opera about Sacco and Vanzetti. Composing, conducting, and jetting around the world, he was more of a signer and endorser than a leader. But his actions were not without consequences. In 1950, he was blacklisted by CBS, suddenly unable to continue the radio and television broadcasts that had fueled his career. Harry Truman banned his music (along with that of Gershwin, Copland, and other progressive American composers) from State Department premises and functions overseas.

119

In 1953, Eisenhower's State Department revoked his passport on the grounds that Bernstein was a security risk, preventing him from conducting overseas at a time when the blacklist was making it increasingly difficult for him to perform at home. To regain his passport, Bernstein wrote and signed a self-excoriating affidavit that, while not naming names, essentially disowned his own leftist activities in the 1940s. He was not a Communist, he swore, and had only ever voted for Democrats or Republicans. His association with anti-Franco Spanish political forces had been "nominal," and his involvement with other anti-Fascist organizations was driven by naiveté, youthful foolishness, ignorance, and a fevered desire to see his own name in print. He was a Jew and an ardent supporter of Israel, he argued, which automatically qualified him as an opponent of the Soviet Union. He realized that in 1949, after *Red Channels* and *Life* had published their accounts of his political activities, he should have immediately "'made a public disavowal' of his unpatriotic organizational associations. He said that he did so now, and he reaffirmed his loyalty to the United States."[24]

Though he described it to his brother as "a ghastly and humiliating experience," the affidavit served its purpose. Bernstein got back his passport, and doors at the Boston Symphony and New York Philharmonic that had been slammed shut and remained closed for five years now reopened. Lenny was back on his way to becoming a star. By the 1960s, perhaps more secure in his status and feeling less vulnerable, he had again begun speaking out, for civil rights and against the Vietnam war, campaigning for a McCarthy victory to "restore some rational humanism" to this "psychotic, power-obsessed world."

Sure, I concede, Tom Wolfe is right—Bernstein did practice celebrity politics. Hell, he practically invented the genre, showing up on the last day of the civil rights march from Selma to Montgomery in 1965 to walk the final four miles of the trek arm-in-arm with Martin Luther King and address the crowd of 25,000 participants. But even that required courage—there had been numerous death threats levied against the marchers, and one of them, Viola Liuzzo, would be murdered by the Ku Klux Klan later that day.

And yes, it's hard not to cringe when Wolfe exposes the exquisite dilemmas that these Upper East Side liberals face in planning their parties for the Panthers (no black domestics) or the Young Lords (no Hispanic ones). But I'm impressed when Bernstein asks Don Cox, a Black Panther leader from Oakland, if it infuriates him to be surrounded by such affluence, if he's embittered by the fact of such wealth. It is, Lenny observes, "a very paradoxical situation."

It's no big deal, Cox says at first. But then he keeps talking, describing how he used to have a job and wear a suit and keep his nose clean and be a "respectable Negro ... But then one day it dawned on me that I was only kidding myself, because that wasn't where it was at. In a society like ours I might as well have had my hair-guard on and my purple pants, because when I walked down the street I was just another *nigger*...see...just another *nigger*..."

Bernstein responds. "Most of the people in this room have had a problem about being unwanted."

Wolfe finds this response to be narcissist, psychoanalytic, and absurd, and veers off into another rhapsody of ridicule. I don't find it at all funny. Of course I get his point—how could the insecurities of some Harvard-educated doyens of Society compare to the daily, random harassment faced by black men? But I also think about Bernstein as the still-closeted gay man; as the Jew trying to make it in a world in which the great composers had, until then, denied their Judaism or converted; as the blacklisted idealist forced to choose between his passion or what would become his shame, choosing shame. I think this gathering, however bizarre, would not have happened in a room where none of the fashionable hosts had ever had the experience of being unwanted. And I think that those who make it from the margins to the glittering center of success make a choice about whether to close ranks and assert their entitlement, and for all of his vacillation, his attempts to take a stand without incurring the cost, Bernstein chose not to.

So even if Lenny was wearing "a black turtleneck, navy blazer, Black Watch plain trousers and a necklace with a pendant hanging down to his sternum," even if the conversation was happening in "a big, wide room with Chinese yellow walls and white moldings, sconces, pier-glass mirrors," at least the conversation was happening. Dialogues like that, however mismatched the players, echo over the years.

Still, why am I getting so worked up about a forty-two-year-old magazine article, written by a fedora-wearing, white-suited white man who is now very old, about a hatless, turtle-neck or tuxedo-wearing white man who has been dead for years? Perhaps I'm seeking justification for having become the kind of checkbook liberal that I once so deplored. Perhaps I'm atoning for mocking my poor Uncle Herbie's banjo lessons, which were, after all, the harmless pursuit of an aging, good man seeking expression for some need that couldn't and wouldn't be satisfied by selling record players. Maybe I'm grateful to Leonard Bernstein for taking a fifteen-year-old girl with big thoughts and bigger feelings seriously at just the moment when I was grasping for the same respect.

Now I am sixty-one years old. I still carry Leonard Bernstein's songs with me. I carry all the songs I listened to over and over again when I was young; the vapid ones with the yellow plastic disc at their core right alongside my beloved *West Side Story*.

From this great remove, I can't chronicle all the turns on that journey, nor can I summon the arguments that steered them. What I now think is that change is driven by snatches of songs and slogans and indelible images on posters and record covers and memes like #BlackLivesMatter and the common sensibility of all who embraced them. What I can plot is a jagged emotional arc from the mid-60s to the early 80s, from excitement to confidence, even ecstasy, to bafflement, rage, determination, and despair. What I remember is Lenny, Che, Huey, and Abbie. Drums, flowers, fists, guns—icons on the walls, the beat of running feet, the scent of the purple Gestetner ink, tangy and bracing and yet somehow sweet.

Nixon's Farewell (1974)

When I got to work that August morning in 1974, I was tired and a little hung over. Richard Nixon, with his scowling face and sour but sanctimonious rhetoric about the justness of our government's murderous ways in Southeast Asia, had announced his resignation the night before. I'd celebrated with my friends and co-workers under a gorgeous starry sky, and only when dawn was approaching did we drop off into the drunken, righteous, and all-too-brief sleep of the vindicated.

Checking in at the nursing station, I learned that a new patient, Duane P., had been admitted. He'd had a small piece of his brain cut out in an experimental procedure a few years earlier, but according to the brief history in his chart, it didn't seem to make much difference. He was still unpredictable, uncontrollable, and undesirable.

I met him in the patients' lounge a few minutes later, where he sat playing *Solitaire*.

"You must be Duane. I'm Julie. I'm a psychiatric aide here."

He chuckled. "I *must* be Duane." He nodded his head slowly and stroked his scraggly beard. "Yeah, man, that's right." His attention wandered up to the television attached to the wall, which featured two top women's roller derby teams live from a nearby rink.

Elizabeth the anorexic (commonly referred to as Thin Lizzy, first by the staff, then proudly by Elizabeth herself once she heard about it) had dropped her knitting and was watching the match. "Cream her!" she yelled. "Cream the bitch!"

"That's disgusting," Duane said loudly. "That shit's terrible, man. Violent. It's terribly violent." He laughed loudly, then laid out a new *Solitaire* hand.

Leo, a regular, came into the lounge, sat down across from him, and silently offered Duane a smoke. Duane accepted, and they both inhaled deeply, then leaned back in their chairs.

"You must be new here," Leo said.

Duane nodded.

"Well, it's not too bad," Leo continued. "Beats the VA hospital, that's for damn sure."

Duane wasn't listening; he was focused instead on the cards lying in sloppy lines in front of him.

"I'd go with the red queen," Leo said, jabbing the card with one hand while deftly catching ash from the cigarette he held between thumb and index finger in the palm of the other.

"You a card shark or something?" Duane asked.

Leo smiled. "No, I've just played a lot of cards in my day." He shook his head ruefully. "And I've played a lot of *Solitaire* since losing my wife and daughter."

Duane looked up, curious. "Oh yeah? How'd you lose them? Did you leave them in a buddy's car? They fall out of your pants in the washing machine?" He laughed, a strange, high titter that was at odds with his raspy voice.

Leo reached into his back pocket and pulled out his wallet. "This is—*was*—my wife, Sherry," he said, holding out a laminated picture of an attractive brunette in her mid-thirties. "And this," he said, flipping to the next photograph in the wallet, "is our darling Alice." An adorable blonde child, as fair as Leo was dark, smiled up from the plastic case.

"So, did you kill them or what?" Duane asked.

Leo shook his head and sighed. "No, they left me. And who could blame them? I was a drunk, a lazy, no-good, sonofabitch slob who took and took and took and never gave a goddamn thing but heartache." He was enraptured by guilt. Duane looked at him, jiggling his knee restlessly, but listening. "The only thing I was good at was excuses," Leo continued. "And Sherry, bless her, she kept forgiving me. She'd reach out with a healing touch, and I'd slap her hand. Little Alice would look to me for someone to respect, and I showed her nothing but sloth and selfishness—"

"But *what* and selfishness?"

"Sloth," Leo answered impatiently. "You know, laziness. General laxity. Anyhow, it finally all came to a head when I forgot Alice's birthday. I'd gotten fired that day, showed up to work drunk, and they sent me home—told me never to come back. So I figured, why go home? I've got a whole day ahead of me, and I'm drunk but I'm not *drunk*."

"Yeah, right." Duane laughed appreciatively.

"So I went to the bar, and I got completely pissed, blotto, drunker than a squirrel in a still." He took a deep breath. "When I finally crawled home that night, there was a Dear John. *Dear Leo*, it said, *I can't watch you destroy yourself anymore. And I can't let you destroy little Alice. I love you, but I never want to see your drunken face again. Hugs and kisses, Sherry.*"

Duane shifted in his chair, then straightened the cards. "So that was that, huh?"

Leo nodded sadly. "That was that. I should've hung on to her."

"By the tits, right?" Duane once again erupted into that silly giggle, then laid down a black jack on the red queen.

Leo lit another cigarette and picked up his newspaper, and they fell into a comfortable silence.

It was all lies. Leo had never been married, never had a child. I'd spent several almost pleasant afternoons with him. He was intelligent and unmedicated—a good conversationalist, but also a pathological liar. He lied about everything. Not only did he have this totally fabricated life, but he'd lie about what he'd had for lunch, about the weatherman's forecast for the next day. Leo had opted out of real life in favor of a warm, state-funded room—sometimes in the hospital, sometimes in a motel—and a life he could make up. He'd created this persona of the man who'd learned the important lessons in life the hard way, the tragic sinner who'd fallen from grace and now wanted only to share his wisdom so that others wouldn't make his mistakes. He'd had stays in practically every hospital in the state and had been in our unit often enough, long enough, to act as its genial host. On

125

most mornings, when you asked Leo how he was doing, he'd answer, "Top of the world." But belying it all were the wife and daughter pictures he'd shown Duane. They were printed on fading newsprint and had come with the wallet.

Carl, a compact young man with bulging muscles and the Parkinsonian gait of the over-medicated, shuffled over and asked me for a newspaper.

Thin Lizzie, whose hearing was as sharp as her skeletal face, yelled, "Sucking up to the teacher, you big pussy?"

Saying nothing, Carl ignored her and sat down. He ran his hand back and forth over his brush cut, and tiny flecks of dandruff fell to his shoulders.

Lizzie, satisfied with her victory, resumed knitting and watching the roller derby. The closer she got to death, the more she cackled and crowed and lorded over people. Although only twenty-six, she'd stopped menstruating over a year earlier; now her papery skin was jaundiced and her breath increasingly putrid as her organs weakened from starvation. The hospital was trying to win legal guardianship so that they could put her on intravenous nutrition, but so far she and her mother had resisted. At this rate, despite our best efforts to police her at meals to make sure she ate, Lizzie was going to die soon, triumphantly in control to the end.

Carl rebuttoned his cardigan sweater and picked up the Home section of the *Springfield Journal*.

"Looking for some flower arranging tips?" Leo blandly asked.

Startled, Carl looked up. His eyes, in a perpetual squint, seemed to be mesmerized by some distant but approaching horror. He didn't answer, just looked down to check the buttons of his sweater.

"We interrupt this program to bring you a special broadcast," Walter Cronkite suddenly interrupted. "President Nixon—former President Nixon—is about to make his farewell speech to the White House staff. We bring it to you live."

"Eat shit and die, you crook," Lizzie screamed at the television.

Duane looked up sharply. "Who you talking to like that?"

"Tricky Dick," she answered, a little subdued. Lizzie wasn't used to being challenged.

"You don't go talking about him like that! That's my man. That's the fucking President!"

"Not anymore," Leo corrected.

"Bullshit," Duane answered. "He can be fucking President for as long as he wants. He's the President. He can drop bombs. He's got his own damn plane. They cook him whatever he wants to eat whenever he wants it. The dude wants a BLT at two in the morning, he can have one. He can do whatever he wants. He can phone fucking George Allen and tell him what plays to call."

Leo hunched forward. "Now I don't abide by that at all," he said gravely. "He's the President, he can run the country, fine. That's his job. Was his job. But you don't tell George Allen how to run the Redskins. That's *his* job."

Conversation dwindled as Nixon, standing in front of a room full of staff and cabinet members, sweating profusely, began to speak.

"I think the record should show that this is one of those spontaneous things that we always arrange whenever the President comes in to speak, and it will be so reported in the press, and we don't mind because they've got to call it as they see it." Mr. Ex-President was still referring to himself in the third person, and his speech had the slow, forced quality of someone heavily sedated. Behind him to his left, Pat stood glassy-eyed, with Julie and her fiancé and Tricia and her husband, flanking the apparently medicated pair.

Lizzie put down her knitting, stood, and walked over to stand directly in front of the television. Normally this behavior wouldn't be tolerated, but Leo and Duane just repositioned their chairs to see around her. Carl continued to look down at the newspaper in his clenched hand, as if afraid to look at the screen.

"...this Office, great as it is, can only be as great as the men and women who work for and with the President. This House, for example—I was thinking of it as we walked down this hall, and I was comparing it to some of the great Houses of the world that

I've been in. This isn't the biggest House. Many, and most, in even smaller countries are much bigger. This isn't the finest House. Many in Europe, particularly, and in China, Asia, have paintings of great, great value, things that we just don't have here, and probably will never have until we are a thousand years old or older. But this is the best House…"

"No, this is the *Big* House," Duane chortled.

"This is not a time for jokes," Carl muttered. "He's going down. He's going down."

Nixon continued, praising his staff and, by extension, himself for their dedication, for all of their excellent service in the past five-and-a-half years.

"…Mistakes, yes; but for personal gain, never. You did what you believed in. Sometimes right, sometimes wrong. And I only wish that I were a—a wealthy man. At the present time I've got to find a way to pay my taxes…"

I could barely stomach it. "Poor, poor Dick," I murmured to Phil, one of the other aides, "having to return to that hovel in San Clemente." He and several patients had ambled into the lounge, having just finished a big bingo game in the dining room. They gradually sat down in a semi-circle in front of the TV, anchored by Lizzie in the middle, and watched raptly as Nixon looked up and fell silent for a moment. His gaze turned inward, and then, as if in a trance, he haltingly began to talk in what was clearly a deviation from his script.

"I remember my old man. I think that they would have called him sort of—sort of a little man, common man. He didn't consider himself that way. You know what he was? He was a streetcar motorman first, and then he was a farmer, and then he had a lemon ranch. It was the poorest lemon ranch in California, I can assure you. He sold it before they found oil on it. And then he was a grocer. But he was a great man because he did his job, and every job counts up to the hilt, regardless of what happened."

Carl abruptly stood up. "I'm not a little man." His chair teetered on its back legs for a moment, then fell to the floor.

"Nobody said you were, asshole," Duane answered.

Phil stepped quickly between them, but Duane had already turned his attention back to the screen, and now Carl, too, was staring at Nixon. His shoulders sagging, his face clammy, Nixon had the haunted, elsewhere look that so many of our patients had.

"Nobody will ever write a book, probably, about my mother. Well, I guess all of you would say this about your mother: My mother was a saint. And I think of her, two boys dying of tuberculosis, nursing four others in order that she could take care of my older brother for three years in Arizona, and seeing each of them die, and when they died, it was like one of her own. Yes, she will have no books written about her. But she was a saint."

"*My* mother was a saint." Leo issued a loud, shuddering sob, and Duane hesitantly patted him on the back, as if burping him. The other patients looked briefly in Leo's direction, then back at the screen. It seemed as if everyone had inhaled and forgotten to exhale, as if their consciousness had fused in a state of breathless anticipation. Or recognition. Nixon was a liar, a self-made man, a paranoid sociopath, a pawn, a victim, a suddenly powerless bully. They knew him, they understood him; they didn't know whether to celebrate his fall or fear it.

Carl stood frozen, his clenched fists now held up to his temples. "My head hurts," he muttered, but we all ignored him, bewitched by the spectacle in front of us.

"Always give your best; never get discouraged; never be petty. Always remember others may hate you, but those who hate you don't win unless you hate them, and then you destroy yourself."

"Ain't that the truth," Phil murmured.

Some in Nixon's audience were visibly crying, and their distress was starting to permeate the TV lounge. So when Carol, the head nurse, stuck her head in to say that it was lunchtime, I was relieved to start shepherding people out of there.

Nixon had wrapped up his speech, Walter Cronkite offered a brief summary, and as I turned off the TV, I got what would be my last view of Nixon standing in the entrance to his helicopter, smiling at some invisible crowd, arms raised like crow's wings and the fingers of both hands arranged, as always, in the V for Victory sign.

And then it was over. The man who had personified arrogance and ruthlessness and senseless destruction was gone and so was my elation from the previous night. The end of his presidency left me feeling slightly hollow and cheap and all dressed up with no place to go. Nixon had been spat out, but the morning had followed its usual routine, and now there were lunch trays to be distributed.

The period after lunch offered a brief reprieve. The patients went back to their rooms while nurses distributed the meds, and I retreated to the nursing station to catch up on charts. Carl appeared at the door.

"I've got a terrible headache," he said. "I need some aspirin." He looked pale, and his eyeballs seemed to quiver like grapes suspended in Jell-O.

"I'm just an aide, Carl. I'm not allowed to dispense any medication, not even aspirin. Why don't you go back to your room and lie down, and I'll get a nurse to bring you some."

He lunged into the nursing station and grabbed the edges of the desk I was sitting at. "My head is going to explode. I need some aspirin now," he moaned. "I've waited long enough! Long enough!"

His face was inches from mine, and I could smell his breath. It was sweet and spoiled like old baby formula. Then he yanked himself upright and screamed. He stood there, and his arms sprung out from his sides, and he kept screaming, a long, hoarse roar. Then he fell straight back to the floor and grimly began twitching and kicking and gurgling.

It was a seizure—a hysterical seizure, one of the nurses later explained to me. Carl was not epileptic—"He just couldn't stand the excitement," she quipped. I couldn't understand how she could be so cavalier. His synapses were literally surging with rage and panic. One minute he was seizing on the floor; the next he was up, calm, and grateful for the aspirin to ease the pain in his head.

Carl had been my first solo admission, and after six weeks, he was still only inches away from the bedraggled, weeping man the police had dropped off in the middle of the night. The cop who brought him in told me that they'd picked Carl up at a bar, where he'd just broken one man's nose and another man's wrist.

"Nag," Carl had moaned when I'd asked him to spell his name for the intake forms. "My name is Nag, not Fag. They all call me Fag. They all laugh at me."

Now, at a "therapeutic" dose of Thorazine, Carl was a shuffling, subdued *dybbuk*—a square and hulking man built for vengeance, but made of clay. He would have no helicopter to whisk him away from the site of his shame, no calming California sun to restore him.

With the fall semester of my senior year just a few weeks off, I also would be going soon, leaving this job with none of the certainty with which I'd started it. Before setting foot in the hospital, I'd believed that with the power of my position, a clear mind, and helpful intentions, I and others like me could make the world a better, more sane place. But I was seeing that goodness and power were rarely coupled. Nixon was only a marginally sane man, and an evil one, both in power and out of it. My patients wandered in and out of their right minds; they engaged in simple acts of kindness and practiced devastating scorn, broke noses one day and were straitjacketed the next. Whether batty or lucid, they were not lovely innocents. I was sane but largely ineffectual, and to my profound shame, I was now frightened of Carl. The juncture of power, goodness, and sanity was nowhere to be found.

After work that day, I walked through the parking lot and peered into the back seat of my car through the window. All clear. I got in, but even after I turned on the ignition and heard the soothing engine sound and felt the car's steady vibration, I was sure that Carl would pop up from where he'd been lying on the floor and fill my rearview mirror with his face and scream.

Then, like everyone else in his strafed and invisible life, I drove away.

Working Average (1976-1981)

On July 3, 1976, at 7:29 a.m., I dragged to my station in Fountain Hill Mill, past dozens of sewing machines and row upon row of middle-aged women in smocks and short puffy brown hair. Long tables were piled high with shirts, some without sleeves, some without collars, lying limp and menacing like stick hangman figures. Dirty canvas bins were everywhere, next to all the chairs, in front of all the machines, abutting all the aisles and straddling cracked and fading yellow safety lines. Clusters of knotted threads, piles of fabric shavings, wads of oily piping scraps already huddled underfoot. Jigsaw splashes of light entered through bare spots on the windows where the paint had fallen off.

Mark and I had moved to Allentown, Pennsylvania, about six months earlier to join the industrial working class. I hated the place, with its small-town suspicion of outsiders, its grid of flat, graceless row houses abutting the sidewalks, its storefront lunch spots touting scrapple and ten varieties of baloney, its gun and ammo stores, its third shift dive bars serving nothing but Pabst and Schaeffer and pickled eggs.

Though I'd had my share of low-paying, pretty menial jobs (waitress, typist, day care worker), nothing had prepared me for the physical demands of factory work. My first job in Allentown, working second shift at a T-shirt printing factory, required me to stand at the end of a production line peering at wet graphics of the television characters Mr. T. and Squiggy, searching for drips, runs, or stains. I'd eliminate any I found with a spray bottle of dry cleaning fluid and a few vigorous scrubs. I hated it. I hated working second shift, spending my daylight hours alone at home in this new town far from any ocean, watching old B-movies on television and preparing

Mark's evening and my own midnight dinner in the crock pot.

Within a month of starting at the T-shirt factory, I found a day-shift job in Bethlehem, on the other side of the Lehigh River, a mile or so from the rapidly emptying steel mills and coke ovens lining its shore. Each day I'd walk from my car past brick row homes planted in the steep hills, with strips of yard lying behind them like licorice sticks. Barely visible at the top of the three-story plant was the sign, "Moyer's Silk Mill, 1894," framed by blue-painted windows and rusty red brick.

On that morning—the day before the American Bicentennial celebration—the horn sounded, and sewing machines turned on like a choir of mechanical gnats, all rumbling and buzzing in different keys. I sat down, popped *Born to Run* into the Walkman and fed the first few inches of red piping into an attachment at the front of my machine. I folded the piping over the sleeve as it passed through it, lining up the straight edge of the first sleeve with the needle and hitting the foot pedal. After a few loud seconds a piped red sleeve emerged, elegant and neat, with its line of twin stitches like high tension lines on a Nebraska highway.

Scissors nestled in my palm, after sewing two dozen sleeves I cut the piping, tore off the cardboard ticket tied to the bundle, and stuck it in the drawer of my sewing table. At the end of the day I'd paste each ticket bearing the price per bundle (typically anywhere from five to fifteen cents) onto a pre-glued sheet and turn them all in to the office so that my day's earnings could be calculated. As a piece-rate worker—paid based on how many bundles I completed each day—I was pathetic, generally failing to produce enough to earn the $2.75 per hour minimum wage they had to pay me. The pros—the competent women with the good work (generally fabrics that fed easily through the machine and didn't gather or fray)—could make double that, some as much as $6.50 an hour. But me, I was what they called "working average"—someone just productive enough to be kept on the job, but not efficient enough to actually make a living wage at it.

As I picked the next bundle out of the bin, I could feel the morning's rhythm developing, a steady rocking into the machine and back, the binful of sleeves providing enough easy work to keep me on automatic until lunch. With the Walkman on, I felt like I was watching TV with the sound turned down. Other people's lips moved, and every so often some sound would penetrate the miniature headphones.

"Who the hell's got my five-inch folder?"

"Marion, I need work!"

"Well there ain't no more goddamn Peacock Blue!"

The bathroom door in front of me was in constant motion. Each time it opened, a gray wave of smoke rolled out, with women trailing in its wake. By midmorning I was breathing through my mouth, trying not to take in the smell of stale cigarettes and sluggish plumbing. Halfway through the day, Marion the floor girl—a non-union job with a bit less authority than a foreman—banged her scissor handles on the Coke machine. She had terrible teeth and a tight face, pulled tighter by a long brown ponytail. "11:30, girls," she hollered.

Normally the women would pull out their lunch bags from under their sewing machines and file outside to lean on the factory wall, smoking or eating. But today, in honor of the next day's Bicentennial festivities, Grace and Marie and Maria-Facenda created some empty space on one of the long sorting tables, and women laid out their pot-luck lunch contributions. Plastic bowls of German potato and macaroni salads, platters of salami and cream-cheese pinwheels, and trays of pigs-in-blankets formed a line down Ronny's sorting table. Between the lunch and a high, floppy pile of shirts lay six inches of bare wood and an Avon catalogue.

"This table's a mess." Grace began scrubbing it with a handi-wipe she pulled from the pocket of her smock.

Grace and Marie could have been twins. Both had pale, doughy complexions beneath brown beehive hair-dos. Both favored delicate floral patterns on their sewing smocks. But Grace wore delicate wire-rimmed glasses when she sewed or leafed through her *Ladies Home Journal* on break, while Marie was twice her size and never appeared to read anything.

Anna, single needle operator and shop chairlady for the union, stepped delicately between bins and set down a large box on the sorting table. Grace and Anna gazed at the cake sitting crown-like inside it, *God Bless America* in oozing blue letters on top.

"What do you girls have planned for the holiday?" Anna asked. Though she worked piece rate like everyone else, the "you girls" gave her away. She was always looking for ways to distance herself from the others, to drop allusions to her steward training sessions in New York and inside knowledge of union affairs, even in her conversations with the plant owners, Nate and Isaac.

"The usual," Marie answered. "Picnic, horseshoes, drag King Keith back to the truck and tuck him into bed, then take care of the other baby." King Keith was her husband, "a useless lug nut," and "the other baby" was the son her daughter had given birth to a few months earlier, much to the surprise of his oblivious grandmother, who had somehow failed to realize that her daughter was pregnant.

"I'm actually going to be marching in Philadelphia," I said nervously. "In a demonstration. Against the government." Grace and Maria Facenda looked at me politely, but Anna's lips pursed in annoyance and Marie flat-out smirked. "You know, for jobs and economic justice," I added weakly. I thrust fliers in their general direction. When nobody reached out her hand to take one, I laid them on the table.

Above an illustration of a multi-ethnic crowd holding a banner, bold red type blared, *We've carried the rich for 200 years. Let's get them off our backs.*

The Bicentennial hoopla is in full swing already and it's going to get worse. Red, white and blue hydrants, license plates, beer cans; Bicentennial minutes on TV; Revolutionary War leaders used to advertise everything imaginable. But behind all these quick-money schemes stands a public relations smoke-screen. The millionaires and their cronies who run this country are trapped in a real economic crisis; these parasites are trying to use the Bicentennial to cover up 200 years of exploitation and convince the people that we have the best of all possible worlds,

135

so that their profit-making system can keep alive.[25]

At this point I was supposed to invite them to abandon their horseshoes and hot dogs in favor of marching through North Philadelphia, demonstrating their anger at the bourgeoisie and inspiring others to join the fight for JOBS OR INCOME NOW! But I knew better than to even try. "We already have jobs," Marie would sarcastically point out. And if I countered that the pay and working conditions were terrible (everyone had chronic sinus infections from the fabric dust and toxic lubricant we'd spray on the sewing machine needles, and the color of our sneezes each night told us what fabric we'd been working with that day), she would reply that "some of us, those of us who actually know how to sew, are doing just fine, thank you very much." If I argued that many people had no jobs, Grace would suggest that "those people should go back to where they came from," and Brazilian-born Maria-Facenda, still desperate after twenty years to prove her naturalized citizen bona fides, would fervently agree.

As a college-educated outsider, I was already strange. They simply couldn't fathom why I was there. Big believers in loyalty, they mistrusted me far more than the union and mill bosses I was trying to mobilize them against. After all, I was a traitor to my class. Who wouldn't want to be a boss if that meant a new car and a trip to Disneyworld, maybe even a cruise, every year? In truth, if I was betraying anyone, it was probably my long-dead grandfather, a failed garment boss in his own right who'd banned his son from ever working in the *shmata* business. Though not an order-issuer himself, my father, with stoic irony, couldn't help but observe an unwelcome symmetry in his daughter's return to the grueling, ill-paid trade that he'd spent his own life fleeing.

"I think it's disgusting," Anna said, picking up a flier, then letting it flutter from her hand back onto the sorting table. "This is the greatest country on earth."

"You tell her," Maria-Facenda nodded with solemn vigor.

"Sure, it's a great country in a lot of ways," I answered carefully. "But that doesn't mean it couldn't get a lot better, a lot more fair."

Marie rolled her eyes. "Everything *could* get better. Take my husband, for example." She winked at Grace, who erupted in surprisingly raucous laughter. "That doesn't mean I walk up and down with a picket sign outside my own house. Family stays together."

"Yeah, but we're not all family," I answered.

But Marie had moved on. "Of course inside the house, that's another story."

"I know. I heard you last night," Anna said. "My husband said, 'What's that? A coyote killing a puppy? But I told him, 'No, that's just Marie talking to Keith.'"

And so it went. When the 3:30 horn sounded that day, Maria-Facenda and Grace and Marie stood, folded their smocks, and dusted their pants. Grace, muttering to herself, rearranged the plastic flowers and photographs on her machine. Maria Facenda wiped away the clusters of thread that lay like painted tears on the cheeks of her plaster Jesus. On her way out, as she walked past me, Marie picked up the stack of fliers still sitting forlornly on the sorting table, and with a broad smile, dumped them in the trash.

Bullied women became bullies, and the piece-rate system was social Darwinism at its most gloriously cruel. My co-workers, incentivized to compete, literally fought over scraps and hoarded the "good" scraps that were theirs, looking down and not around them. Like kids not picked for the starting team, they turned on those lower in the food chain to inflate their own sense of worth.

But knowing that didn't help. Humiliated and angry, I picked up my bag and wore my filth past the senile guard and out into the muggy afternoon.

The next day's *Rich off our Backs Demo*, as it came to be known in our small circle, was a pale knock-off of the massive anti-war and anti-Nixon *Throw the Bum Out* demonstrations I'd grown up on. Small contingents of fellow leftists from New York, Philadelphia, and Baltimore gathered in a Germantown park, joined by a slightly larger brigade of Vietnam Vets Against the War from throughout the East coast. Among the crowd, numbering in the hundreds, were some students, even some real workers. But the people we seemed to attract most were the homeless and the half-mad, emaciated men in tattered army jackets, and bearded, weather-beaten, toothless ones, aged beyond their years by amphetamines and sleeping on sidewalks.

Still, as we snaked our way through the bombed out, largely black neighborhoods of North Philadelphia, the embarrassed despair I'd felt when we first rallied started to dissipate. The notoriously brutal Philly police were largely deployed to the officially sanctioned red, white, and blue celebrations and parade around Independence Hall. We were just a minor distraction. As we chanted our slogans and waved our crimson banners, people trickled out of their row homes to watch and listen. Many smiled and gave us the fist; some even joined our scrawny procession. Opening our throats, shouting in a shared voice, we were no sillier than the Mummers parade. Our words had far more real gravitas than anything else being intoned from televised podiums that day.

It was one of the few times during all our Allentown years that I remembered the joy of rebellion.

Despite my loneliness, I wasn't totally isolated. I'd made a handful of friends. Ruth, one of the few black women in the plant, was also one of the few to embrace the idea of class struggle without any help from me. I'd met her in my first week or two at Fountain Hill Mills, when one day at lunch she raised her eyes and looked at Anna, who was earnestly conferring with Nate, one of the plant owners. "That Anna, she kiss any more ass and she'll be as brown as me."

I laughed.

"She should have some pride. I don't know what that woman does for self-respect. My kids give more thought to their pet mouse than she do to the whole damn shop full of people she supposed to be standing up for."

"You can say that again." *Please do*, I thought. *Say it louder.*

"And how about Kojak?" she said, jerking her thumb toward Nate. He was a big man, with a shaved knobby head and a fat cigar in his mouth, wrapped in tight size 40 jeans, a black satin cowboy shirt, and a heavy silver belt buckle with *Levi* spelled out between the legs of a rearing bronco. A gaping hole between shirt snaps exposed a fold of pale flesh. "I don't know about you, but I just wet my pants every time he comes into view."

An honest-to-god proletarian hero, I thought to myself, and quickly got to know Ruth. We'd hang out at lunch, smoking and talking about the state of the world, and she even came to a few political events. But as a mother of three, with a husband who worked second shift ("He gets them by day, I get them by night. I'm the lucky one."), Ruth's time was scarce. And when she moved from the sewing floor to the cutting room in the building next door—one of the few women to succeed in fighting for that higher paid, higher skilled job—I saw even less of her. Productivity trumped all. Ruth was fast and unfailingly accurate in dissecting the big bolts of cloth.

At that point, I started spending my lunches with Martha, a quiet redhead my age, and a presser named Jay. Sometimes we'd go to Martha's apartment after work and watch *General Hospital,* or accompany her to see her boyfriend's band play Springsteen and Bob Seger covers at the Legion hall. Jay, a guitar player with a ponytail, piercing eyes, and a community college degree in Culinary Arts, had a cover band of his own. When the weather was warm enough, we'd hang out in the parking lot listening to the car radio, or walk around the neighborhood, where Martha would guess the price, number of bedrooms, and wallpaper patterns of every house we passed.

"Are you practicing to be a real estate agent or what?" Jay finally asked her.

"There's worse things to be," Martha answered. "I wouldn't mind going in and out of people's houses all day and just looking at their stuff."

"You mean their mail, or pictures of their kids?" I asked.

"No, I don't give a shit about that. I mean furniture, curtains, mirrors, you know, their stuff."

"Personally, I never saw the point in having real estate agents in the first place," Jay said. "I mean I don't see why you can't just talk to the person who owns the house and work it out. I don't see why you need this person in the middle going 'he says this' and 'she'll settle for that.' It's like having a translator when you're both speaking the same language."

Martha began throwing Tic Tacs into the gutter, one at a time, delicate little tosses, arcing from her fingertips to a crescent of rotten leaves rimming the sewer grate. "Realtors exist because left to their own devices, people won't work it out." Martha wasn't ignorant. Her credo was: Drop out and turn on. When I'd try to enlist her to come to a lecture or a demonstration, she'd flash a patient smile, roll a joint, and tell me that outlaw country singers Waylon Jennings and Willie Nelson were her political heroes.

"Oh man, I don't believe that," I protested. "I think that if people could get over their petty differences and see that it was in everyone's interests to work together ..."

"And how are you going to make that happen?" she asked.

"I don't know exactly. But I think—"

"That's right," Martha said grimly. "You don't know, because it can't be done. You just wake up, come into work, go home, fuck your boyfriend, watch TV. Just like me. We're like a line of hens at a Perdue chicken farm, you know?"

Jay laughed. "Man, that's harsh." He stuck out his chin and bobbed his head.

Martha chirped, "*Bawk, bawk bawk bawk,*" taking the first high-footed step back to the plant.

The pathetic peak of my organizing efforts at Fountain Hill Mills came about a year later, when I succeeded in persuading Jay to run for shop steward. Despite his habitual sarcasm, he still had aspirations— to get paying gigs for his band, to eventually get a Bachelor's degree, to accomplish something for someone.

With the earnestness of a Student Council election committee, a few of us developed Jay's campaign materials. We taped up posters featuring his picture captioned with a big bold demand to *Take*

Back the Union! We wrote leaflets decrying the piece-rate system that drove workers to produce more and more while fellow workers were jobless. And when the election results were announced, Jay got 23 votes out of the roughly 250 cast.

There had been a severe thunderstorm that afternoon, with gusty winds that blew down one of the electrical lines leading into the plant. One end of the dangling wire curled on the sidewalk, hissing and jumping. After punching out, everyone gathered around it. The security guard dug into the tool box in his trunk and came out with a metal washer. He threw it at the downed wire, but the wind caught it and it sailed over the spitting tip. Then came nuts, bolts, and connectors that hit their target, making the wire writhe. The circle grew, and the women all watched, as if taunting a caged and dangerous animal, grateful for its liveliness, excited by its helplessness.

I left Fountain Hill Mills for a series of jobs in electronics factories soon after. They were as clean as the garment mills were filthy. I earned a low but stable hourly wage, and there was something aesthetically pleasing in assembling the multi-colored transistors and resistors, loading them into printed circuit boards, and soldering them into place. Though I didn't understand the physics of electronics, I loved the poetry of its language, the transmission and capacity of current, the easy flux of solder from glowing liquid to solid. I worked mostly with men. While they could be just as cruel to each other as the women in the garment mills, their jabs were funnier. Many of them had been in the military, and went to New York regularly, even if just to see Yankees games. Their worlds were bigger.

Mark and I had gotten married, had a baby, and established a small but reliable social circle. Occasionally we'd have barbeques with the couple next door, a hairdresser named Cindy and her dumb but sweet husband, Harmon, who worked at the Sunoco station. Domingo, a chain-smoking Dominican, down the block, always sitting on his stoop or working on his car, ambled over whenever we stepped outside, to talk about the Iranian hostage crisis or the Panama Canal Treaty or Mohammed Ali's loss to Leon Spinks.

Mark had befriended Ken, a guy at the Caloric stove factory where he worked, and through him, we loosely folded into a group of people our age that had grown up in the Lehigh Valley. On summer days we'd cheer at Ken's softball games or go swimming in the local quarries where the water was clear and the sunfish were so plentiful and fearless that they'd nibble on our toes. We had lazy, long evenings at the drive-in, where we learned to bring lawn chairs and coolers and have moonlit picnics.

But most nights we watched television, prepared our lunches to take to work the next day, cut grocery coupons, worried over the bills, and cared for our daughter. "What is to be done?" I'd murmur to her every night (echoing Lenin's famous 1902 tract), then answer with a singsong litany: "First we change your diaper. Then put on your jammies. Then we feed you dinner. Yummm...milk again." *What is to be done?* I'd ask myself the next morning as I reeled through my checklist: *diaper bag, lunch, purse, keys.*

I felt less and less like a poser as our days took on the same silhouetted routines as everyone around us. We'd made a life not so different from those of the people we'd come to rescue, one of yawning tedium and small pleasures, but also marked by a nagging despair at our own inertia. We'd been to college and knew how to fit in among highly achieving people. We read books and the *New York Times*, had been to Europe, didn't say "ain't," and had good teeth. A road back to an easier, more stimulating life beckoned to us.

But taking it, resuming the lives we'd been born into, felt shameful, even though we no longer believed what we'd probably never believed—that the American proletariat would rise up and make a better world.

John, the Pottstown auto worker who embraced his role as boss of our New Left cadre with all the passion and avarice of Gordon Gecko at a junk bond auction, always suspected that the siren song of our own privilege called to us. Smart but bitter, frustrated by the mindlessness of his day job, he loved to quote Stalin, and his droopy mustache even resembled Uncle Joe's. He'd abandoned the Russian

Orthodoxy of his Serbian parents for the Marxism of a guy he used to drink with, and as one of the few proletarians in an organization of middle-class kids who aspired to be downwardly mobile, had risen rapidly through the ranks. He was a sneering, self-important martinet, but as dislikable as he was, John was actually right in his conviction that when I moved to Allentown, I was a spoiled middle-class girl, fundamentally just hoping that somehow we could all just be nicer to each other. Allentown was supposed to cure me of that and expand my horizons, immerse me in the *real* world.

The biweekly meeting of our cadre was now down to eight or so people, six of whom were tired of our own voices. I commented about our latest directive. "On the one hand..."

"On the one hand!" John interrupted. "So you're going to tell me there's another hand?"

"Um, yes."

He laughed at me. "You're still the same petit bourgeois you were when you came here. You've got two books on the shelf."

"Two books on the shelf?"

"Yeah, you want to consider *all* the possibilities." He squealed "all" in a falsetto. "You don't want to commit to the correct path, even though Mao says that when it comes to the science of revolution, you only need one book on the shelf."

I wish I'd stood up then, said "You're right—I want a shelf full of books," and stormed out. But though John's dogmatism helped push us out the door, as much as we longed to return to a big city, one where we had old friends and new possibilities, we were scared. We'd been off the expected path for several years, during which our college friends were becoming doctors and lawyers and social workers. Unattached and childless, they were going to clubs and had taken up jogging.

Mark and I were still drawn by their gravitational field, but ours was a cold, dark orbit. We felt more remote with each passing day.

What was to be done?

We felt as though we had come across something that people did not understand or did not recognize but that's the season that we were going into, not for three months but for an extended period of time. A lot of the folks who represented summer and spring and fall had been killed and assassinated. The only season left was winter. ...

- Gil Scott-Heron, discussing the origin
of his 1974 album, "Winter in America"

Winters (1978-Present)

We were driving west on I-84, on our way back from Boston to Allentown, and on the radio, Bob Seger was singing *Against the Wind*, wishing he knew as little now as he did when he was young. Mark and I joined heartily joined in the chorus when we saw two helicopters overhead. I ejected the tape from the cassette player and turned on the radio.

"After 444 days in captivity, the fifty-two American hostages have just touched down on American soil," the newscaster intoned. "After being greeted by President Carter—excuse me, *Former* President Carter—at the U.S. Air Force hospital in Wiesbaden, Germany, where they received medical check-ups and debriefings, they embarked on their final leg home."

We pulled onto the shoulder just before the first exit to Newburgh. On this gray, bone-chillingly damp January day in 1981, many more copters approached, swarming like black flies. The choppers' staccato penetrated the car microseconds before we then also heard it on the radio at a slightly higher pitch. Though I could see the helicopters through the windshield, somehow the broadcaster's trebly chronicle filling the car felt more real.

"And now—yes, they are deboarding at the Stewart Air National Guard base in Newburgh, New York, and boarding buses to West Point," the newscaster continued. It was strange to be so near to such a highly anticipated event, to hear what was happening only a mile away but to see only the watchers in their choppers. "There, throngs of grateful Americans are already lining the streets to greet them."

The day before, sitting in my parents' living room, we'd glumly watched Ronald Reagan's inaugural address, which unfolded as the hostages were being led to the MedEvac planes that would take them from Tehran to Athens to Algiers, and finally to the U.S. Air Force base in Germany. As the final affront to Jimmy Carter's decimated dignity, the Iranian regime ensured that the hostage release would not happen while he was president. And perhaps they already recognized that they'd have a friend, albeit a covert one, in the new president.

"We must act today in order to preserve tomorrow," Reagan had said, his rouged cheeks glowing. "In this present crisis, government is not the solution to our problem, government is the problem."

"It is now," Mark muttered.

When Richard Nixon had defeated George McGovern in a landslide victory eight years earlier, I'd at least had enough spirit to get blazingly drunk with my brother and a few friends, and throw a boot out the car window on our way home. But on the night that Reagan beat Carter by a margin almost as large, I couldn't even bear to watch the returns. I left Mark slack-jawed on the couch, climbed upstairs with our two-year-old daughter in my arms, and went to bed. Katie slept with us that night; I sought comfort in her soft splayed form in footsy pajamas and her deep surrender to sleep. I was seeking sanctuary as much as giving it.

The 1960s ended in 1975. By the time Saigon fell in April and U.S. Marines frantically air-lifted the remaining Americans out of Vietnam, the anti-war movement and all it carried in its wake was spent.

As usual, it was the artists who'd absorbed the zeitgeist, naming what so many of us felt. "Winter in America," poet Gil Scott-Heron called it on his 1975 album. Songwriter Jackson Browne knew it too. "Running on Empty," he sang in 1977.

And like him, there were Mark and I—running behind. As we

traipsed from house to house, job to job, and from one anemic protest to the next, we were increasingly mute. Political splits, defections, and just plain fatigue caused lifeboat-based friendships to drift apart. One by one, we were being submerged.

In March of 1979, when Katie was five months old, Three Mile Island, a nuclear power plant about eighty miles west of our house in Allentown, threatened to blow up. News reports were conflicting and vague: There had been a partial meltdown or there hadn't; there was cause for "concern" but not "alarm"; radioactive steam may or may not have been released into the air; radiation levels were or weren't elevated; the increased radiation levels weren't a danger to public health, but 140,000 pregnant women and children were being evacuated from a twenty-mile radius of the plant; cows were toppling over in the fields around Harrisburg or lactating with their usual sluggish contentment, confined to their barns or free to graze. The situation was, according to Governor Scranton, "under control" or "more complex than MetEd first led us to believe."

Should we leave town, which would have cost us our lousy, poorly paying, but scarce jobs? Should we stay, choose to believe what reassurances were being issued, and just hope everything would be okay? I watched Katie nap, knees tucked and arms outstretched like a tiny frog. Was her paleness just the normal March pallor? And was she suddenly napping longer? By the third day of the crisis, when a hydrogen bubble had developed within the reactor's dome, we were done vacillating. We stocked up on infant formula and drove our baby to Mark's sister's house in Long Island. She spent one very long week there—great fun for my young, newly married and unemployed sister-in-law, but wrenching for us. When we brought Katie back home, it wasn't with relief so much as fatalism. Recession, contamination, apathy followed by jingoism —we were fucked.

Almost exactly a year after Three Mile Island, in March of 1980, I began my automotive day doing the only thing that would enable my car—a massive burgundy Olds Delta 88—to start. I opened the hood, unscrewed the wing nut on the air cleaner, lifted it out, then inserted the hard plastic head of Katie's toy elephant, trunk first, into the throat of the carburetor to prop open the butterfly valve. Once the engine was running, I reassembled the air cleaner, closed the hood, tucked the elephant into my glove compartment, and headed off to work. At the end of the day, I repeated the process as my amused co-workers at Colbourn Instruments stood in the parking lot looking on. ("That chick sure knows how to give head," Dwight would sometimes say, earning a rare reproof from the other guys, who didn't approve of sexually crude comments pertaining to women they knew.) After pulling out onto West Tilghman, I'd gun the engine, hoping to catch a green light at the top of the hill so that my wheezing old car wouldn't stall out.

We'd bought this enormous vehicle (for "a song," the Pottstown used car dealer assured us) after my oil-gushing Subaru, which had boycotted the reverse gear for months, finally refused to shift into first gear as well. It held over twenty gallons, and at almost a dollar per gallon, a fill-up was unaffordable.

Thanks to gas rationing, at least once or twice a week I got to end the workday by waiting in a crawling, exhaust-spewing parade to top off my tank. April 21, 1979, was an odd date of the month, and since my license plate number ended with a three, I was eligible to buy gas. Me, and the fifty or so cars in front of me snaking around Liberty onto Ninth Street. Since the gas line wasn't moving, like most of the other drivers, I got out of the car to stretch my legs and have a better view of the inaction.

Two guys leaned on the bumper of the black Ford Pinto in front of me.

"This is just like '73," the redhead in the dark blue, oil-stained jumpsuit said. A Mack Truck logo was emblazoned over his left chest pocket. "Fucking OPEC is at it again."

"No, they're not," retorted his buddy, an older guy with a leathery face and a missing tooth. "They're on our side this time."

"Bullshit," redhead answered, emphasizing the second syllable, as if to distinguish this bull product from others. "Haven't you seen them fucking towelheads on the news?"

He was referring to the fist-pumping Iranian crowds demanding the extradition of Reza Pahlavi from the United States. A month earlier, the U.S.-installed Shah of Iran had been overthrown and fled the country, eventually landing in New York to be treated for the cancer that would kill him a few months later.

"The protests are in Iran," his friend patiently explained. "Iran's the country that's exporting less oil to us. All them other Arab countries are in OPEC, and they're picking up the slack." He laughed, shaking his head. "Don't you get it, man. There *is* no gas shortage, just high prices and panic-buying."

The guy in the jump suit bowed in mock deference. "Well, excuse me, Professor. It's hard to keep track of who hates us this week."

"They're mad about us sheltering the Shah." The older man laughed. "Try saying that three times fast. Sheltering the Shah, Sheltering the Shah…" He seemed to be trying to coax his buddy into good humor.

"Enough, man. I get it. And I'm not laughing. Jesus Christ." He smacked his car's dusty black trunk. "We're using up all the gas we're buying just waiting to buy the next round."

"What kind of mileage does this thing get when it's not exploding?" his friend asked, now trying to change the subject. "Eight, ten miles to the gallon?"

"What does it matter, asshole? If that pansy Carter hadn't invited that shit-eating Shah here in the first place, we wouldn't be having these problems."

"I don't think *I'm* the asshole, sunshine." He was done cajoling. "It's not Carter, it's not the Shah that's our problem. It's Exxon and Mobil and all the big oil companies making up this phony shortage."

"You're calling *me* sunshine?"

I'd heard accounts of fights breaking out when a car tried to cut in line or fill a gas can in addition to a tank. One gas station attendant got kicked to the ground for imposing a five-dollar maximum on every driver. It was a necessary but dangerous time to make the case for American Imperialism being the enemy, and not the crowds of chanting, bearded Iranian men we were seeing on the news every night. So although I had leaflets in my car, I wasn't about to hand them out in this fuming queue.

From about 1978 until the early 1980s, I was chronically scared. During the 1960s and early 1970s, the political demonstrations I had been in were peaceful and huge. We were the majority, and though our chants may have been angry ("Hey, hey, LBJ, How many kids did you kill today?"), we eschewed violence. Even at Richard Nixon's counter-Inaugural, the protestors outnumbered the people there to cheer Tricky Dick's second term.

But by the late 1970s, the clock had been turned back twenty years, and small, mean, angry mobs were once again in vogue. In 1975, before we'd left Boston for Allentown, a teenager in a small white crowd protesting the desegregation of the schools, was immortalized in a newspaper photograph. Grimacing, legs planted wide apart, he grasped a long pointy flag pole and tried to impale a black man with the Stars and Stripes.

One Saturday night in November, 1979, Mark and I sat on our blue plaid couch in Allentown, facing the living room wall that the previous owner had painted in purple stripes and bordered with pink roofing shingles. We'd seen the tail-end of *Jeopardy* ("What is Lake Baikal?" we shouted to each other in unison, then tallied up the money we would have won had we been contestants), and were awaiting a rerun of *Laverne and Shirley*.

But before it did, the familiar logo of the network's News Brief filled the screen.

"Five people believed to be members of the Communist Workers Party were shot and killed today in a protest in Greensboro, North Carolina," the newscaster announced. Mark and I froze. Though we didn't belong to that group, it was possible, even likely, that we knew people who did. "Their 'Death to the Klan' rally and march were disrupted by several vehicles filled with men believed to be members of the Ku Klux Klan and American Nazi Party," he explained as video from the incident played.

The protest had been small—a cadre of mostly white people in blue hard hats chanting "Death to the Klan," curiously observed by the residents of the housing project they were parading by. A procession of cars drove up alongside the marchers—a big, pale-green one with a confederate flag decal on its front bumper and looming dorsal fins over the back wheels, a blue car, a red van, a long white pick-up truck. The marchers seemed to be hitting one of the cars with their signs. Two of them pulled over, and passengers pulled rifles out of the trunk of one of them. They scrambled down the street, shooting at the marchers in front of them. They did this for about thirty seconds—running, aiming, shooting, before going back to the car and returning the weapons to its trunk. The camera panned a little, showing one body on the grass beside a flat, ugly building with a cross over its door. On the ground behind a parked car, someone else twitched his foot.

Mark and I stayed up for the eleven o'clock news. We needed to hear the marchers' names. We didn't know any of them, but it seemed as if we should. They were people just like Mark and me and those in our isolated, diminishing circle. One marcher was a black nurse; two were white doctors (one of whom had quit his medical practice to organize textile workers instead). One was a Cuban immigrant who'd graduated magna cum laude from Duke University, another a graduate of the Harvard Divinity School. Professionals and radicalized do-gooders, their silly slogans had been punished by death. (Over the course of the next several years, their murderers would be twice acquitted by all-white juries.)

So there was a certain inevitability to events closer to home in 1979, when the Syrian immigrants who populated the garment mills and auto body repair shops of Allentown were attacked by gangs of young white guys. And when fifty-three Americans were taken hostage by Iranian students, it was open season on foreigners and the malcontents who sided with them. Patriotic fervor reached such a peak in the wake of the U.S. hockey team's 1980 Olympics victory over the Soviet Union that people took to chanting "USA" not just in international sporting events, but driving down the street waving the Red, White, and Blue outside their car windows. The "true" Americans—those who had felt marginalized or left behind during the 1960s—were taking their country back.

On a rare night out in February, 1980, Mark and I drove to Philadelphia to see The Clash. *London Calling* had been released a few months earlier, and replaced Bruce Springsteen's *Darkness at the Edge of Town* as the default on our record player.

Married young, already parents, Mark and I were too old for slam dancing or mosh pits. But in the emerging party culture of pop music, in a landscape studded by the puerile stuttering of *My Sharona* or the glitzy camp of *YMCA,* punk—especially The Clash--kept streaking through my peripheral vision. Against Mick Jones' slashing guitar, Joe Strummer's savage glee at the imminent demise of London and civilization as we knew it was disturbingly resonant.

Springsteen's poetry moved me, but punk's nihilism, while alien, broke through all that sorrow now and then, fueled by some bright red blood coursing through it. So we were excited as we slogged through Philly's slushy streets, past the small neighborhood movie theatre whose marquee boasted the unusual double bill:

Jesus Christ, Superstar

Creature from the Black Lagoon

"See, I told you that religion's monstrous," Mark roared.

I poked his shoulder. "Shh…" I said, gesturing to the surrounding working class Italian neighborhood. "Pay attention to where you are."

"Oh, for Christ's sake," he muttered. "Can't a man even be heretical in peace?"

"In peace, just not in public." I couldn't believe how cowed I'd become.

When we got to the theatre, we joined a crowd of leather-clad eighteen-year-olds. The lights went down and out came an opening act—the old, stooped Lee Dorsey, accompanied by a pianist and a bass player whose combined age didn't equal his. He'd had a couple of hits in the mid-1960s—the New Orleans-influenced "Ya Ya" and the far-funkier "Working in a Coal Mine." This song about an honest-to-God worker is probably why The Clash had invited the singer to open for them. But gray-tinged and brittle as a twig, Dorsey was an antique on display in a very obscure museum.

When he shambled off stage, nobody called for an encore. And when instead of The Clash, a young black guy in dreadlocks and a knit Rastafarian hair-do cap came out carrying a huge boom box, the crowd booed. Seemingly undaunted, the guy pressed play, propped the boom box up on his shoulder, and started to rhyme against its sputtering beats. His voice was nasal, the reverb on the mic turned up all the way, and we could barely make out his name—Mikey Dread—let alone his lyrics. In England, he was already a chart-topping Dub performer and sound engineer, but in this crowd of white punks, Mikey Dread was just mystifying. We were witnessing the birth of Hip-Hop, but to me, curmudgeonly at twenty-seven, this wasn't music. Why would he willfully subjugate his voice to the hollow thumping of a machine, replace live musicians with muddy looped recordings?

When they finally arrived on stage, The Clash hewed tightly to script. Each song sounded like the record, note for note, without any of the looseness I'd expected. And though it was invigorating to be one with a singing crowd, the macho, violent lyrics to "Guns of Brixton" left me feeling both queasy and foolish.

I was in a crowd that I didn't quite belong to, listening to a boom box and a live performance so relentlessly routinized that it could have been recorded. Unmoved, isolated from the newest wave of cultural rebellion, I felt a new kind of alienation.

In April, 1981, after six years in Allentown, we decided to move back to Boston. My father had just been released from the hospital following an episode of ventricular fibrillation that had caused his heart rate to climb dangerously high. ("Sell if it reaches 180," he claimed to have told the EMT sitting in the back of the ambulance with him. Given my father's powers of denial, I almost believed him.) I was worried about being so far away from him. I wanted Katie to know my parents and to give them the pleasure of being grandparents. But mostly, I wanted to go home, not just to my family, not just to my old college friends who had migrated in droves to the Ann Arbor of the East, but to myself and to all those artistic and intellectual aspirations that had not a damn thing to do with the class struggle. We were tired of being lonely and marooned, and if we were going to be broke, we at least wanted to be broke in a city with decent public transportation and free concerts.

On our first night back, we went to the Wordsworth bookstore in Harvard Square, which stayed open until midnight. On our first weekend back, we took the subway to the Aquarium and sat outside it with Katie, watching the seals frolic in their outdoor pool. And in December of that year, we went to see the newly opened *Reds*.

Part documentary, mostly romance, Warren Beatty's epic film ostensibly documented the lives of revolutionary journalists Louise Bryant and John Reed. Beatty and his co-star, Diane Keaton, were impossibly gorgeous; Keaton's clothes were stylish even when meant to be ragged. Still, how affirming it was to see a story about intellectuals joining a real class struggle. How much cooler to point to handsome Warren Beatty and beautiful Diane Keaton, both utterly charming, and say to our friends, "*That's* what we were doing in Allentown."

At intermission—probably the last major American movie to have an intermission—Mark and I walked up the aisle toward the lobby. As we approached the back row of seats, somebody called our names. There sat a row of our old political friends, people whose first sojourn in Boston ended when ours did, when we had fanned out across the country to more industrial locales.

"Fancy meeting you here," said Nate, as his wife Nancy rose to give us both hugs. Lou reached out to offer a handshake only slightly less elaborate than the kind he'd routinely dispensed six years earlier, then introduced us to his new wife, Sandi. Bruce, a big guy stuffed into a small seat, struggled to stand, then settled for a friendly wave.

"When did you come back to Boston?" Mark asked.

Everyone chuckled and exchanged glances. "The last party split kind of did us all in," Nancy answered. "And honestly, without political work, why stay in Schenectady?"

"Why indeed?" I felt giddy to be back in time, back with people who needed no explanation.

"We all kind of staggered back within the past two years or so," Nancy continued, bringing us up to date. Bruce was working in a hospital and had recently been elected shop steward in his union. Sandi was a guidance counselor at a university. Lou and Nate and Nancy were all back in the kind of quasi-professional social service jobs they'd had before their pilgrimage to the factories.

"Now we organize each other to go out on Saturday nights," Nate quipped, gesturing to the half-empty theatre. "We unite with the masses at the movies."

What soon made us so passive? The demands of working and raising two small children? Perhaps it was just fatigue in the face of the culture of the decade. One of the top-grossing movies of 1982 was *Rocky III*, in which a once-dominant, now-complacent boxer loses a big bout and must regain his mojo. That was exactly Ronald Reagan's message in those early years of his presidency. Enough self-doubt or complacency—America needed to once again show the world who was boss. Two years later, running under the slogan of *Morning in America*, Reagan would be re-elected in a landslide. But when I think of his tenure, I think only of wintry dusk.

One August we went hiking and camping in Alaska, at a time when our kids were entering their own adolescence, when the sky turned violet but never black, and the sun skimmed along the horizon after midnight but never set.

"Alaskan Brown Bears—better known as Grizzlies—mate in late spring," a placid ranger in Katmai National Park told us. "The cub embryo grows for a month or so, then stops—or at least grows at such a decelerated pace that it seems to stop. From May through October, the bears gorge themselves, consuming as much salmon and berries and carp and tender shoots as they can forage and catch."

We believed him. We'd seen dozens of honey-colored bears— massive and silent—dive deep into the frigid lake and surface with fish wriggling in their jaws, swat salmon out of the air as they leapt or catch them in their open mouths like party performers. We'd watched the bears plant themselves on their haunches and systematically suck every blueberry off the dense, prolific bushes.

Alaska in August was crowded with life—swarming insects, bounding herds of caribou, rivers so clogged with fish that you couldn't take a step without being butted in the shin by one. Even what looked like lacy moss below our feet was actually an inch-high forest growing on the tundra.

"If by November the mother bear has amassed enough body fat, the cub embryo will resume growing throughout the winter," the ranger explained, "gestating throughout the mother's next cycle of hibernation. If not—if the mother bear hasn't been able to nourish herself enough, then she'll spontaneously abort."

In the 1980s, nourishment was scarce. When I struggle to remember who I was then, I think of the accounts I've read about freezing to death. People describe the hush of it, the sleepy enchantment.

In that decade, I surrendered to the notion that my ideals had been as acute and short-lived as a child's first teeth. Two decades later, in the wake of the 2008 recession, I looked around and saw cooperation manifesting itself in new ways. Zip cars and bike sharing, localism and community-supported agriculture, a do-it-yourself, artisanal movement borne of economic necessity but sustained by conviction—these second-world solutions to first-world problems were being created by my children's generation. Looking at the lives of my daughters and their friends, I saw their backyard chicken coops and guerilla knitting circles, at how volunteering their time to food banks and inner-city arts troupes was as routine as going to the gym, at how they shared what they couldn't and didn't want to buy.

They were taking on the ills of the world in subtly powerful ways. Maybe we had transmitted more than we'd realized. In the dismal decade of their birth, below our feet, in the thin layer of soil above the permafrost, tiny trees were sinking delicate stems.

But now, a year into the Trump presidency, I'm realizing that reaction is as tenacious as revolt. The Reagan years—what I'd thought of as the last gasp of those who can only feel tall by grinding down others—were just a preview. Some of the American Nazis who pathetically paraded in Skokie, Illinois in 1977 were undoubtedly alive to cheer forty years later when another of their Klan in Charlottesville, Virginia, mowed down an unarmed protestor with his big fat car. In 1976, some Americans referred to Mexicans as "spics"; forty years later Donald Trump sneered and blustered his way to the presidency by calling them "murderers and rapists." In 1991, Reagan's vice-president and newly elected president, George Bush, nominated a man to the Supreme Court who had sexually harassed Anita Hill; twenty-five years later a self-professed pussy grabber was voted into office by those willing to overlook this and dozens of other peccadillos.

I could go on, but if you're still reading this, you know all these details. You know that those who feared that their privilege, already limited, was draining away and some of those who rightfully resented the cronyism of the ruling class, astoundingly found their enraged voice in the inane braggadocio of a narcissistic, vicious, arrogant prick. Those who found it intolerable to have been led for two terms by a black president, who would have felt still more emasculated with a white woman at the helm, instead elected a self-serving mockery of a human being. And voila, we're back in the bad-old-days of robber barons and America First, of giveaways to the rich and decimation of the safety net for the poor, of inviting church into the state and curtailing women's right to choose.

I can't remember any point in my lifetime, any point in American history, where the ruling elite has been so ready to sacrifice the planet and lives of younger generations to satisfy their own limitless greed and consuming zeal. I've never encountered leaders so bloated with hypocrisy and so contemptuous of the future.

Yes, their ideology and actions are being countered by #BlackLivesMatter and #MeToo, digital movements that are transforming into physical ones. The Women's March and counter-Inaugural, the self-forming army of young people taking action within and outside the electoral process—these are sources of solace, reasons to hope. But the work that they and we must do will be harder, often more joyless, and take many more generations to develop roots that are sufficiently deep and durable.

On days like this one I wonder if I still have it in me.

The Cost of Goods Sold (1999-2003)

Prologue

When I got to work on September 26, 2002, I was surprised to see my boss, Cheryl's, Z3 convertible parked out front.

I stuck my head in her office. "I thought you were going to see Jennifer in Atlanta today."

Cheryl looked up, her bright-red nails matching her lipstick, and complementing her dark-blue wow-the-clients suit. "A terrible thing has happened. Jennifer's brother was killed in a surfing accident yesterday. She flew out to California last night."

I fought to suppress the grin I felt breaking out and retreated to my cube. Within five minutes my colleague Sandy came to my desk.

"The timing is really uncanny," she whispered.

I confessed that I was about to start searching for surfing accident stories in the California newspapers and obituaries.

"I already did," Sandy said triumphantly. "Nothing. Nada. Zip."

Scott, our chief financial officer, ambled over to the entrance of my cube, where he stood, gray and bland as always, intently peeling his banana. He took a big bite.

"So," he said and then chewed deliberately. "Do you think Jennifer even *has* a brother?"

April 1, 1999 (1 Brattle Square, Cambridge, 2500 sq. ft.)
In which my eyes are opened and grow wide

Eight colleagues and I sat in the office, rereading the termination letters we'd just received from the parent company that had acquired us, then dumped us.

"Surely we can put our heads together and invent something new," urged Don, founder and president of our newly deceased company. Don, a self-described "serial entrepreneur," was my Pied Piper into the business world, a worldly, curious man with the twin gifts of ego and ideas. He was the classic entrepreneur, a supreme schmoozer, trend-watcher, and visionary—the guy who could excite the troops not with bravado but with a sense of fun. And for me, on that day, the moon was in "Why Not." Before going to work at Don's firm, I'd made a living as a freelance writer for several years. If this spring skit—Hey, Let's Start a Company!—didn't work out, I felt confident enough that I could go back to contracting.

On the spot we decided to pool our efforts and our eight weeks of severance pay and start a new company. Coopernation was born that day and nurtured in our living rooms over the next couple of months. It was to be in the business of hosting and running online communities, private places on the web where companies could collaborate both internally and with their customers.

At the beginning, our company was a piece of improvisational theater. We drew pictures, built ideas out of color-coded Post-its, and did research into the ethnography of workplace learning and online communities. We put together PowerPoint presentations, software prototypes, and market matrices, and within a matter of weeks, our enthusiasm and leadership's track record with past businesses were enough to get us our first $900,000 in angel capital. Unlike venture capitalists—squinting, lean people who took big risks in the expectations of big rewards—angel capitalists were soft and nurturing. Sure, they expected a substantial return on their money someday, they told us, but they were really just benevolent guardians who were there because they *believed* in us.

Until this point, I had no idea of how businesses actually got started. But in our first few months of operation, I learned. The "Friends of Don" were, like Don himself, smart, often liberal Ivy League Business School graduates who defied my more adolescent stereotypes of all business men resembling Richard Nixon, physically and morally. Raising our initial round of angel capital seemed to be primarily a process of sitting in meeting rooms talking about the possibilities, which were infinite in those heady end-of-the-century days. We'd serve coffee and make the pitch to one of Don's buddies from B-School or from *Ground Floor Angels*, a group of angel capitalists that met once a month to evaluate new supplicants.

And after looking at the PowerPoints, clicking on a few links, and listening to our vision, a millionaire named Nick or Hal or Alex would stretch out his lanky legs in front of him, roll up his Egyptian cotton shirt sleeves, place his hands prayer-like on the table in front of him, and ask, "So how much are you looking to raise?"

"Well, I'm thinking about $1 million to start, in increments of $100K," Don would answer.

"Sounds about right." Nick would nod. "Who else are you thinking about approaching?"

"Well, I thought I'd talk to Ted, maybe Ken."

"Yup, makes sense. I know Ken is looking around, so your timing's good."

And that was that.

Of course only a small portion of these dollars went to actual product development. Our investors told us we had to exploit our "first mover" advantage, to spend big marketing bucks to carve out our niche as not just "the *first* online community software and services company for business," but as "*the* online community software and services company for business." So we auditioned for several marketing communications firms, pulling out all the stops to prove that we were worthy of their talent and their willingness to accept our money.

Led by a stubble-cheeked, black turtle-necked Steve Jobs wannabe named Miles, the team we ultimately hired spent several days interviewing our clients, our prospects, and us; researching our potential competitors, and then weeks devising logos and taglines. When I objected to their proposed logo because I thought it illegible, Miles patiently explained that logos are to be recognized, not read. "They're iconic," he instructed. "You don't actually *read* IBM." (*Ibim*,

I thought instantly.) "No, you recognize the brand; you take in the gestalt."

Miles hired naming specialists to help us come up with a better corporate moniker. After spending two days brainstorming verbs ("Is 'zoom' a verb?"), adjectives ("Which is hotter—'hot' or 'cool'?"), adverbs ("Anything ending in 'ly' is lame"), and then in stringing them all together in different combinations ("Green Light Express?" "Daily Zoom?" "MindPartner?" "PartnerMind?"); after scouring the web and discovering that every good domain name had already been taken and was either in use or for sale for some ridiculous sum; we ended up once again deciding on Coopernation. But this time, with conviction.

This process of redefining ourselves, or rather, of burnishing our definition to more brightly shine in the marketplace, took months and burned through hundreds of thousands of dollars. But meanwhile, we were doing real work as well—developing and testing software, implementing it, and learning by doing.

Much to my own surprise, I was fired up as never before. We were preaching what we practiced, marrying technology with mutual respect, honest expression, and an appetite for learning. Our quest was not only to live the values of cooperation, fun, and irreverence, but to prove the financial merits of those values. I was, for the first time, allowing myself to believe that it was possible to create capitalism with a human face, a face with middle-aged wrinkles and laugh lines. And though I tried not to, I couldn't help thinking that maybe I'd get rich.

November, 1999
(1 Brattle Square, Cambridge, 2500 sq. ft.)

In which we meet Jennifer, who is the Real Deal

With that first infusion of cash, we also hired Cheryl to be our CEO, and within months she had raised $10 million in venture capital to fund us in transforming our slides and wireframes into a working online environment where people could come together to have discussions, brainstorm ideas, and share pictures and documents.

In her mid-forties, Cheryl was smart, charismatic, and driven. She was flirtatious with men and women alike, seductive in her ability to elicit and listen, and to create the feeling that you shared a common sensibility and set of goals. She intimidated me, but I couldn't dislike her and I absolutely couldn't disrespect her.

Six months younger than me but lifetimes ahead in terms of business knowledge, she was something of an anomaly in the boardrooms of the venture capitalists. She was not some would-be-Internet-millionaire-before-the-age-of-thirty. She was not like my husband's former boss, the bright but oblivious twenty-seven-year-old man who, when asked how he felt at the end of the day on which his company went public and earned him six million dollars in eight hours, had the stunning audacity to say, "I feel vindicated. I feel just fine. After all, I poured two years of my *life* into this company." No, Cheryl was a grown-up, and she recruited salespeople like herself—smart, informed, straight talkers, who were relentless in pursuit of the right sale, but willing to walk away from the wrong one. They had integrity.

Cheryl had worked with Jennifer at a prior company and lost little time in hiring her to bring the same skills and Rolodex to Coopernation. Based in Atlanta, Jennifer came up to Boston for several days of meetings and training. Having expanded as a company from ten people to fifty over six months, we'd outgrown our conference room, and our Tuesday morning staff meetings had become hot, crowded, standing-room-only affairs.

But Jennifer was cool bordering on frosty, all five feet of her; with glossy blonde hair pulled back in a simple hairband and cascading almost to her waist, she stood before the group, seven months pregnant with her second child, firing off as many questions about the business model and technology as she was answering about herself, taking copious notes about current and potential competitors, and generally impressing the hell out of us. At the end of her last, long training day in town, a few of us took her out for dinner, and I tried to get to know her a little better.

She shared her professional history, but only in headlines. She'd worked her way up in the world, from a clerk at United Parcel Service to the director of sales at a multinational training and organizational development firm. Somewhere along the way she'd married and had a child, but the references to her family—indeed, to anything personal—were rare. Finally, in an attempt to make some sort of a connection, I asked, "Do you have a picture of your son?" I never particularly liked looking at pictures of other people's kids. But Jennifer was such a cipher, a cool, dark, granite wall reflecting only my own image back at me, that I was looking for a way in.

"No," she answered. "I always think it's tacky to pull out pictures of your kid, don't you?" A small, tight smile came and went. "Say, do you think I could have another Diet Coke?"

Then she said something to Cheryl, indicating that our conversation was over. Okay, I thought. A pregnant bottle blonde who has Diet Coke for dinner isn't exactly my soul mate anyhow. She's smart, she can sell. It takes all kinds of people to make a business work.

February-September 2001
(1 Arsenal Place, Watertown, 15,000 sq. ft.)

In which we acquire ample office quarters but meager revenues

The company quickly outgrew our space, and after briefly subletting a grease-infused, bug-ridden office over a Chili's restaurant, we moved into our new quarters—a parking garage that had been converted to open plan offices. The place was huge—far too big for us—but given the extraordinary demand for commercial real estate, we were confident that we'd sublet half the floor in no time. With its psychedelic color scheme and foosball table in the cafeteria, it had all the accoutrements of dot-com culture, which I viewed with a mixture of pride and unease. Pride, because I wanted our company to be egalitarian and irreverent; unease, because I struggled to see riding scooters around the office as anything *but* an affectation.

In February, at the end of her maternity leave, Jennifer returned to work. A month later, Wall Street came crashing down from its Internet high. Despite everyone's best efforts, revenues were paltry and our now panicky investors, the ones who'd told us to go ahead and rent our capacious, barely furnished office and to spend, spend, spend, now told us, "Cut your burn rate by fifty percent in the next month, reduce your COGS, and grow your top line faster." I quickly learned that this was financier-speak for laying people off, lowering the Cost of Goods Sold (the labor and dollars we invested in order to deliver the product and service that our clients purchased from us), and increasing our revenues.

This was our first major test, and true to our principles, we did not do the standard pack 'em up and move 'em out. The management team did not hole up in a room, assemble a list of names, and then lay-off half the staff and escort them out of the building in the course of a single bloody morning, as had become the norm. Instead, we called a company meeting. Cheryl distributed the cash flow spreadsheets and explained them. She illustrated all the ways in which we were hemorrhaging money—the unleased office space, the payroll that vastly exceeded revenues. Then she asked everyone present to volunteer for salary reductions or cutbacks in hours worked.

"Don and I are not going to draw any salary for the next six months," she announced. "We don't expect that everyone can do the same, but we are asking you to take a hard look and tell us what you can afford to do." Then she looked around the hushed room, and with a trembling voice said, "You are the most talented, committed group of people I've ever worked with in all my years in business. There's nobody in this room who is dispensable. But the fact is that we're not going to get out of this without some layoffs. If we all put our hands in the center, if we all pool our creativity and our willingness to sacrifice, we can save some jobs. And with each and every sale we make, we'll be able to save more jobs down the road."

People filed out of the conference room—the first room we'd ever had that was big enough to hold all of us—and back to their desks to talk to their spouses on the phone, to run numbers, to group in small clusters and frantically devise job-sharing schemes. And when the management team reconvened on Thursday, we learned that forty-nine out of our fifty employees had volunteered payroll and time cuts that in aggregate would save us close to $100,000 per month. Two programmers had independently approached Cheryl and offered to be laid off if it would save the job of a third, a recent immigrant whose wife was eight months pregnant. Another two people had volunteered reductions in hours, finding a grimly silver lining in the fact that this would give them more time to spend with their recently laid off spouses. All told, the voluntary cutbacks had saved twelve jobs.

The next day, we laid off eight people and explained that if sales didn't pick up substantially, we'd have to repeat the process in three months. "So this is it for now," a pale and subdued Cheryl told the staff. "Go back to work if that's what'll help you feel better. But my suggestion is that you just take some time to be with the colleagues we have to say goodbye to today, and then go home to your friends and families. Let's not pretend this isn't wrenching. But let's come back to work on Monday with renewed energy to make this company work."

That week, the honesty and decency and self-sacrifice that pervaded it, fueled my commitment to the company like nothing else ever had. This wasn't about the business, I told my husband that night, holding back the tears. It was about making room in this world for new, more humane, more mutually responsible forms of organizational culture to take hold. I was in it for keeps.

Meanwhile, on the sales front, Jennifer was leading the charge. She was tireless and we at headquarters responded in kind, forming a short-lived SWAT team to help her close sales with several prospects, all of whom were on the brink of signing.

It seemed to pay off. By September Jennifer had brought in signed contracts totaling $598,000—not bad for six months' work. But on Monday, September 10, as we reviewed the numbers at the start of our sales meeting, it was clear that we were still about $200,000 shy of our goal for the quarter that would wrap up in just under three weeks. Our investors, Cheryl informed us, had made it clear that another round of financing—a round we could not survive without—was contingent on us making our targets.

We fell into a grim silence that Jennifer finally broke by saying, "Well, you know we salespeople don't like to talk about anything before it's real for fear that we'll jinx it, but I'm actually expecting delivery of a signed contract from Delta tomorrow."

The next morning's meeting started routinely, with updates on the testing of the new software release ("Only about seventy-five bugs, which isn't as bad as it sounds," our chief technical officer announced) and the quest for tenants to share the costs of our newly leased space ("Maybe we should rent the office out for children's birthday parties," I suggested).

Then, with a Cheshire Cat grin, Cheryl innocently asked, "Any sales updates?" and Jennifer casually tossed a FedEx envelope on the table.

"Just this little contract from Delta Airlines for two customer communities amounting to $178K," she said quietly.

We burst into applause. Cheryl pulled a shiny gold Burger King crown from her briefcase and ceremoniously placed it on Jennifer's head. Sandy handed her a small packet of glitter ("Fairy dust," she said with a big smile), which Jennifer regally scattered around the table. Then, sitting upright at the head of the long conference table, Jennifer held a pencil up like a scepter, the oversized golden crown surrounding her gleaming blonde head, and we all scraped and bowed in mock thanks and supplication at her feet, frozen in the pose until the flash of someone's digital camera flared twice.

We resumed our seats and had begun to circulate slices of coffee cake when someone came into the conference room and handed Cheryl a note. She read it with a puzzled look, then announced,

"Apparently there's been some sort of accident. A plane has crashed into the World Trade Center."

"God, I sure hope it wasn't a Delta plane," someone murmured.

October-December 2001
(200 Talcott Ave., Watertown, 3000 sq. ft.)

In which we learn how to live under water

In the dazed horror and economic paralysis following September 11, most of our new contracts stalled and our pipeline—the pool of serious prospects who were close to signing—dried up. Sales still had a long gestation period, and those that Jennifer had made in the last quarter were advancing at a glacial pace. Although we had signed contracts from several of her accounts, we could not actually bill until we started the series of client meetings to plan the community, and we could not realize the revenue in our books until we'd recruited consumers and that community was up and running.

But we were having a difficult time getting to launch. Delta, not surprisingly, was too focused on survival to have much energy for us. Jennifer's client contact at NDC Health lost a brother in the World Trade Center and was out of commission for several months. Bell South, like many telecommunications companies, was hit especially hard by the economic decline and had put our project on hold. Then once again, at zero hour, just before the close of the fourth quarter, Jennifer finally won a $240,000 contract with Rare Hospitality, the company behind a string of steakhouse chains.

That was good enough for our investors, who agreed to give us enough additional money to keep us afloat for another ten months. In a spectacularly non-festive company meeting in February, 2002, they sat eating pizza (no more tote bags with gourmet sandwiches, two kinds of side salads, and Belgian chocolates for dessert), and shared with us the angst of venture capital. Uncharacteristically tie-less, in a rumpled shirt, our lead investor Jim told us that we were one of the few companies they'd invested in to have grown at all in the past six months.

"We took a look at our portfolio," he said, "and we divided it into an A-list and a B-list. We're pulling the plug on the B-list companies altogether." He paused and picked the pepperoni off the pizza while letting that sink in. "You guys are still on the A-list," he said, drawing out "still" like an executioner drawing out the plunger on his poison syringe, "because you're making sales. You've got revenue coming in—not enough, mind you, but more than a lot of other companies who got off to a much splashier start."

In exchange for their support, they gave us a term sheet ensuring that if and when the company was sold or went public, they would receive three times the value of every share they owned before anyone else received a penny. Given that the valuation of our company had dropped from $30 million to $6 million in the past year, this meant that all of the rest of us—the founders, the CEO, and all the employees—were almost guaranteed that our stock options would be valuable only to clean windows or wrap fish. Our bereft state, I now learned, was referred to as being "under water." Ironically, this was the price we paid for staying afloat.

February 2002
(200 Talcott Ave., Watertown, 3000 sq. ft.)

In which Jennifer redoubles her efforts, and we pull together as one

Our rainmaker threatened to leave. Jennifer submitted her resignation to Cheryl, telling her that she wanted to be near her brother and ailing mother in Southern California. She'd been offered a sales job there with a company called Accomplish Now, who was willing to pay her more and to relocate her. Cheryl made her a counter-offer. Jennifer could open a new territory in the Los Angeles area, and Coopernation would cover her housing and relocation expenses, effective the following January.

Jennifer accepted and we congratulated ourselves on keeping her. In fact we took her assent as a sign of confidence. I'd always been told that salespeople followed the money, so if she was staying with us, it must mean we were doing something right. Emboldened, we once again pooled our efforts to provide her with enough sales support to keep her dizzying number of prospects afloat.

But although we could see the products of her labor—proposals, signed letters of intent, contracts, emails from Jennifer to us and our new but still unmet clients in Atlanta—Jennifer herself began to feel more and more remote to us. Like so many companies at that time, we'd frozen all but the most essential travel, and our geographically dispersed salespeople were just tinny voices coming through the speaker phone.

Jennifer's voice was precise, tired, but determined as she recounted the delays in launching her signed contracts and strategized around how to get them off the ground. Her thought, effort, and bad luck were evident in the hundreds of pages of detailed call reports, weekly narratives to the management team, and pipeline reports that all the salespeople used to track and report on imminent sales.

At Ryder Trucks, Jennifer's client, Dorothy, was diagnosed with stage 3 breast cancer, and when she returned to work, priorities had changed and we needed to re-spec the contract. At UPS, implementation of our contract was delayed while the company negotiated a new contract with the Teamsters, and there seemed to be several staffing challenges despite a few good telephone conversations we had with Rob, Jennifer's client there. ("Hang in there," Rob told my colleague Sandy. "We're slow to get started, but once we do, we move fast and we see a lot of future potential for you guys here.") At Delta, Jennifer reported spending freezes—hardly a surprise.

At least at Rare Hospitality, things were plodding along, if just barely. Jennifer had arranged a conference call with our new client, Harry Day, the VP of Business Research, to get the member recruitment and community launch process underway. But a half-hour before it was scheduled to start, Jennifer called, sounding grim and breathless, to say that her husband was having chest pains, and she was taking him to the hospital. "I can't be on the conference call," she said, "but you go ahead without me. I'll tell Harry to call you directly. I am so, so sorry…"

Amazingly, she followed through. Harry, a terse man with an exceptionally low voice, called from his cell phone as he was in transit between meetings.

"I know Jennifer wanted to be on this call," I said as we were signing off, "and I'm sure she'll move mountains to join us next time."

"Yup, she's a real trouper," Harry said.

August – September, 2002
In which bad luck stalks the worthy

In the year following the 9/11 attacks, we, like most people in the country, felt breathless and claustrophobic, like we were hiking on the ocean floor and literally moving at a snail's pace. Nonetheless, by the end of August, Jennifer brought in signed contracts from Home Depot and Coca-Cola amounting to another $500,000 in business, making her once again our most successful salesperson in a slack and skittish market.

But then Heidi, our new client at Coke, didn't have time for us because Coke no longer had time for Heidi. "She's been laid off," Jennifer reported in a phone call in early September, her voice quivering with frustration. "She was one of a bunch of people laid off, and our project is back in limbo while they redo their marketing budgets."

She wasn't the only frustrated one. In fact a few of us were confessing our suspicions to one another in hushed conversations.

"It's just too weird," Sandy insisted. "Jennifer's like Pig-Pen. She's got this permanent cloud of chaos swirling around her."

The next week Cheryl had a half-day conference call with Jennifer in which they reviewed each of her accounts in detail. Cheryl was tough, insisting that Jennifer supply Sandy's team with the names and contact information for every client so that we could work with them more directly and efficiently. She also persuaded Jennifer to get some of these clients to agree to be billed in advance to compensate for the cost of their delays.

This meeting seemed finally to yield results. On Jennifer's instructions our bookkeeper, Janet, mailed out invoices to three clients. She scheduled two trips in the upcoming two weeks for Cheryl to come to Atlanta to meet senior client contacts.

But on September 20, Jennifer cancelled the first of Cheryl's two meetings. "Schedule changes," she explained, and forwarded to Cheryl an email containing the client's apologies. Then on September 26, the date of Cheryl's second set of meetings, Jennifer left her a frantic message that her brother had been killed in a surfing accident, and she was running to be with her family in California.

Some of us whispered, some flat-out snickered, but Cheryl took word of this tragedy completely seriously. The company sent Jennifer flowers, and in a silent reproach to us for our cynicism, Cheryl forwarded to all of us the tearful voice mail Jennifer left her in response.

"I got home to Atlanta this morning and saw the flowers you sent, and it just unlocked all the tears I'd been holding in all last week in California," Jennifer's hushed message began. "This has been so hard," she went on, her voice breaking, "so hard," she sobbed, "and I can't begin to tell you how much everyone's support has meant to me. I'm blessed to be working with a company like this."

"Well, color me *asshole*," I wrote to Sandy in an email after listening to it.

"Maybe, maybe not," she shot back.

October 17, 2002

In which an investigation is mounted

Cheryl was not immune to the skepticism that had mounted from a whisper to a steady murmur and issued a memo to the management team. She began by stating the facts—that Jennifer had basically closed about ten accounts for over $1.5 million, and yet none of those accounts had generated any revenue or cash yet. Needing to feel that she understood the worst-case situation, Cheryl had worked with Scott to create a financial scenario in which several of Jennifer's clients just disappeared and others continued to stall. The result was alarming. Within six months, we'd need a series of miracles, including an additional infusion of venture capital, in order to make payroll.

She acknowledged what so many of us had begun to express, but upon digging into the details, concluded that:

"... there is sloppiness here on Jennifer's part, related to nailing down dates, etc. However, I have worked with Jennifer for a long time, and she has always brought in solid numbers. Most of the time, the more I dig in and press for information, the *better* I feel."

October 23, 2002

In which the shit hits the fan

Six days later Jennifer called to say that the kick-off meeting with our newest client, America's Finest Chicken (AFC), had been postponed.

Cheryl was out of town, but in her absence the rest of the management team conferred and decided that Janet should call the person to whom she'd sent the AFC invoice on the pretext of introducing herself and see if she could figure out what was going on.

An hour later Scott signaled us to return to the conference room.

"They've never heard of us," he said without preamble and without affect.

"They'd never heard of us?" Sandy asked in disbelief.

"Nope, and a half-hour after we called, their lawyers called us back and warned us to cease and desist from trying to collect payment or we'd face legal action," Scott answered flatly. "I've told Janet to go through the list and call the accounting department at every single one of Jennifer's clients to see if any of them are real."

We arranged to reconvene at 1:30.

"Ten for ten," Scott announced a few hours later. "They're all fake." He ticked off what he and Janet had learned about each of these "clients" in the past few hours. Most were actual people, high enough in their companies that their names and titles could be harvested from corporate websites. Others were completely fabricated.

Contracts were forged. The total $1.5 million in sales was made up.

Our investors had financed us and we'd based spending on contracts and revenues that we didn't have.

October 24, 2002

In which the truth becomes inescapable

At a company-wide meeting the next morning, I scanned the faces across the table from me. All eyes were on Cheryl as she broke the news, some jaws already visibly tightened, torsos erect, like people watching an execution. Meg began to shake her head in disbelief. Cheryl paused for a sip of water, and I could hear Lynn's chair creak beside me—nothing else.

"I wish I could tell you why she did it," Cheryl said, "but I can't. She blames it on obsessive-compulsive disorder. I don't think that explains it."

"Was she getting commission?" I asked.

"No, that's the strange part. She was, however, working for Accomplish Now for the last ten months during which she was also working for us."

"No way!" Sandy gasped.

Cheryl looked at her, grinned tightly, and nodded.

Scott's usually gray face turned strawberry red as he asked, "But how did she do this? Did she have collaborators or conspirators or—what's the word—accomplices? Did she have accomplices? I mean we spoke to Harry Day. We spoke to Heidi at Coke. We spoke to all of these clients. How did she do this?"

"Well, she—" Cheryl suppressed a hysterical giggle. "I told you this was an amazing story, right? She had a speech synthesizer that she attached to her telephone."

"Shut up!" squealed Sandy, while the programmer next to her started to sing *The Twilight Zone* theme. But others snapped instantly into shocked silence. Another programmer sitting at the back of the room hugged herself and quietly chanted, "That is so sick. That is so sick."

"But what about the invoices I sent?" Janet asked. "I mean some of the names on these contracts, some of the people I sent invoices to, were real people!"

"Yeah, well, Jennifer would tell you to send the invoice, then she'd call the client—or rather, *not* the client—and tell them that you'd made a clerical error, that they were going to get an invoice from us, and that when they did, they should just throw it out."

"Son of a bitch," Janet exploded.

The meeting continued in bipolar fashion, with the mood swinging wildly from barely contained hysteria ("Maybe I should call Jennifer and say, 'Hi, this is Harry Day,'" Meg suggested) to fear ("Are there going to be more layoffs?") to horror ("She's got *little kids*. What kind of household are they growing up in!") People peppered Cheryl with questions, but most of them were variations on the same theme: How could this have happened? How could Jennifer have gotten away with it for so long? And above all: How will she be punished? Will we sue her? Is it a criminal offense? How will she be made to *pay* for this?

But I found myself unable to share in this lust for revenge. Somewhere in Cheryl's narrative I'd realized that if Jennifer hadn't made up these contracts, we probably never would have gotten our last two rounds of financing. Without her fraud our company would probably have collapsed a year earlier. So instead of speculating about whether bogus email constituted interstate mail or telephone fraud, about whether she had enough assets to make suing her a worthwhile endeavor, I found myself looking guiltily around the room, feeling more like a collaborator than a victim.

Epilogue

Jennifer's case finally came to trial in 2005. She was charged with wire fraud, and after blaming Cheryl in her trial for putting too much pressure on her, after thanking God and her pastor for helping her see the way back to the light, she eventually pled guilty. She was given three months' house arrest, five years of probation, and ordered to pay $70,000 in restitution to Coopernation.

But the outcome does nothing to explain the cause. Was Jennifer a sociopath? Was she so successfully able to defraud Coopernation and Accomplish Now because she lacks some essential genes or synapses needed for a conscience?

Perhaps, but that only explains *her*. How did *we* let this happen? How did we let her get away with it for as long as we did? And why, according to newspaper reports, did Accomplish Now continue to employ her even after being informed by federal prosecutors that she was under investigation, and later pay her $43,000 in commissions on two fictitious contracts she claimed were worth more than $400,000?

It was hope, irrigated by a subterranean stream of self-interest. We all watered Jennifer's twisted roots for so long because we needed her to prosper. And in late 2011, as we stumbled through the economic ruins wrought by systemic greed and self-deceit, it was a dynamic that looked increasingly familiar.

In response to an online post about her trial shortly after it ended, Jennifer wrote: "I know God knows the truth and I know that God has forgiven me, regardless of those who have not and will not. I am very thankful that I have only one judge in this life and it is not the media or people who are mad at me for the mistakes I have made in the past."

Jennifer looked to God for much the same permission that we, her enablers, offered her. But sadly, she didn't have to look skyward. She'll find that kind of license much closer to home.

Laterna Magika (2009)

Over forty years after Expo 67 ended, I finally got to visit the Czech Republic, on a trip that was almost a pilgrimage. Of those members of my Aunt Anne's family who didn't die in Auschwitz, many did so in the Czech concentration camp of Theresienstadt. Visiting that city, seeing her family name in haunted, spidery script on the wall of victims in the Pinkas Synagogue, seemed like a way to honor her memory. And walking through the old cemetery in the Jewish Quarter, I honored my father's as well. One of the consequences of being confined to a ghetto was that the Jewish residents quickly ran out of burial space. So, in the one graveyard that was permitted them, the tombstones cluster and tumble, and an estimated 100,000 people are buried in layers, fifty centimeters apart, twelve layers deep. But the serenity of the place is uncanny, and like an ethnobotanist who imagines entire societies from ancient seeds and pods, my family— aunts, uncles, grandparents, and parents—made a new kind of sense to me. Standing in the old cemetery ten months after my father's death, some odd dissonance about him finally clicked into place. He *knew* that he straddled the old and new worlds, knew that he carried and had to find a way to honor both the suffering of his ancestors and his right to self-invention.

Prague and invention—the two were coupled in my mind. Kafka had lived there, shaking off the weight of his father's expectations and inventing a new genre. The Golem—a mythical Frankenstein-like creature who protected the Ghetto Jews from anti-Semitic attacks—had been shaped from riverbed clay there. The democratic movement that had flared there—the Prague Spring, in 1968—had been doused but not defeated, and triumphantly revived. This was a country that had elected a playwright as president.

176

And Czechoslovakia was the birthplace of the Kinoautomat, which after all these years, had only gained luster in my memory. On our second night there, my husband and I went to the Laterna Magicka, which had been the inspiration for Kinoautomat. With its crinkly gold façade, the building looked like a wrinkled Easter egg wrapper. The décor also teetered between cool and simply gaudy. Stairways were bordered with lapis-colored glass, spear-like lights hung from the ceiling like stalactites, and hammered metal sculptures in the shape of snail shells and other organic forms rose up out of the floor and newel posts, glowing with dimpled amber light.

Next to it stood the National Theatre, gold-domed, stately and grand—the architectural opposite of Laterna Magika. I was struck by the duality of Prague. Castles and spires and charmingly crooked facades of four-hundred-year-old houses lined the old city's narrow, winding, and climbing streets. But surrounding the fairy tale quarters, where the poor and working class people lived, the wide roads were pocked by Soviet-era cinder block housing and stores, boxy and beige, adorned only by the debris of candy wrappers blowing in the gray wind.

We felt that desolation, a sense of the modern turned shabby, witnessing the performance that night. Through music, dance, skillful lighting, and films of looming rock and pounding ocean and listing ships projected onto multiple screens, we were shown the story of Odysseus, without words and with considerable drama. Had I not been expecting magic, I probably would have admired the harmonious coupling of artistry and technology. But I was childishly hoping that the dancers would enact what had only ever been true in my imagination—the miracle of two dimensions hatching a third, the sight of a human being emerging from the screen, listening to what we in the audience had to say, and then melding back into it to do our bidding. Instead, I was simply an audience member viewing a performance.

At intermission, my husband and I sipped wine and half-heartedly praised the production, neither of us quite ready to surrender to our disappointment and leave the theatre. Instead, we wandered around it. Dotting the lobby and staircase walls were photographs, most in black and white, commemorating the Velvet Revolution that overthrew the Czech Communist Party in November and December of 1989. Most of them showed encounters on a small, intimate scale. I looked at the young men gathered around a large urn of hot coffee under a streetlamp, admiring their looks, wanting to be in their energetic company, and the gap in age and decades disappeared. I felt that same sense of shifting time looking at another photo of a young man standing on a roughly assembled wooden stage, smile wide and fist high, addressing the crowd.

In the picture above him were three older men in caps and a middle-aged woman, her tufty blonde hair blowing in a wind so frigid it almost pierces the picture frame, facing off in somber debate. They were my age too, my age now. Their seriousness moved me, as did that of an old lady in another photo, hunched but immaculate in a stylish leather car coat and knit hat, striding purposefully toward the camera, unstoppable.

This theatre had been the headquarters for the Civic Party, a loosely structured, non-hierarchical group formed in large part by the dissidents who had been calling for freedom of speech since the Prague Spring of 1968, and been imprisoned and harassed ever since. On November 17, 1989, riot police had violently suppressed a student demonstration on this street, just outside this theatre's walls. By November 20, the protestors' ranks had swelled to half a million.

We must hold on, we must be cautious, we must intensify the pressure on the governing circles, said a framed translation of a manifesto issued by the Civic Party on November 25. *It is the only possible way the half-opened door can be opened wide. We believe that the social movement in our country is irreversible, that the desire of our citizens to live in freedom and dignity will prevail.* On November 27, practically the entire population of the Czech Republic held a two-hour general strike. On November 28, the Czech Communist Party relinquished power and called a general election. A month later, Vaclav Havel, whose plays, essays, and imprisonment had celebrated and inspired this rebellion, was sworn in as president.

In the last picture in the exhibit—the only one in color—a ring of people surrounds an enormous circle of flowers that have been laid on the street. In the center of this floral installation, Vaclav Havel, in jeans and a suede jacket, with hair longer and hipper than any twentieth-century American politician has ever had, adorns a small tree, wispy and so laden with ornaments that it is almost dwarfed by the Czech flag that has been planted beside it. In rich and vibrant color, there at the edge of the glass stairwell, I saw a man and a fragile tree, encircled by circles of living beings. This is what artists can do, I thought.

Susan Sontag once wrote. "Photographs that everyone recognizes are now a constituent part of what a society chooses to think about, or declares that it has chosen to think about. It calls these ideas 'memories,' and that is, over the long run, a fiction. Strictly speaking, there is no such thing as collective memory… But there is collective instruction."[26] Looking at these photos, that fiercely proud tribute in that garish theatre with its fading rugs, I felt instructed and revived.

"Hope is definitely not the same thing as optimism," Vaclav Havel would say some years after the revolution. "It is not the conviction that something will turn out well, but the certainty that something makes sense, regardless of how it turns out."[27]

In 1967, as I merged, untethered, with the crowds at the Czech exhibit on Ile St. Helene, I was hopeful. What I felt that summer and would feel for much of my young adult life, was that I was involved in something that made sense, that I was a single thrumming cell in a larger organism with a shared intelligence and common breath.

Was that belief as illusory as the power I felt pressing my red or green button?

Yes, and No.

Corporate Giving (2010)

On an October morning, I got up earlier than usual to go to a 7:30 a.m. fundraising breakfast for Horizons for Homeless Youth. I parked in a downtown garage, and emerged from my car to the echoing click of sensible but stylish high heeled shoes and a parade of women in tailored suits and pearls filing into the Westin.

I was there as a guest of my CEO, a member of this worthy organization's Board of Directors. She is smart, passionate, and absolutely driven, approaching philanthropic fundraising as relentlessly and with as much personal investment as she brings to driving us toward our bookings targets and revenue projections. And over the years, she has given me entrée into a sub-culture of high powered business women, a small but growing elite.

As I stood in line to register, I looked at the tags pressed on the silk and wool and cashmere-clad chests of the women around me. The individuals' names meant nothing to me—it was the company identifiers in equally large font that marked this crowd. State Street Bank, Choate Hall & Stewart, Hale and Dorr, Fidelity Investments, Talbots, Crabtree and Evelyn, Digitas—every major financial institution, corporate law firm, advertising or marketing agency, and retailer catering to women was represented there. And the representatives were a tastefully presented bunch. Their make-up was subtle, the manicures pearly and not brash.

Inside the ballroom, PowerPoint presentations on two enormous screens on either side of the dais displayed rotating images of black and brown and white children—on playgrounds, at story time, drinking milk, clutching a jump rope in their mittened hands as they were herded down the sidewalk. They were uniformly adorable with their gap-toothed grins, wide eyes and puffed out chests as they prepared to blow out candles, hurtle down a slide, or climb to the top of a snow bank.

As the lights dimmed, I sat down at our company table and removed the goodie bag full of tchotchkes from various corporate sponsors from my plate. The hall filled with the amplified sound of pre-school aged children singing "The Wheels on the Bus," and this morning, as they did every year, these small but boisterous voices with their mispronounced R's and active hands driving the bus as its wheels went "wound and wound," instantly caused me to well up with tears. Something about their fierce pleasure in singing, their obliviousness in that moment to the fact that they were kids, that they were homeless, that their bold and happy voices were being broadcast to a ballroom of the penitent privileged, broke my heart this year as it did every year.

Liz Walker, a former newscaster and now an ordained minister, bounded onto the stage.

"You're here because you know that goodness is manifested in your deeds," she said, allowing just a hint of black preacher cadence into her speech. "You're here because you know that your caring, your action, your generosity make a substantial difference in the lives of those less fortunate." She paused for the silent *Yeah* that this crowd might have felt but wasn't schooled in uttering. "You're here because words alone, mere expressions of concern are not enough. You're here to make a difference, and just by being here, just by buying your seat at the table—a table with a lovely centerpiece generously donated by Crabtree and Evelyn—and I just learned that their name is pronounced 'Eeevelyn'—you've already made a difference. So please, before we turn our attention to this morning's speakers, give yourselves a hand."

As warm and genuine as the Reverend Liz seemed to be, my applause was limp and brief. I was embarrassed by this request.

"Tonight over 1,200 families will be staying in publicly funded family shelters," declared this year's chairwoman, a graying lawyer from a downtown law firm. "Compared with low-income housed children, homeless children experience more health problems, developmental delays, increased anxiety, depression, behavioral problems, and lower educational achievement." Her delivery was matter of fact, but with a hint of the indignation to come. She must do litigation, I thought.

The facts were appalling; the worthiness of the organization undeniable. But as always, my outrage was undercut by the sight of the enormous corsages worn by the speakers and all of the Board members, as if we were at prom and this year's theme was *Homelessness!* Even the organization's Executive Director—a committed, unpretentious, and hard-working woman whose daughter had gone to school with mine—looked faintly ridiculous with the giant carnations engulfing her pale neck.

I picked at my breakfast. Cross-sections of kiwi and starfruit dotted with blackberries formed a happy face emoticon in one quadrant of the plate.

Reverend Liz stepped back to the microphone. "I'd like to introduce you to one of the hundreds of mothers who have been helped by Horizons for Homeless Youth in the past year. Please give a warm welcome to Lucelia."

We clapped vigorously as a young Hispanic woman in a tailored navy pin-striped dress walked out of the wings. The applause tapered off and we waited for Lucelia to speak.

She cleared her throat. "Excuse me, I'm very nervous," she began, then stopped.

"Take your time," I heard Reverend Liz urge her from the wings.

"Let me try again," she forced out in a quivering voice, then again fell silent, her fingers audibly clawing at the index cards she held in front of her. Her face, projected to the thousand-person audience on two 5' x 7' screens on either side of the stage, was damp, and her eyes were welling up with tears.

"You're among friends," someone yelled from the audience.

Lucelia looked down at her notes "I'm glad… I'm very glad…" She stopped again. Reverend Liz began walking out toward her, but stopped when Lucelia turned, held up her palm, nodded to herself, took a deep breath, and began again.

"I'm glad to be here," she declared. We all clapped encouragingly. Lucelia smiled with relief, her enormous brown eyes beaming out over the crowd. "I'm no good at public speaking, so I never thought I'd be talking to a big room full of people." Her voice was low and breathless. "But then I never dreamed I'd be homeless either. Three years ago, I was just like you. I had a job in the Medical Records department at St. Elizabeth's Hospital. I lived with my husband who worked at a garage, and we had an apartment where my little boy Raffie had his own room."

Just like you. I knew that the children of at least two women at this table had bedrooms that were probably the size of Lucelia's entire apartment. And yet I believed that Lucelia believed her own words. She was, after all, a working woman with a home, just like all of us.

"But then my husband started to drink. A lot. He began to miss work so much that he lost his job, and then he drank even more. It was impossible to pay for our apartment on just my salary, and it wasn't good for Raffie to see his father like this. So I took Raffie and we moved in with my mother-in-law—just me and Raffie, though my husband, we said he could visit now and then until he got himself together."

Many of us nodded. This was a good plan, a sound course of action.

"But my mother-in-law's place, it was even smaller than ours. And then her daughter needed to move in with her baby, and my mother-in-law, she's a nice lady, but she told us we had to go."

Lucelia's story continued—a grim and predictable downward spiral as she moved from home to home, couldn't pay for daycare, couldn't get a job because she had no daycare, finally landing in a homeless shelter. She paused and looked up, finally in her groove, and got to the punch line. "Horizons for Homeless Youth changed everything for me. With Raffie at the Play Center I could get to work on time. And he did great, you know? He…" she paused, looking down at her notes, and said with great pride, as if mastering a foreign language, "He flourished there. He'd come home—well not home, because we was still in the shelter so it wasn't home —and be singing songs and recognizing his letters and stuff that he didn't do before. Every day watching him was something new. It was like a little treat for me every night."

"My treat's a glass of red wine," someone at my table said. "Hers is better."

"With Raffie taken care of, after a few months I was able to transfer to another, better paying job at St. E's, and now I'm training to be an ultrasound technician."

The crowd clapped in acknowledgment of Lucelia's career advancement.

"And best of all, me and another mother I met at the shelter—her little girl Lena is in daycare with Raffie—we was able to find an apartment in Dorchester that we could afford, right near the T— so we have a home again. Our own home. Thanks to all of you."

This was our cue. We stood, not a dry eye in the house, and clapped wildly as the Executive Director walked back on stage holding the hand of a skipping, waving, unawed little boy who briefly flirted with the massive audience, then charged into his mother's thigh, where he buried his head, then comically wagged his rear-end.

After Lucelia picked up her son and bestowed us with a radiant and relieved smile, after she was awarded a bouquet of flowers and embraced by the line of speakers who preceded her, Reverend Liz returned to the stage to introduce a procession of earnest and eloquent Play Center volunteers. Then she brought the breakfast to a close.

"I know that you've got appointments and phone calls and meetings to make. But before we wrap up…" She held up her hand like a crossing guard, "…first I've got to ask you to take a look at the gorgeous centerpiece in the middle of your table and remember why we're here. We are here to help this worthy organization with the gifts of our time and our influence and our lobbying and our dollars. Under that gorgeous centerpiece is a stack of pre-printed envelopes that make it easy for you to sign up to help in any and all of these ways. Table Captains, please blindly draw one of the envelopes from the pile. The lucky winner will get to leave with the Crabtree and Evelyn goodie basket. Now I ask you: Does it get better than that?"

I hoped so.

Still, with a feeling approximating relief, I pulled out my credit card. I knew I'd love to volunteer at a Play Center, but only later, when I was no longer working fifty hours a week. But giving money—I'd gotten good at that, gotten better each year in inverse proportion to my appetite for doing anything more direct or personally taxing. As my income had risen, my political energy had waned, only occasionally flaring from its chronic brown out, surging through manic binges of door-to-door canvassing and check writing. I did it with the ease and privilege and impersonality reserved for those who could say to themselves, *It's only money.*

When Reverend Liz incited us to give ourselves a round of applause, I felt sick. The rich breakfast frittata settled heavily in my stomach.

Then, of course, I won the centerpiece.

This perky basket of everything lavender—soaps, bath oils, fabric softeners, exfoliating cleansers—was now mine.

"Does anyone else want this?" I asked lamely, but most of my tablemates were already picking up purses and preparing to bolt. I fled the ballroom, lugging my purse, coat, goodie bag, and lavender basket down three escalators and one elevator to the sanctuary of my car. I wanted to be at work, where every moment was busy and none of them counted.

Back in my office, I looked in the goodie bag. An unbearably appropriate stress ball from Bank of America, a handy USB stick from Price Waterhouse PLC, a business card case from a Human Resources consulting firm, a ballpoint pen from Fidelity that had pleasing heft, and a spa-branded pedometer to show me how far and fast I'd walked away.

Satellites (1945-2015)

In the early 1970s, while working at the Circle Pines summer camp, I saw the Northern Lights. It was around midnight as Ian and I walked back from the staff house to our tents. At first we thought the glow in the sky was sheet lightning. But as we emerged from the pine woods, we saw that the big meadow ringed by cabins was crowned by liquid green light. Stalactites of yellow and green and pink light formed a spikey dome in the sky over us.

We raced to the cabins, woke the campers up, and herded them, still dazed and shivering in the cool night air, into the center of the meadow. Some lay on the damp grass; others simply stood hugging themselves, heads back, mouths opens, staring at the luminous swirls above us. It's like whipped cream, one kid said. No, like the topping on a lemon meringue pie, said another. Like the fringe of hair around a bald guy's head.

To me the swooping ripples and twisting sheets of light were like curtains blowing in the cosmic wind. But not curtains—something animate. You could see the particles streaming into and through them, shaping and twirling. And as a fold of light began to fade, I saw its dancing shards, dropping and spiking like lines on an electrocardiogram, like the pulsing heart of the universe.

A decade later, late one night while visiting my parents' summer house eighty miles north of Montreal, we saw an extremely bright light, low on the horizon, moving quickly through the sky. It looked like a star, but bigger, and flying too low to be a jet. After watching it for a few minutes, we could tell that it wasn't flying so much as orbiting at a very high speed.

After a hurried search, I found the binoculars and aimed them at the brilliant white object. It was unlike anything I'd ever seen before—bowtie shaped and covered in a crosshatched pattern of what appeared to be mirrors. We took turns studying it as it moved across the sky. My mother frantically drew what we were seeing on a napkin so that we wouldn't forget any of its details.

I called the provincial police. "There is a strange object on the ceiling," I said in my fractured French, never strong to begin with and rusty after so many years of living in the U.S. "Can you see it?" I asked.

They asked me if I'd been drinking. They asked me if I'd ever seen an airplane.

"*Non*," I answered. "*Ce n'est pas un avion*," I said in frustration. "*C'est quelle sort d'un* UFO," I went on, as embarrassed by my French as by the words I was daring to say in it.

(A few years earlier, I'd been at the house with an American friend and locked my keys in the car. Unable to remember the word for "locked," I eventually told the police what would literally be translated as, "My keys are in the car and I am not." They came within ten minutes, clearly grateful I'd equipped them with yet another Stupid Anglo story.)

But the night cop at the other end of the line this time was not amused. He'd make note of it, he told me, and that was all he could do.

We watched the object for another five minutes or so. Eventually it sank below the horizon. We went to bed, telling ourselves and mostly believing that whatever this thing was, it was probably man-made. But though fear eventually dwindled to unease, I was still shaken. My infant was sleeping in the next room; my husband was hundreds of miles away. From the deck of our little Laurentian house, this thing in the sky was a polka-dot, dwarfed by the bounty of stars. But I imagined the perspective from up there, where surveillance was constant and half the earth would make a luminous target.

The object that my mother had sketched on that napkin was a communications satellite. In 1966, when Frank Mannors saw his

UFO over Dexter, Michigan, there were about thirty satellites in orbit, but what they did and who for was unknown to all but a few scientists, business people, and spies. As I write this today, there are more than three thousand. If we think of them at all, it's when the football game on our satellite television turns into a dithery mass of pixels and we shake our fists at the heavens for obstructing our view of the replay.

As with so many innovations, the orbiting communications system was the step-child of military technology. In 1945, science fiction writer Arthur C. Clarke suggested that satellites in high orbit could beam telephone and television to everyone on the planet. In an article for *Wireless World,* Clarke proposed that a relay satellite sent 22,300 miles above the earth's surface would take exactly twenty-four hours to complete one orbit. "It would remain fixed in the sky of a whole hemisphere and, unlike other heavenly bodies, would neither rise nor set."[28] Clarke's expectations were incredibly prescient. He predicted that such satellites would inspire a huge and highly targeted range of television programming and enable people to work from their homes. "One of Clarke's more frightening thoughts," *Time* magazine wrote in 1965, "is that every man on earth will eventually have his own telephone number and will carry a personal apparatus that will permit him to be called, even by people who have no idea where he may be."[29]

That "personal apparatus" has made McLuhan's global village a reality, supplanting drums and smoke signals with geotags and mobile apps that make instant sharing across geographies and time zones the new normal. But in April of 1965, COMSAT Corporation's launch of the Intelsat I communications satellite (nicknamed Early Bird), was anything but routine. This extraordinary 76-pound device enabled instant, continuous television, radio, and fax transmissions between the United States and Europe for the first time in history. Within a month, President Lyndon Johnson used this new capability in service of the Cold War. To counter the Russian media blitz in honor of the twentieth anniversary of V-E day, and in violation of diplomatic protocol prohibiting the leader of a country from directly addressing the citizens of another without prior notification, LBJ broadcast an anniversary address of his own to the people of Britain and Italy.

That same year, 1965, one of that satellite's inventors, Dr. Harold Rosen, proposed a special Educational Television Satellite for NASA. "The benefit to mankind of such a system staggers the imagination. It may well be the major return to humanity of man's venture into space," he said.[30]

Two years later, Early Bird was one of the three satellites enabling *Our World*.

Our World would turn out to be The Beatles' last live, real-time performance. Ask any music fan of my age what was the first music video released in the United States, and they'll instantly tell you that it was "Strawberry Fields Forever," the B-Side to "Penny Lane." Mark, his lifelong friend, Gil, and I can't agree on whether this video debuted on The Ed Sullivan Show or on The Smothers Brothers Comedy Hour, but we all remember the puzzled disappointment with which we watched it.

With its somberly psychedelic special effects, the black-and-white video was kind of cool, even by today's standards. But we were expecting to see them perform *live* on television. I'd delicately adjusted the rabbit ears antenna on our TV that night, hoping that the right combination of angle and touch would once again transform the snow on the screen to a clear image. I'd been anticipating a shared experience, with John and Paul and George and Ringo, and with the millions of other kids just like me. Sitting alone, cross-legged on my parents' bed with its golden, pilled polyester quilt watching a short movie, didn't qualify as one. This was the first time that a televised performance on a live show was canned. Our music was being served up as a product that could be replayed, rebroadcast, unchanging.

Of course now that's precisely the allure of the Internet. Each of us is a market of one, calling up what we want, when we want it, amplifying our solitude as we dial up entertainment. It's not all dancing cats and sneezing pandas; people create and watch more than clever commercials and newlyweds competing with other unknown, online newlyweds for who can perform the most jaw-dropping First Dance at their weddings. But as I spend hours at my computer, looking to YouTube for memories and diversion, I sometimes fear that we're becoming inert clams, sustained by simply filtering the plankton-rich culture that continually flows through us.

"What we're trying to do is save the world," Harold Rosen had said in describing his goals for the satellite system he was creating. But in 1967, when *Our World* aired, I would have found that sentiment laughable. We would save the world through protest and celebration, by condemning and persuading, embracing and rejecting. Saving the world was an essentially human pursuit, incompatible with anything that had a metallic, industrial sheen. Then, I believed technical and military pursuits to be intimately, inextricably bound. Any technology was a gear in the war machine. Then, I didn't think of the car I longed for or the television I watched as machines.

Now, though, I live by and through technology. And as I surf through the indiscriminate torrent of tweets and posts and videos about Starbucks and the Syrian civil war, about hurricane victims and Zappo's shoes and Iran's nuclear program and Black Friday sales and laughing babies, I better understand both Rosen's utopian vision and McLuhan's dystopian one.

Digital technology alienates us from our *own* experience, causes us to see lives—even our own—as films, with poor pacing and disturbing discontinuities, with plots that are too formulaic or too unsettling. On some days, I look at my youth and young adulthood as my favorite movie, the one I never tire of, and am mystified by the sequel, the one in which I feel I'm masking as a corporate sell-out, working for The Man. On other days, I regard my job as a way to turn "consumers" back into people in the eyes of the frantic advertisers and marketers vying for a piece of their nervous system, to reveal the humanity beneath the scrolling digits. But the speed that this same technology now enables, makes empathy scalable, turns us back into a culture where the sensory experience of someone else's suffering or joy is as immediate as a flame, as tangible and sharp as a paper cut.

I am much older than I was in 1967, but I still love to look at the sky. I know that for every light emanating from a used car lot, there is one showing the world what joyful rebellion in a city square looks like. The points of light arcing through it have, over time, made me curious, awed, and anxious. For every surveillance satellite—masked and silent—there are millions of particles colliding, the conflict in their charges producing a gorgeous illumination.

To Be of Use (2011)

My corporate office is across the street from the Federal Reserve, and catty corner from Dewey Square in the city's financial district, where the Occupy Boston movement set up its tent city. Every day I'd walk over there for lunch and go exploring. The signs were more eclectic than in my day, ranging from *End the Fed* to *Bring our Troops Home* to *Keep the Lexington School Committee Independent.* I found no rigid adherence to a narrow platform there. *As one people, united, we acknowledge the reality: that the future of the human race requires the cooperation of its members,* read the Statement of Purpose accepted by Occupy Wall Street's New York City General Assembly in the disturbingly balmy fall of 2011:

... that our system must protect our rights, and upon corruption of that system, it is up to the individuals to protect their own rights, and those of their neighbors; that a democratic government derives its just power from the people, but corporations do not seek consent to extract wealth from the people and the Earth; and that no true democracy is attainable when the process is determined by economic power.

Or, as one particularly pithy sign in Zuccotti Park noted, *Shit is Fucked Up.* Not as metaphorical, perhaps, as *We've carried the rich for 200 years; let's get them off our backs,* but the Occupiers' actions generated much more tangible hoopla. *We are the 99 percent* arose as a mantra of the Occupy Wall Street movement, memed its way out of New York to other Occupy encampments, into public consciousness and casual conversation.

In Dewey Square, the causes people championed were quirkier and more personal than those championed by our stilted rhetoric from the 1970s. But the mix of people was familiar—vegetarian students, grizzled old lefties for whom leafleting was as natural as breathing, and homeless people reveling in the library tent and volunteer-staffed clinic, the three meals a day and the nightly concerts and lectures. As I picked my way through the paths between tents, I'd read the life stories hand-lettered on the sides of cardboard boxes, chat with the people basking in the autumn sun, drop money in the Donations tin, sign petitions, and study the daily schedule of activities: *Meditation at 7:30, Lecture on "The False Promise of Capitalism" at 10, Free Clinic at 11, Class on Nonviolent Resistance at 2, Protest at State Street Bank at 4, free concert at 6:30*. It was as if Jerry Garcia and Howard Zinn had teamed up to run a day camp.

And though electronic amplification was allowed at the Occupy Boston site, sometimes the squatters chose to use the "human microphone" method of communication developed at Occupy Wall Street. *Recycle your soda cans, Free Guam, We are the 99 percent, Bagels for breakfast* —the short, declarative sentence would start with a single person, then be passed through Dewey Park by small groups relaying what they'd just heard at the top of their lungs, like an improv troupe playing Broken Telephone.

Thirty years after leaving Allentown, little more than a protest tourist, I took my daily constitutional in this encampment. Then I'd return to the lobby of my office building, pass my employee photo ID in front of the sensor on the granite reception desk, and ride the elevator up to my seventh floor cubby with its coveted window view. Only then did I feel like an imposter.

On the wall behind my desk, adjacent to the Amnesty International calendar and the corporate style guide, hangs a yellowing Marge Piercy poem, one I've carried with me to every job at which I've had a desk.[31]

To be of use
The people I love the best
jump into work head first
without dallying in the shallows
and swim off with sure strokes almost out of sight.

They seem to become natives of that element,
the black sleek heads of seals
bouncing like half-submerged balls.

I love people who harness themselves, an ox to a heavy cart,
who pull like water buffalo, with massive patience,
who strain in the mud and the muck to move things forward,
who do what has to be done, again and again.

I want to be with people who submerge
in the task, who go into the fields to harvest
and work in a row and pass the bags along,
who are not parlor generals and field deserters
but move in a common rhythm
when the food must come in or the fire be put out.

The work of the world is common as mud.
Botched, it smears the hands, crumbles to dust.
But the thing worth doing well done
has a shape that satisfies, clean and evident.
Greek amphoras for wine or oil,
Hopi vases that held corn, are put in museums
but you know they were made to be used.
The pitcher cries for water to carry
and a person for work that is real.

I no longer have the "massive patience...to move things forward"
and probably never did. But what I miss—and felt during those walks
in Dewey Square—is the sense of moving in a common rhythm. I've
never wanted to go skydiving or run a race, let alone win one. My
dreams have always been to sing in a gospel choir, to dance in the
chorus of *West Side Story*; to bring in the harvest, any harvest.

So when the protestors were finally evicted from the park, leaving
not through gradual attrition but, like everything today, all at once, I

was bereft. By the next morning, their colorful mosaic of tents and food trucks and handmade signs had vanished, leaving behind just yellowing grass, cast-iron fencing, and a few barren benches.

Beacons (2015)

With its vaulting, poured-concrete ceilings, faux marble floors, aisles wide as boulevards and almost as long, Chicago's convention center—McCormick Place—looks like a set from *Triumph of the Will*. As I hobble down its empty length in my dress-up shoes, I envision it holding tens of thousands of uniformed men, clones with pale faces and chiseled square chins. The vastness is overwhelming; in the unused exhibition hall in the south wing, the forklifts look like Tonka Toys, their hard-hatted drivers little Lego men.

MccormickPlace.com informs me that the complex offers 2.6 million square feet of exhibit space alone—not including its 173 meeting rooms, four ballrooms, and 18,000-person assembly hall. But for all its capacious mass, what lies inside it is utterly ephemeral. Central American waitstaff bustle into improvised dining rooms defined by movable walls and curtains, whisk food on and off tables—then disappear. Cookie plates, baskets of salty snacks, urns of coffee and fruit-infused water appear on tables strategically placed mid-exhibition hall for the duration of each "expo break"—then vanish. Entire food courts pop up or evaporate based on the size and number of events going on in a given day.

I'm here to attend and speak at the annual Consumer Insights Today! Conference. An aerial view of the 600 of us—some of whom I now recognize from countless meetings and conferences like this one—would look like a tiny smudge, a stain on the floor of one of McCormick Place's many corridors. Eerily, we seem to be the only conference in the joint.

In the first presentation of the morning, a guy with a shock of white hair, thick-framed hipster glasses, black shirt, black jacket, black pants, black shoes, and no socks stands before a slide displaying a dramatically bifurcated silhouette.

"People, especially young people, are paradoxical." His voice, quiet and effeminate, is at odds with the boldness of his graphics and attire. "They revile consumerism but voluntarily watch ads on YouTube; they deplore Nike's sweatshops but breezily buy iPhones made under similar working conditions. And as a nation, we like our celebrities to reflect our conflicts."

He advances the slides through a series of portraits: Sexy but child-like (Marilyn Monroe); virile but vulnerable (Johnny Depp); brainy but degenerate (James Franco); Aryan but inclusive (Heidi Klum). But dialectical or not, members of this cohort need a single name so that pundits can discuss them and agencies can specialize in marketing to them.

"The Torn Generation, I call them," he says.

Why, I wonder. Isn't contradiction—the longing for novelty and familiarity, for challenge and comfort—characteristic of every generation, fundamental to being human? And today, in the twenty-first century, isn't everybody of every age over thirteen always as ambivalent as I am?

The presentation dwindles to an end, and I flee the darkened room in search of coffee. Outside the window-lined corridor, the fog has lifted to reveal Lake Michigan, a deep and gorgeous blue on this early June morning. But it, too, is strangely vacant, bereft of sails, tugboats, any sign of the Chicago shore life that I know must be stirring a mile or so north of where I stand. For a second, I wonder if one of those science-fiction movie plots has come true, if overnight some lethal virus has struck down all but those of us encased in the nation's largest convention center. Or perhaps it's the opposite. Perhaps we're the dead ones, unknowingly incapable of seeing actual life.

Reluctantly, I turn away from the big, silent view and plod to the next session, where a drab man from AniMate ("Brand Matchmaker for Today's Consumer!") explains the neuroscience behind the merchandising of cookies.

"Our unconscious emotions direct our conscious thoughts,"

he explains in a gentle sing-song. He could be telling us a bedtime story. "And our unconscious is still really primitive, based on animal responses like hunger and anger and fear. That's why we feel aroused in the grocery store, and if we succumb to unhealthy or socially undesirable impulses—and, I mean, who doesn't?—it's also why we feel ashamed after leaving it."

No surprise there. Of course our emotions around sweet snacks are complex. (I suspect that this is a man who's never bought his own groceries.) No, what's unnerving is *how* the AniMate researchers arrived at this conclusion. In-store beacons, little devices on store shelves that sense your presence via a signal generated by an app on your phone, capture how long you stand in front of the cookie shelves, determining whether you're spending more time considering the Oreos or the Pepperidge Farm Milanos. Then they can send you offers and promotions, or, in this case, images of the products you're already studying, accompanied by positive and negative adjectives describing them. If it's a positive adjective—*healthy*, for example, or *delicious*—you're instructed to swipe the screen toward you. You swipe away if a negative adjective like *sugary* or *overpriced* is displayed. The theory is that if you really believe Milanos are tastier than Oreos, you'll swipe toward yourself on *delicious* more quickly when the Milanos package appears on your screen.

Come to me, we're signaling with one swipe. *Get away from me*, says another.

"Imagine the possibilities," the AniMate guy croaks, his anemic delivery at odds with the inspirational words some brand matchmaker has probably written for him.

I do, and it exhausts me.

At lunch, I scan nametags before sitting down, looking for people from prospect companies, the people I know I should be trying to meet. But this shopping for tablemates is difficult and rude, and I quickly settle for the first vacancy I can find.

To my right is a woman in her late twenties who works as a market researcher for Subway sandwich shops. She confirms that yes, weight-losing Jared, the Subway spokesman, was trusted up until the day he was arrested, but no, they don't spend much time doing qualitative research into the needs of Subway guests, preferring to infer it from the relative volume of Meatball Marinaras and Classic Tunas sold.

On my left is a woman of similar age and complexion to the Subway researcher. She's a Consumer Insights Associate for HomeAway, the vacation rental company that, I learn, also owns all the other online vacation rental companies I assumed were its competitors. Yes, Airbnb certainly is a competitive threat—though a bigger problem for hotel companies than for hers—and no, she hates living in Texas and fervently hopes to leave as soon as her boyfriend finishes graduate school there.

Together, we trundle off to the keynote speech of the day. It's by another agency guy with a cool office in downtown Chicago. ("It has an old school Pac-Man console!" his introducer breathlessly informs us. "And the guy in Birkenstocks and the Death Cab for Cutie T-shirt who's the champion player turns out to be one of the smartest big data analysts in the country!")

He begins with a story—this one about his son's birthday party. Although he and his wife had barred weapons ("real or toy") from the festivities, the kids found a way around the prohibition by dropping their pants, flashing their *Fast and the Furious* underwear at each other, pointing their index fingers, and shouting "bang." After the party ended, he sat his son down for a talk.

"Not *the* talk—he's still too young for that—but *a* talk." The agency guy puts his hands on his knees and bends toward an imaginary child at his side, lowering his voice to a gentle scold. "Dylan, you know that we had a rule against even pretending to hurt other people, and you and your friends broke the rule." Then he straightens up, pauses, and once again directly faces us, readying us for the punch line. "But every little consumer is smarter than his parents. My eight-year-old son—did I mention that he's eight?—he knew who he was talking to. Without skipping a beat, Dylan sat back on the couch, crossed his arms over his chest, and said, 'Dad, you're old enough to know that boys will be boys.'"

A few titters percolate in the otherwise silent auditorium. The guy sitting next to me scrolls through his email in an iTrance. I stare at the broad-backed person in front of me. She has stuck her right hand down the back collar of her shirt—a synthetic, glistening plaid of lemon, orange, and strawberry sherbet-colored squares— and is scratching her shoulder. I'm mesmerized by the wriggling fabric, imagining a ferret on her back, or a mole, gleaming and blind, frantically seeking a way out.

I'm in Boston, sitting in the company cafeteria with my twenty-something colleague Martin, preparing for a workshop we're going to be leading next week. The session will be held in 7 World Trade Center, a new building in the original lower Manhattan complex. In attendance will be about thirty-five chief executive officers, chief marketing officers, and other executives from fifteen agencies in the "family" of agencies owned by our parent company. Our mission: *Learn about how digital and data are transforming the retail technology! Mix and match with sister companies to outshine and out-perform the competition!*

Martin will be opening the half-day session with the obligatory relationship-building exercise.

"We want to kick off the afternoon with an exercise that will hopefully help you let down your hair a little and create a climate of trust." Martin's rehearsing his opening. "I'd like you to break into pairs and tell each other a professional fact about yourself, along with a more personal fact that you'd be willing for your teammate to share with the rest of the group. For example, my professional fact is that I worked for a yacht manufacturer in Naples before joining my current company. My personal fact is that my father owned several bakeries and *cannoli* was my first word."

Martin pauses for my feedback.

"Here's the thing," I say. "If we're doing this personal sharing to break down some defenses and get people talking more freely,

I wonder if your personal fact should have a bit more emotional content."

He looks at me, puzzled.

"Like, for instance, speaking for myself, I'm actually a bit freaked out to be in the World Trade Center."

"Ooh, that's good," Martin answers. "Maybe I'll use that."

Behind his head, the wall-mounted video screen is cycling through a series of company announcements. *Welcome our Chinese colleague, Ching Ling!* says one against a backdrop of the Shanghai skyline. *Got a question? HR is here to help.* Outside the window, I see employees of the government building across the street ambling out onto their roof garden for lunch. It's the perfect day out there, sunny and breezy, warm but not hot. I feel for the guys in black suits and navy uniforms perpetually guarding the place, so enclosed and unavailable to the tangy air blowing in off the water.

I will my attention back to Martin.

"So now, I want you to share something private, something that you wouldn't normally tell a stranger within the first few minutes of meeting them," he continues. "For example, my private fact is…. Shit, I haven't figured out what my private fact should be."

"Remind me—why are we doing this?"

"The point of revealing the private thing is to break down barriers and show how we all carry around stuff that shapes us."

"That's ambitious," I say.

"To accomplish in five minutes? Yeah, you think?"

He's getting flustered, and I realize I should try to be helpful. "Okay, so let's think of a private fact that illustrates that point. For example, imagine you had a stutter as a kid. Even once you learned to stop stuttering, you might still be very deliberate in your speech. You might still hold back a little and internally rehearse, just being a really careful, intentional sort of person."

"Oh, that's also great. Maybe I'll use that, too!"

"We're so fucking authentic, aren't we?"

We both laugh. *Don't forget Corporate Social Responsibility week! There are many ways to give back,* flashes the PowerPoint behind Martin.

Between meetings, waiting for a coffee pod to release its goodness into my *Luminoso: Shed New Light on your Data* mug, I join the other smartphone checkers. Just the usual string of messages seeking urgent help with this client project or that sales opportunity, and a missed call from Mount Auburn Hospital.

I go to an unused telephone room and call Liz, a nurse practitioner. I'd met her two days earlier, immediately after a needle biopsy in my breast.

"The news is mixed, but mostly good," she says. "The pathologist didn't find any malignant cells." My heart leaves my throat and settles back into my chest. "But there's some atypical tissue, a papilloma that really should come out, just to play it safe. So, I'd like to schedule day surgery for you, an excisional breast biopsy so that we can remove it, just to make absolutely sure it doesn't turn into cancer."

Having gone through a similar drill fourteen years ago in my other breast, I dread the procedure. I've done my research since being told the previous week that the mammogram showed a small mass ("probably nothing, but just in case"). As I've studied my own films and ultrasounds in ignorance and fearful curiosity over the past few weeks, I've seen striations of white against the conical gray of each breast, the marbled markers of weight and time. And now, I once again consider the pros of early information against the cons of simply too damn much of it.

Swipe away.

It's my last meeting of the day. Two finance guys from the parent company are making the rounds of all seventy companies within our corporate division on a tour they call "Spend Together, Grow Together!"

"Now, we're not here to tell you how to run your business," the tall, cheery one reassures us. "We just want to introduce you to the capabilities of your sister companies so that if you're spending on printing or advertising or public relations, you can keep those dollars within the family. After all, a rising sea lifts all boats!"

Then his skinny, ghostly partner starts going through the list of all our expenditures that could have gone to a preferred vendor or a parent-owned company and didn't. He goes to great lengths to say that we *may* have had good reasons for choosing other suppliers— just as there *may* be a justification for fratricide—but for everyone's sake, he'd urge us to look within the family first. He concludes with a video he hopes we'll find inspirational.

It's an animated movie. Against a soundscape of upbeat, synthesized music—a formless but repetitive collection of chords that sounds like an early version of a Diet 7Up commercial— a young man with a perky voice explains how the world works. "Doing business within the family creates jobs," he begins, and pictures of happy new employees fill the screen. "Creating jobs increases wealth"—though he neglects to mention that our corporate overlord is already a $15-billion company—"and greater wealth *should* lower taxes. Lower taxes puts more money in people's pockets!" We can see that. Like an amazing rewind, money is spurting out of dollar-sign-adorned bags and streaming into the pockets of the happy new employees. "When people have more, they spend more on the things they want. That makes them happy. Happy people are peaceful people. And isn't that what we all want—a peaceful planet?"

The video ends. I don't dare make eye contact with anyone else at the table. My mental jaw is hanging open to my chest, and I'm too stunned to know whether to laugh or cry.

On Monday, seventeen of my colleagues are laid off. I knew this was coming, and for a time I thought I'd be among them. This company, which took shape in my old office and living room, which was partially funded for a few months by the earnings I brought in as a freelance writer, has long since outgrown any claim I might have had on it. Real business people, people who have MBAs and track records, who know their bookings from their revenues, their margins from their COGs, who care deeply about "growing the business," have long since taken over its leadership. I'm still valued, of course—as a smart person, a nice person, maybe even as someone with a degree of wisdom appropriate to her age (which is a couple of decades more than most of the young marketers and ad agency graduates swarming into management)—but I'm a luxury now, a sentimental attachment, a favorite aunt whose company is still welcome on Thanksgiving but would never be invited to go out to a bar, let alone to a vacation home.

The confidential memo those of us in management received last night in preparation for the layoffs advises us to be proactive in checking in with the survivors, to be empathetic while still projecting an air of stability.

The one vice president getting the axe in this round was notified at the end of day Friday, given the chance to pack up and walk out after the office had largely emptied. The one or two more VPs on the chopping block will ostensibly get to leave of their own volition a few weeks from now, when "family" or "exciting new opportunities" will draw them out of our orbit. But apparently the dignity of the more junior people isn't quite as protected. For many of our millennial employees, this will be the first time they'll see a person they've worked next to for months or years stagger out of a conference room like someone concussed, who'll then discover that packing boxes were placed on her desk while she was having a "check-in" with her manager. This will be the first time they've had to choose whether to hug, offer consoling words, or avoid the gaze of the normally wiseass colleague whose eyes are now swimming and whose cheeks are aflame with rage and humiliation.

Be positive, but be genuine, the memo advises. *Acknowledge that this is an emotionally difficult time, but demonstrate confidence in our future.* For those unsure of how to achieve this delicate balance, it offers some suggested phrases: *This was a hard decision that we were reluctant to make, but this short-term pain will put us on a much better footing for the long-term. And rest assured that we will do our best to support your colleagues in their future endeavors.*

Meanwhile, in a conference room at the other end of the building, seventeen new summer interns—college seniors or brand-new graduates working for ten or fifteen dollars an hour—are assembling for the start of their Professional Development Day. We've gotten an email about this, too, which outlines the agenda for the session that our head of Learning and Development has put together. It features training in how to become a better face-to-face communicator, including a small-group workshop on *How to Win your Clients' Trust* and another on what it takes to *Own Your Awesomeness!*

I feel like I'm in that scene in *The Godfather*, the one where Michael Corleone stands in church as his newborn nephew is baptized while his hit men are out executing the family's enemies. As reverential music soars, the camera cuts back and forth between the rays of sun streaming through the cathedral's stained glass windows and Moe Greene being shot through the eye as he lies on a massage table, between the gentle kisses being planted on the silky head of the baby boy and the machine-gun bullets pulverizing the gangster stuck inside the revolving door of the St. Regis Hotel.

Emily, the snub-nosed young woman who had only been working at the company for a couple of years comes to our pod to say goodbye to Mike, the almost-thirty-but-still-very-very-young man who I think she's had a crush on all this time. She makes no effort to hide her tears, and one of her coworkers—accompanying her as a friend, guard, or both—feebly pats her shoulder. Mike gives Emily a hug, then sits down, ashen-faced, and immediately resumes work. Inside his kelly-green Celtics T-shirt, his back is rigid.

"It's tough, isn't it?" I say.

"Yeah," he mumbles, still not quite daring to look up.

"Don't worry," I tell him. "Your job is safe. If any of us were being laid off today, we'd know by now."

His shoulders sag. "Phew." Then blushing, he turns to face me. "I mean, I feel bad for Emily and the others. Who were the others?"

I violate the explicit instruction to not reveal those names—a stupid edict, given that it's just a matter of time before word will spread—but otherwise try to honor Tip #3 in the memo about helping staff cope with layoffs: *If asked who's being laid off and no one on your immediate team is affected, reassure them that while this is a difficult day, your team is safe. If jobs on your team are being eliminated, say everything but the part about your team being safe.*

#helpful

But here's the thing. It's all true. These were difficult decisions that will, at best, disrupt the lives and confidence of hardworking people, but will also save the company money and prolong the jobs of those who remain.

I can't find a villain here, at least not a human one. Our parent company is demanding higher margins. And why? I don't know if anyone even in the parent company's boardroom could answer that question beyond paying a vague homage to "growth."

This is how the system works. I'm just not sure I can bear to be a part of it for much longer.

Martin, our colleague Jenn, and I pull up a block away from 7 World Trade Center. After signing in and being issued photo IDs, we head up to the thirty-second floor. The view is spectacular. The copper cupolas of the Woolworth Building gleam, as do the shoes of the women who greet us. We're welcomed as experts, as stars in the craft of facilitating conversations. I feel vaguely queasy, and as every good workshop leader knows to do, steer clear of the arugula-adorned tuna-salad sandwiches offered for lunch. Never eat anything with mayonnaise before getting up in front of people.

The room has a wall of windows facing out over the Hudson, and as at McCormick Place, I get momentarily lost in the silent blue outside the glass. But this is no time for reflection. The execs are taking their assigned seats, Martin and I are being fitted for our lavalier microphones, the English woman who leads Corporate Learning is introducing us.

Make it a great performance, I think, planting myself in front of the giant ficus tree. Gliding from one slide to the next, I tout my company's services and give an overview of the day.

"Before hearing from the first speaker, we're going to do a short team-building exercise," I say, then rush to add, "I can see you rolling your eyes. Don't worry, it'll be short and high-impact, but no Koosh balls, no trust falls."

They laugh appreciatively. My nervousness has passed. I speak authoritatively, though I occasionally and disarmingly confide my ignorance about things that don't really matter.

I hand off to Martin, whose coppery hair, crisp delivery, and obvious smarts evoke a young, corporate Jude Law, at least to every woman in the room. But he plays it straight and confides his sample secrets with disarming sincerity before instructing the attendees to pair off and share their own professional and private facts.

The room gets as noisy as a pick-up bar. People are eager and willing to share, to generate some interpersonal spark that will make their next few hours together a bit more fun. In the share-out, we learn who likes to surf, who has just had a new baby, who has just moved from one coast or continent to another and misses the weather or friends or housing prices or taco restaurants of their old homes. They seem like nice people.

We introduce the first round of speakers. A brilliant Brit talks at length about how our purchasing data, RMV records, and browsing data are triangulated so that companies whose business is to measure the return-on-investment of advertising can determine who is seeing what and how it correlates to who is buying what.

"It's anonymized, of course," he says smoothly, but the net is that "marketers can do amazing things with this incredibly valuable information. You can see that the people living between East Fiftieth and East Fifty-Fourth who watched *Dancing with the Stars* didn't change their behavior after seeing your ad, but those who saw it while watching *South Park* went out and bought a new pair of your sneakers sometime within the next three weeks."

"The holy grail," a paunchy man next to me murmurs to his female companion. "Measurable ROI on creative. The agency guys must be shitting their pants."

"And this is just the beginning," the Brit speaker concludes with something approximating animation. "Five billion people are already walking around with the Internet in their pockets. I believe the applications of Big Data are infinite and transformative."

Wow—concepts once reserved for God and natural selection. And here I thought we were just talking about selling stuff. Who knew?

On the break, Jenn sidles up to Martin. "I had no idea you stuttered as a kid. Really, you're such a great public speaker, I never would have guessed it."

Before he can respond, one of the conference conveners gives Martin a warm hug. "Don't worry," she says, "the World Trade Center is the safest place in New York City."

Stricken, Martin flashes me a wide-eyed look over the woman's shoulder.

I'm going to hell, he mouths.

The next two speakers do me in. Not only have they put beacons on store shelves, but they have placed them on benches and trash bins throughout Manhattan.

"Imagine it," says the one in the yellow shirt. The room is hot, and he's sweating profusely. "Once enough apps have enough beacon receptors, we should be able to know who's walking by a given store every day and feed that data to merchants, so that I could say to Sal at Sal's Consumer Electronics on 10th Avenue, 'Hey Sal, there's this guy who I know is in the market for a cell phone 'cause he's been searching Best Buy and Walmart and researching different brands, and he's walking past your door at around 5:10 p.m. every day, Monday through Friday, and I bet that if you were to beam him a great deal on one of your phones, that business could be yours!'"

"Hyper-localization, hyper-personalization, hyper-contextualization," intones his partner. "These are the characteristics of Data Driven Personal Retail, and it's not just a dream. It's a reality. When you're sitting at a red light near a KFC and an ad for Chicken Littles shows up on your Waze screen, you're seeing it in action."

In many accounts of near-death experiences, people describe the sensation of levitating and looking down on their own bodies lying on the floor or the operating room table, often surrounded by the people trying to revive them. I'm feeling that strange but powerful mix of curiosity and disbelief right now. Here I sit, the Hudson shooting shards of light through the windows behind me, in a room full of nice people with dogs and dinner plans and a recorded episode of *This is Us* awaiting them at home, hearing about how these other really smart people have developed extraordinary technology to merge physical and digital experience, to intercept people with enticements to act on ideas they barely knew they had, to harness the exceptional power of having the Internet in one's pocket, all in the service of getting people to buy more stupid shit that they don't need.

I'm frantically taking notes for the obligatory report-out when I get back to the office, every insane story of mobile-commerce, every malapropism ("let's be proactive and not reactionary!"), all the new words like *omnichannel* and *pretail*; each and every example of how you can see a virtual image of a store on a subway wall, touch what you want, and discover it delivered to your home five minutes after you get there. My writing is getting smaller and smaller as scenarios cascade out of the perky coral-hued mouth of Google's "retail imagineer," stories about how shoppers can connect with product experts in Google Hangouts, make their purchases with Google Wallet, which then passes user data to retailers who rely on Google Express to fulfill the purchases. I record that the Me-Ality app installed at select Bloomingdale's locations somehow scans your body and recommends items of clothing based on your measurements. At least I think that's what it does, because I'm writing so fast that my cursive is illegible. It looks like it's come from someone else's hand.

Tonight, back at LaGuardia, Martin, Jenn, and I drink. We talk about music and the World Cup and vacations.

As the jet lifts off and the New York City lights unfurl beneath my eyes like a breaking wave on this hot summer night, I rest my sweaty cheek on the cool plexiglass porthole. Tomorrow, I'll have my breast surgery, wondering until I go under why I've subjected myself to another wound—another excised warning that will simply confirm what I already know.

A line from a Mary Oliver poem comes to mind and won't leave. *Tell me, what is it you plan to do with your one wild and precious life?*[32]

Burn like Oak (Present)

Summer 2016

To celebrate my birthday, I take a vacation day from work and head out to Walden Pond before the parking lot closes. It is the hottest day of the year, and by 10:30 a.m., the beach is already dense with strollers, umbrellas, small tents, and sticky bodies of all ages.

Out near the farthest buoy line, an overweight tattooed man with a shaven head and big bristling beard is cavorting with his wife, also large and adorned with inky pictures of eagles and lightning. He pulls her toward him, she splashes him lightly and pushes him over, and he provides a running football broadcaster's narration of their frolic. Their kids are tossing a ball nearby, their son making diving catches in the water. They are buoyant; they jostle and bounce, freed from the greedy pull of gravity. They look like Hell's Angels or Idaho militia members, like the couples you see in news photos of American flag-draped Trump supporters or Second Amendment defenders.

Of course these are caricatures; I know nothing about these people except that they have an outlaw fashion aesthetic. But I also know that regardless of what they think about firearms or candidates, whether they appreciate diversity or want to take "their" country back by any means necessary, right now they are simply enjoying the blessing of cool clear water on a blistering day. As their leaping son practically knocks over a small Indian girl nearby, the woman quickly apologizes to the child's mother and father, and the man chastises his boy. In heavily accented, lilting speech, the Indian parents assure them that no harm's been done, that their daughter is startled but not hurt, and the four parents smile wryly at each other, united in the challenge of keeping their children both lively and safe.

Maybe the white parents are celebrity chefs or software engineers,

211

though I doubt it. But even if they are true to the stereotype I've assigned to them—even if they are struggling to make ends meet, feeling angry and disenfranchised and blaming exactly the wrong people for their hardships—today, right now, they are just grown-ups enjoying simple, childish pleasures. Except for the handful of triathletes in wet suits grimly trying to improve their mile times, so are all of us dunking, paddling, floating mammals here today. In this instant, I can't imagine that they are thinking about banning immigrants or protecting the right to own automatic weapons or denying the fact of climate change. No, in this sun-baked, water-splashed moment if I were to ask them why they held those beliefs and why those convictions were so important, I think that they would look at me in blank puzzlement, unable to remember why they're so aggrieved. But ask them tonight, when they're back in their overpriced rental or heavily mortgaged saltbox house, and they'll once again channel the vitriol that's been scripted for them.

I swim away, out to the middle of the pond. Looking back on this, my birthday, I'm angry that in my lifetime, not enough has changed. The poor are poorer, the exiled are finding no safe haven, and the ruling class is still all too successful at pitting the have-nots against one another. But looking ahead, I'm not quite despairing, and find a strange hope in the riot of colors dotting the shoreline. Thermoses, beach umbrellas, insulated baskets, backpacks, kayaks, brightly packaged tubes and bottles of sunscreen—these are the human inventions that enable us to be mobile, to protect ourselves and our children while adapting to a rapidly changing environment. They are the mundane but profoundly practical products of imagination and skill that people centuries from now will dig up in deserts that once were lakes.

And all of them were created by the people who populate the pond, the people without summer homes who rediscover their shared humanity on days like this.

Winter 2017

Late in the 2016 Republican presidential primary season, Donald Trump's campaign engaged in a breathtaking feat of denial. His leading opponent, the equally reprehensible Ted Cruz, ran an ad featuring a 1999 television interview in which candidate Trump declared himself to be "strongly pro-choice." In response, Trump's campaign sent Cruz's a cease-and-desist letter charging Cruz with defamation for running an ad "replete with outright lies" for suggesting that Trump was, well, pro-choice. In other words, Trump pointed to Cruz's use of documentary footage showing him declaring his support for abortion rights as evidence of his opposition to those rights.

Now that flagrant inversion of reality has become the norm. This morning's *Guardian* ran a story about Pete Hoekstra, the now President Trump-appointed U.S. ambassador to the Netherlands, who was interviewed by a Dutch television journalist.[33]

"You mentioned in a debate that there are no-go zones in the Netherlands," said reporter Wouter Zwart, "and that cars and politicians are being set on fire in the Netherlands."

"I didn't say that. This is actually an incorrect statement," Hoekstra replied. "We would call it fake news."

Hoekstra was then shown a video clip of himself saying those exact words.

"You called this fake news," Zwart said. "Obviously—"

"I didn't call that fake news," Hoekstra interrupted. "I didn't use the words today."

"No?" challenged a remarkably composed Zwart.

"No," Hoekstra answered belligerently. "I don't think I did."

I suppose I should no longer be astounded by such brazen falsehood—not just the original lie ("I didn't say that... We would call it fake news"), but the lie about the lie ("I didn't call that fake news.") After all, in a recent interview that Trump did with the *New York Times*, fact-checkers at the *Washington Post* clocked twenty-four false or misleading statements made by the president in twenty minutes.[34] And that's just a half-hour out of one day.

But I am. Amazed and terrified. Having capitulated to the "filter bubble" that is the Internet, having surrendered to the notion that by default, Facebook and Twitter and Instagram and every other social "news" site is going to serve us what some algorithm thinks we'll like and shrink our world rather than expand it, we're now in danger of giving up on facts and the notion of some shared, objective reality altogether.

I've watched in fascination as journalists struggle with how to handle falsehoods when they emanate from the President and Commander-in-Chief. Should the press simply ignore tweets such as those about the "millions" who "illegally" voted for Hillary Clinton? Present them as assertions with no evidence. Or call them lies?

"Reality is beside the point," Dallas Woodhouse, the executive director of the North Carolina Republican Party, told the *New Republic*, in reference to his state's efforts to limit voting rights. "Whether there's widespread voter fraud or not, the people believe there is."[35]

Belief—based on aspiration, on rage, on aggrievement, on impossible hopes, on the fundamental *desire* to believe—is the currency that fuels the sale of products and of candidates. And creating beliefs through the conscious manipulation of unconscious emotion has long been the province of advertisers, marketers, and political campaign strategists.

But up until twenty or thirty years ago, belief was a product of how one interpreted fact. Now it is replacing it.

This phenomenon didn't begin with Trump. In a prescient 2004 article, Ron Suskind wrote of George W. Bush, "… he's a believer in the power of confidence. At a time when constituents are uneasy and enemies are probing for signs of weakness, he clearly feels that unflinching confidence has an almost mystical power. It can all but create reality."[36]

Bush advisor and Republican strategist, Karl Rove, made autocratic sureness his guiding political principle. Here's how Suskind described it: "The aide [Rove] said that guys like me were 'in what we call the reality-based community,' which he defined as people who 'believe that solutions emerge from judicious study of discernible reality… That's not the way the world really works anymore. We're an empire now, and when we act, we create our own reality. And while you're studying that reality—judiciously, as you will—we'll act again, creating other new realities… We're history's actors, and you, all of you, will be left to just study what we do.'"

Bush, Rove, and their fellow actors led us into a war based on a lie. And now, twelve years later, here we are, studying the tweets of a man whose campaign and supporters seemingly summon new realities at will, and trust that through confidence and virality, they'll stick until it's time for another, more convenient new reality.

Twitter makes this easy. So do scrolling tickers at the bottom of our television screens, and our reliance on pictures over words, sound bites over substance. We are entering what Joe Wiesenthal has described as a "post-literate age," noting that, "Before the invention of writing, knowledge existed in the present tense between two or more people; when information was forgotten, it disappeared forever. That state of affairs created a special need for ideas that were easily memorized and repeatable (so, in a way, they could go viral). The immediacy of the oral world did not favor complicated, abstract ideas that need to be thought through. Instead, it elevated individuals who passed along memorable stories, wisdom and good news."[37]

The 2016 presidential campaign tale of a child sex ring being run by Hillary Clinton and John Podesta out of the basement of a Washington D.C. pizza parlor was certainly a memorable story. That's why Michael Flynn, Jr., son of Trump's disgraced-turned-informant National Security Advisory, tweeted even *after* a man walked into this restaurant firing his AR15 rifle, "Until #Pizzagate proven to be false, it'll remain a story."

Social media enables liars to lie at unprecedented scale. It lets manipulators invent and amplify hashtags and phrases, hateful tales that are so quickly so ubiquitous that they infuse our consciousness despite our best efforts to elude them.

"It's a beautiful thing, the destruction of words," says Syme, a

215

loyal servant of the Party, early in George Orwell's *1984*. He goes on to extoll the virtues of language that's increasingly simple and lacking in nuance. Who needs the word "bad" (let alone "flawed" or "erratic" or, heaven forbid, "multi-dimensional") when you can simply describe someone or something as "ungood." When your aim is to police thought and enforce submission, the more blunt and binary your vernacular, the better. After all, as Orwell noted, "... if thought corrupts language, language can also corrupt thought."[38]

Like all great demagogues before him, that's a principle that Donald Trump understands, and his communications channels of choice—Twitter and Fox News—embrace.

"I'm a better person than the people I'm running against," Trump declared while campaigning. "I'm really good at the trade," he crowed at rallies. "I'm really good at the borders." Assert anything often enough and with enough vigor, Trump believes, and people will accept it.

But he goes a step farther than his equally cynical brethren in this and past political contexts. Trump has intuited that by constantly repeating that he's a winner, that people love him, that his poll numbers are better than anyone else's, he can marginalize the non-believers. If the majority of people say that he is the best, then that is the de facto truth, just as in Orwell's Oceania, if the party says 2+2=5 and enough citizens repeat it, the dissenter—the statistical outlier—is, by definition, insane. After all, in Oceania and presumably in TrumpWorld, "Sanity is statistical."

"Today there were fear, hatred and pain, but no dignity of emotion, no deep or complex sorrows," Orwell wrote in yet another pithy summation of Oceania's ethos.[39] He could have just as easily been describing ours. Political discourse throbs with rage, reproach and hyperbole. Not just hyperbole, but the biggest, boldest hyperbole the world has ever seen.

"I love Mexico, I love China, I love many of these countries that rip us off because we have leaders that are incompetent and don't know what they're doing," Trump frothed on the campaign trail. "China in particular—that's the big one. The greatest abuse of a country that I think I've ever seen financially—China....What they've done to us is the greatest single theft in the history of the world. They've taken our jobs, they've taken our money, they've taken everything."

Who "they" is and what they've taken does, of course, depend on the day, the state, the audience. "... The rage that one felt," Orwell wrote of the *1984* ritual he dubbed the Two Minutes Hate, "was an abstract, undirected emotion which could be switched from one object to another like the flame of a blowlamp."[40]

We all know it now, feel it multiple times over the course of the day, that surge in outrage that flares, then leaves us depleted. Yes, we share it with others, but our "community" burns like paper—hot and fast. What we need is to burn like oak, slowly, long-term. And even when the flame subsides, we need to smolder long enough to ignite another log.

Summer, 2017

I'm studying a picture from the summer of 1976. My parents, my Uncle Herbie, and my Auntie Anne are in their bathing suits, arrayed on deck chairs, smiling into the camera. More likely, they are beaming at the scene that lies behind the photographer—the large, rugged contours of Quebec's Lac Archambault, the small island within swimming distance of the dock where a pine tree juts out over its rocky face like a jaunty hat.

Then in his early fifties, Herbie, my father's brother, was the oldest of the quartet. My mother, at forty-seven, was the youngest. Until a few months ago, she was the lone survivor. Now she too is gone.

But then, my God, you can't imagine four people more full of life. The intensive parenting years are behind them; my cousins, brother, and I are by then all in college or have launched from it. They are all employed, but not consumed by their work. The best of friends, they are together in the spot on this planet that nourishes them most with its evasive sun, temperamental water, rounded green mountains, and haunting family of loons that glide across the lake every evening at dusk.

Today, on a deck chair behind the gym tucked between a condo complex and a body shop, I think mournfully of that picture. The house in Quebec has long since been sold. None of the five of us cousins live in the same city. Some of our children know each other more through Facebook than through live encounters.

Sitting alone, scrolling through the news on my phone on this melancholy morning, I'm bombarded by reports on crumbling glaciers and rising seas, increasing temperatures and climate refugees, false and incendiary tweets about nuclear weapons, fire, and fury, videos of Nazis and white nationalists parading through the streets of Charlottesville.

I miss those people in the picture. And I want to be them— fearlessly soaking up the sun, surrounded by family, embracing the day with unmoderated joy.

But of course I'm idealizing the past. My father and uncle had grown up during the Depression, moving from one apartment to the next, and in each, anxiety permeated the home as much as the smell of chicken fat. Anne had started her life in Vienna, and when she left that city as a young teenager, it was on one of the last Kindertransport trains, with her mother and father and all the other doomed parents left behind on the platform waving heartsick goodbyes.

"Jews will not replace me," the Unite the Right demonstrators chanted in Charlottesville. I see them in a tiny window on my phone.

Our parents had no Twitter, but they were just as scared and appalled by the lunatic rantings of a powerful leader spewing out of their radios. Their wars were not fought in remote lands and shown to the public only in censored, sanitized pictures. Herbie had been an Air Force radio operator in England, where he met Anne. My father had served in the Canadian army, and though my mother only knitted lumpy scarves for the soldiers, she was no different from the other three in her knowledge of people who went away and didn't come back, or came back changed, and not for the better. They hadn't known nuclear weapons existed, but then saw them used.

By the time the cheery summer picture was taken, the four of them had already been orphaned—to concentration camps, to cancer and heart disease and Alzheimer's. They'd lost jobs, faced bankruptcies, started anew over and over again. They'd worried about our safety, about our poor judgment and bad choices and still, always loved us unconditionally. They'd taught us the hatred of racism and war that my generation would claim as uniquely ours.

Despite their tanned, relaxed bodies, despite their barefooted comfort on that dock on that day, their lives were not perpetually sunny. They'd lived through the cataclysms that so frighten me now, and handled them with no more or less grace than anyone else. Now older than they were in that picture, I know all the pain that seethed and tumbled with all the joy inside them.

But they knew something I haven't yet grasped. Somehow they mastered the feeling of helplessness that is so new to me and so corrosive in this strange new/old world.

Having grown up in hardship, did they have a stronger sense of their own agency? Having weathered enough calamities—both routine and extraordinary—had they lost their fear?

Neither, I think. Those four parents simply loved life's essentials—food, water, sun, and a herd to huddle with—with a blazing fierceness that parched despair before it could take root.

Studying their picture like it's the Torah, like it's the cure to all diseases, like it's my child's face, I wonder: Can I learn to love like that?

This All-at-Onceness (1967-2015)

Now this strange, new, all-at-once situation in which everyone experiences everything all at once creates this kind of X-Ray mosaic of involvement and participation for which people are just not prepared. They have lived through centuries of detached ... of non-involvement. Suddenly they're involved, and it's a big surprise, and for many people, a kind of exhilaration. Wonderful.

- Marshall McLuhan, in a interview at
the start of *Our World*[41]

In the final segment of *Our World,* we hear the satellite's steady, electronic heartbeat as the screen dims, briefly goes to black, then illuminates a man standing at the foot of what the zooming out camera reveals to be one of two radio telescopes.

"The sun is below the Eastern horizon," he says in an Australian accent, "and it's a cold and dewy morning as the astronomers here at the Parkes Radio Observatory are preparing to take us on a voyage to the limits of the universe, a trip to the edge of time."[42]

Inside the control room, two scientists are about to capture signals from a quasar. Dubbed 0237-23, it is, in 1967, the most distant object known to man. "It may not seem like anything dramatic," the correspondent tells us, "but when the mechanical pen on the chart of John Bolton's recorder begins to shiver its way up to the right, and when we hear a hissing noise, we'll be seeing live the signals from something ten thousand million, million, million, million miles away, the farthest reach of human experience. So now, let's watch."

The camera zooms in on what looks and sounds like a bulky old electric typewriter as it bursts into chattering life. "Here it comes..." the correspondent says. We hear it—a surge in crackling static— and the plotter pen rises up, up, forming a perfect parabola, then returning to its level course. "...And there it was."

As *Our World* draws to a close, the broadcast signal hops from one satellite to the next in a montage of scenes from the sites that the show has visited. We zoom out to a model of earth in its solar system. Simulated satellites, like cherry tomatoes on toothpicks, revolve around it.

Now most of the journalists who made *Our World* are dead. Looking back at their forty-four-year-old vision of the future, I think that they were so wrong about what they thought they knew. Their earnest portraits of public works projects, fish farming, agribusiness—all of these artifacts of planning, these steady markers of development— weren't silly; the number of people living in abject poverty, squalor, and ignorance has declined. But the change the show's producers envisioned hasn't happened gradually, or originated from any of the expected quarters. It isn't what they chose to show in *Our World* that ultimately mattered, but simply that they were able to show it.

My first really good writing teacher challenged me with every submission. *Why are you writing this?* she'd scrawl on the manuscript. *And why are you writing this now?*

"It's about simultaneity," I'd written in my early notes for this project, "and simultaneity creates a sense of urgency." Now, as I assemble and rearrange pages, build collages out of pieces of memory, I realize I've been looking backward as intently as the show's producers had tried to peer into the future, as interested in my rear view mirror as in the spattered and pitted windshield in front of me. But it's the present that's revealing my past—the Arab Spring and the Occupy movement, WikiLeaks and Anonymous, the spirit-lifting YouTube videos of flash mobs breaking out into song and dance at an airport in Beirut and an unemployment office in Madrid.

This is where hope and satellites have taken us. I'm at an age and living in an age where I don't think the great milestones in history or an individual life—the torch being passed to a new generation, the Summer of Love, the thirteenth birthday, the first cigarette— trigger or even signal the moments of profound societal or personal shift. The beacons are embedded in McLuhan's "humming, buzzing confusion"—shared images on the screen, the simultaneity of laughter and horror, the confluence of past and present, braided together in each individual's snaking narrative of what could have, did, might happen.

Marshall McLuhan's crazy interview at the start of *Our World* is like a great surrealist poem. While its words can't be meaningfully parsed, they are marbled with truth and prophecy. They were also fueled, at least in part, by an enormous brain tumor that, three months later, was finally removed in what was, as that point, the longest recorded neurological surgery in medical history. McLuhan retained his speech, his ability to write and to think. But he lost great swaths of memory, and with it, his capacity for any creative work.

She never lost her memory, but toward the end of my Auntie Anne's life, she seemed to achieve some sort of armistice with her demons. On her seventieth birthday, newly widowed, she consented to being feted in the private upstairs dining room of a Chinese restaurant in a Montreal suburb. Trailed by a boisterous line of adoring grandchildren and great nieces, she marched around the faux gold pillars and under the garish red streamers, singing a silly song in her shrill Viennese voice. Once again crackling with energy, she had become our children's Pied Piper. It seemed in that moment that she had finally survived the pummeling shame of having lived more years than her exterminated mother.

My mother's creative life also flourished with age. By her mid-eighties, she rarely painted, but was instead a collagist, working in a form that's not about reproducing or depicting, but about synthesizing. She moved slowly, and paused frequently, not just to regain her balance, but to pick up interesting bits of rock or bottle caps from the ground, or to peel pieces of poster off buildings and fences to use in her art. Her hands trembled from Parkinson's disease except when she applied glue or paint or scraps of borrowed images.

Her vision took shape on much smaller canvases than she used to work on. But still, she tried to make something entirely new.

Two years after *Our World*, I visited San Francisco for the first time. I was about sixteen years old, the Bay area was still the hippy Mecca, and I'd finally arrived (even though it was with my parents). While they went off to do something boring, they gave me permission to wander.

Somewhere near Fisherman's Wharf, a young man in jeans, peasant shirt, Peruvian vest, and floppy leather hat, was selling the *Berkley Barb*. The sun danced off the water. I gave him a quarter for the paper. After pocketing it, he kissed me. I felt his downy beard on my face, and his tongue was as sweet as cinnamon. *All you need is love.*

Past, present, future—these tenses aren't points on a continuum. They're not points at all, no more than light is. After all, what is memory if not this all-at-onceness, this thrumming sense of who-you-were embedded and inseparable from who-you-are?

I swear that the electric goodness of that kiss persists. Its charge has lingered, reignited as I pluck this moment out of the ether as easily as I can see millennia-old history in the light of a star, just by looking up.

Endnotes

[1] In *McLuhan's Wake,* Kevin McMahon and David Sobelman (Canada, 2002), DVD.

[2] Burton, Pierre. *1967: The Last Good Year* (Toronto: Doubleday Canada, 1999), 114.

[3] Ibid., 120.

[4] Duncan, David Douglas. *The Private World of Pablo Picasso* (The Ridge Press, New York), 1958.

[5] Ibid., 38-9.

[6] McLuhan, Marshall. *Gutenberg's Galaxy* (University of Toronto Press, Toronto, 2011, First edition, 1962), 37.

[7] "French-English Expo Effort an Example for Canadians," *The Ottawa Journal,* May 2, 1967.

[8] McLuhan, Marshall. and McLuhan, Eric. *Laws of Media: The New Science* (Toronto: University of Toronto Press, Scholarly Publishing Division. September 16, 1992).

[9] Culkin, John. "A schoolman's guide to Marshall McLuhan," *Saturday Review* (March 18, 1967): 70.

[10] Diski, Jenny. *The Sixties* (New York, Picador, 2009), 37

[11] "The Council for a Summer of Love," *The San Francisco Oracle* (April 1967)Vol. 1, Number 7.

[12] "The Hippies: Philosophy of a Subculture," *Time* Magazine (July 7, 1967).

[13] The Doors. "When the Music's Over," words and music (all rights reserved, Doors Music Co., 1967). Used by permission of Alfred Music.

[14] Kilbanoff, Hank. "The Lasting Impact of a Civil Rights Icon's Murder," *Smithsonian Magazine* (December, 2008).

[15] Ibid.

[16] Congress on Racial Equality. "King Holiday 2009 Slideshow," http://www.coreonline.org/Events/mlk_celebration/photos/mlk2009/mlk_2009_slideshow.htm.

[17] O'Neil, Paul. "A Well-Witnessed Invasion – by Something," *Life* Magazine (April 1, 1966) Vol. 60, No. 13.

[18] Baulch, Vivian M. "The Great Michigan UFO Chase," *The Detroit News,* http://info.detnews.com/history/story/index.cfm?id=210&category=life.

[19] Mathis, Jo Collins. "UFO Mystery Still Haunts Some (1966)," *The Ann Arbor News* (March 20, 2006), http://www.ufocasebook.com/michigan1966revisited.html.

[20] Freire, Paule. *Pedagogy of the Oppressed: 30ᵗʰ Anniversary Edition* (New York, The Continuum International Publishing Group, 2006), 54.

[21] Mathis, Jo Collins. "UFO Mystery Still Haunts Some (1966)", *The Ann Arbor News* (March 20, 2006)..

[22] Ian, Janis. "Society's Child (Baby I've Been Thinkin')," words and music (Taosongs Two (BMI), 1967), exclusive worldwide print rights for Taosongs Two administered by Do Write Music, LLC All Rights Reserved. Used by permission.

[23] *New York Magazine* (June 8, 1970).

[24] Seldes, Barry. *Leonard Bernstein: The Political Life of an American Musician* (Berkeley and Los Angeles, University of California Press, 2009), 70.

[25] "Unite for Bicentennial Action." *The Veteran* (December 1975/January 1976) Vol. 5, No. 7.

[26] Sontag, Susan. *Regarding the Pain of Others* (New York, Picador Press, 2004), 85.

[27] Havel, Vaclav. *Disturbing the Peace* (New York, Vintage Press, 1991), 181.

[28] Clarke, Arthur C. "Extra-Terrestrial Relays – Can Rocket Stations Give Worldwide Radio Coverage?" *Wireless World* (October, 1945).

[29] "Electronics: The Room-Size World." *Time* Magazine (May 14, 1965).

[30] Ibid.

[31] Ibid.

[32] Oliver, Mary. *New and Selected Poems* (Boston: Beacon Press, 1992).

[33] Belam, Martin. *The Guardian* (December 22, 2017). US ambassador to Netherlands describes own words as 'fake news.

[34] Kessler, Glenn. *The Washington Post* (December 30, 2017). In a 30-minute interview, President Trump made 24 false or misleading claims.

[35] Yeoman, Barry. "The North Carolina GOP Has a New Suppression Tactic: Voter Defamation," *New Republic* (December 2, 2016), https://newrepublic.com/article/139111/north-carolina-gop-new-suppression-tactic-voter-defamation.

[36] Suskind, Ron. "Faith, Certainty, and the Presidency of George W. Bush," *The New York Times* (October 17, 2004).

[37] Weisenthal, Joe. "Donald Trump: The First President of Our Post-Literate Age," *Bloomberg View* (November 29, 2016).

[38] Orwell, George. "Politics and the English Language," *Horizon* (April, 1946).
[39] Orwell, George. *1984* (New York: New American Library, 1950).
[40] Ibid.
[41] McLuhan, Marshall. Canadian Broadcasting System introduction to *Our World* (1967).

[42] *Our World*, 1967. Burke, Stanley (25 June 1967). "Our World – Five continents linked via satellite," *CBC Archives* (Toronto: Canadian Broadcasting Corporation).

Acknowledgments

Most books are collaborative efforts, and this one is no exception. It was born and took shape under the extraordinary mentorship of several Lesley University MFA faculty, most notably Jane Brox and Alex Johnson. They teach both through how they live and how they write. I'm deeply grateful for Jane's kindness, candor, and clarity, and for Alex's passionate, incisive critiques and guidance. She was my literary midwife, and I couldn't have been in better hands.

Along the way, many chapters of the book were workshopped—sometimes multiple times—by the members of Cow Skulls, my longstanding writers' group. Thank you for your feedback and patience, my colleagues and friends: Carol Aucoin, Cindy Dockrell, Kevin O'Kelly, Kathleen Tibbets, and Debbie Sosin.

I can't adequately express my gratitude to Simon and Glorianne Wittes, who were as loving and encouraging a set of parents as anyone could hope for. Their lifelong encouragement and the palpable joy they took in seeing me develop as a writer was a form of manna, and I have reason to silently appreciate that and so much more almost every day. Layla, your pride and encouragement, and that from almost everyone in my family has been a vital, motivating force. I love and thank you.

This book wouldn't have been written without the support, keen editorial eye, and neck rubs from my husband, friend, cheerleader, and beloved companion Mark (who's no slouch himself in the writing department). Thank you from the bottom of my still wildly pounding heart.

Finally, this book wouldn't have been published without the leap of faith shown by Jaynie Royal at Regal House Publishing, by Frannie Carr Toth at *Cognoscenti*, and by the editors who published many of these essays in the past eight years. Thank you all.

Permissions and Previous Publications

"Signs" was originally published in *Journal of War, Literature, and the Arts*, Volume 27, 2015, http://www.wlajournal.com/

"Detectives" was originally published in *Pangyrus*, Issue 3, Jan. 2017, http://www.pangyrus.com/voices/detectives/

"Aliens" was originally published in *Shenendoah*, Volume 63, Number 1, http://shenandoahliterary.org/631/2013/09/30/aliens/

"Power Lines" was originally published in *Crack the Spine*, Issue 134 http://issuu.com/crackthespine/docs/issue_134/22

"Nixon's Farewell" was originally published in *Eleven Eleven*, Issue 9, 2010

"Our Wed and Unwed Mothers" was originally published in *The Summerset Review*, Winter 2015, http://www.summersetreview.org/15winter/wed.html

"The Cost of Goods Sold" was originally published in *Talking River*, Issue 34, 2013
http://www.lcsc.edu/talkingriver

"PhotoShocked" was originally published in *Cognoscenti*, http://cognoscenti.wbur.org/2014/02/25/google-image-search-julie-wittes-schlack

"Beacons" was originally published in *Talking Writing*, http://talkingwriting.com/beacons

Portions of "Winters" and "Burn like Oak" were originally published in *Cognoscenti*.

http://www.wbur.org/cognoscenti/2016/07/19/that-which-unites-us-julie-wittes-schlack

http://cognoscenti.wbur.org/2016/02/24/make-oceania-great-again-julie-wittes-schlack

http://www.wbur.org/cognoscenti/2017/08/16/looking-to-a-generation-past-for-mastering-these-anxious-times